Murder She Wrote

Murder She Wrote
A Study of
Agatha Christie's
Detective Fiction

Patricia D. Maida
Nicholas B. Spornick

Bowling Green State University Popular Press
Bowling Green, Ohio 43403

Library of Congress Catalog Card No.: 82-73346

ISBN: 0-87972-215-0 Clothbound
      0-87972-216-9 Paperback

Contents

Devon: Agatha Christie corrects proofs of her latest book, January 1946
(Photo courtesy of United Press International)

Preface

The novels of Agatha Christie have reached sales numbering in the hundreds of millions of copies. She is the second most printed author in English—next to Shakespeare. According to a 1962 UNESCO report, her works have been translated into 103 languages (at least a dozen more than the works of Shakespeare).[1] This polyglottal distribution is matched by an unbelievable quantity. She was acknowledged by UNESCO to be "the most widely read British author in the world."[2] Nancy Blue Wynne points out that Agatha Christie is likewise "the most translated crime writer."[3]

The enormous flood of Christie novels flowing from presses of grateful publishers washed away any chance of obtaining an exact reckoning of her sales total. We are told that even "her publishers have lost count of her total sales."[4] Certainly Christie herself lost count of the total number of books she had written (if she ever cared). Astonishing as it is, one must rest with the fact that no one knows the exact number of copies, printed and sold, copyrighted and pirated, of her total output of detective novels.

Lowenthal estimated that some of her American editions in paperback went into a 10th or 15th printing. The Pocket Books edition "has had sales of 5 million copies in a year."[5] In the 1960s her total sales was placed at an excess of 350 million while in 1975 it was said to be probably more than 400 million copies.[6] Bemused by her vast output of titles and by the exploding astronomical sales distribution, Christie was moved to term herself a "veritable sausage-machine."[7] This was a highly lucrative sausage-machine spewing forth riches for its readers, its inventor, her publishers, her family and the coffers of the Inland Revenue, but above all, providing works of enjoyment for millions of readers.

Christie's popularity and critical acclaim peaked in the thirties and the forties, when she was at the height of her creative powers. The post-war years saw her diligently producing at least one new thriller a year, often more. While the critics agreed that her powers were fading and the books of the fifties and sixties reveal a decline in invention, freshness and originality, the ranks of loyal and new readers kept increasing and the sold volumes of her novels rose into the hundreds of millions.

The profits from all this endeavor were also astronomical, raising Agatha Christie into the ranks of the "scribbling" millionaires. It is estimated that after 1926 she never received less than $10,000 a week in royalties from short stories, novels, plays and movie rights, even in the worst years.[8] Her yearly income alone was in the six figures: this placed her for decades in the ranks of the super-rich, a position she obtained solely through her pen.

By right of authorship, wealth and social position (she was a Lady twice-over, once through marriage to Sir Max Mallowan and once through the conferring upon her of the title "Dame" by the Queen), Agatha Christie enjoyed a great popularity, a reputation which spread over the world. However, early in her career this shy writer was one of the world's most elusive women who led a strictly private, even secretive, personal life.

For a woman in her position, Agatha Christie had almost no public exposure. She presented no lectures, shunned radio and television, avoided public functions and dinners, refused to write about her private life, and granted fewer than ten interviews in her lifetime—and then only to select reporters who were certain to ask the same questions and receive the same superficial answers. As a result, little was known about the life of this intriguing writer, even less about her family. Christie, her family and her publisher were united in a conspiracy of silence—they programmed her interviews, controlled press releases and refused appeals for assistance from scholars. The much awaited publication of her *Autobiography* in 1977 provided some of the missing facts necessary for an adequate understanding of Christie's family background, her values and interests, as well as the range of literary and social forces which shaped her development. However, even the *Autobiography* is elusive at times as the reader catches glimpses of Agatha Christie over a period of more than three quarters of a century.

Various accounts of Christie's life and art have attempted to fill obvious gaps in the available information concerning the "Queen of Mystery." Among those focusing on biography are G.C. Ramsay's *Agatha Christie: Mistress of Mystery* (1967), Jeoffrey Feinman's *The Mysterious World of Agatha Christie* (1975), Derrick Murdoch's *The Agatha Christie Mystery* (1976), Gwen Robyns' *The Mystery of Agatha Christie* (1978) and Kathleen Tynan's *Agatha* (1979). Appraisals of Christie have also appeared in the standard histories of the genre (Haycraft, Murch, Symons); in critical studies (Bargainnier, Cawelti, Grossvogel, Maggowan, Manley); in journals (Auden, Holquist, Calder); and in a few interviews (Bernstein, Dennis, Snowden, Wyndam).[9] Nancy Blue Wynne's *An Agatha Christie Chronology* (1975) and Russell Fitzgibbon's *The Agatha Christie Companion* (1980) provide other bibliographical material. *Agatha Christie First Lady of Crime* (1977), edited by H.R.F. Keating, offers multiple views of Christie presented by her peers. And *The Bedside, Bathtub and Armchair Companion to Agatha Christie* (1979), edited by Riley and McAllister, cavorts lightly over the Christie canon.

In our study of the Christie legacy, we have chosen to focus on her detective fiction, for this is the genre to which she made her greatest contribution. Although detective fiction was less than a century old when Christie entered the field in 1921, critics had been attacking its pretensions as art, pinpointing its faults and foibles, and prophesying its demise as both a viable and a marketable commodity. Yet critics agree that the modern detective story reached a peak of development in the twenties and thirties of this century, a period which has since been deemed "The Golden Age" of detective fiction. During that time, Christie rose to become the world's most famous author of detective fiction, surpassing her competitors in popularity and sales. Why was Christie so successful?

In examining the forces which shaped Christie as both a person and a writer, we have considered significant biographical and historical matter. We have looked closely at the fabric of her fiction, which frequently was woven from the very stuff of her own experience. And we have analyzed components of the works themselves—the puzzle, the detectives, the policemen, the environment—to discover the uniqueness of her detectival structure. Essentially, our approach has been to explore the inter-relationships between Christie and her works to seek the wholeness in the Christie experience. We perceive an integration in personal experience and moral and aesthetic values between the woman and her art. Though the mystery which has continued to enshroud her person may persist, we believe that Christie reveals herself in her art. A shy woman with a natural gift for story-telling, she achieved success through a combination of *seemingly* artless effects which combined to produce some outstanding detective fiction. Thus her readers would not allow her to pension off Hercule Poirot, demanding their "Christie for Christmas" for over fifty years, participating with millions of enthusiasts who play the game of detection with Agatha Christie.

Chapter I
Agatha Christie: The Beginning

The Queen of Mystery—Agatha Christie—who was responsible for devising hundreds of murders and related crimes, created her own personal mystique. By resisting any intrusions into her private life, she effectively created an aura of mystery about her own person. Although readers clamored for years to become better acquainted with the "real" Christie, they met with little success. A shy person uncomfortable in the public eye, Christie avoided interviews and public appearances. And with what seemed a conspiracy of silence, those who knew her best guarded her privacy and protected her. Her natural shyness and abhorrence of public scrutiny combined to build the mystery surrounding Christie's character.

Though reluctant to reveal herself personally, she found her medium in the written word. Writing became for her an outlet for self-expression; even her mystery fiction bears the stamp of her attitudes and values. The public awaited Christie's *Autobiography* (1977) with anticipation of great revelation of life and character—but again Christie was elusive. She clarified some issues, clouded others, and simply overlooked a great deal. We feel that although the *Autobiography* is useful, the work that reflects the real Christie is still her *Unfinished Portrait* (1930), an autobiographical romance published under the protective pseudonym of Mary Westmacott. Critics have pointed out the autobiographical strains of this work before, yet its candid reflections are now strongly reinforced by the revelations in the *Autobiography*.

By examining *both* sources one gains a greater understanding of the hidden Christie and the public Christie; for she emerges as a vulnerable individual who could be both romantic and realistic, a person shaped by the forces of family and environment and imbued with the pervasive values of Edwardian society.

5

I. Family

A dominant social structure is the primal English family unit with its extensions, its milieu, its struggles for survival while pursuing its ritualistic duties, social patterns and pastimes. Part of the Christie literary heritage is her careful delineation of evolving upper middle-class English family histories during the first sixty years of this century. So strong is her fascination with family that it becomes a force working its way through the major portion of her novels while revealing that she herself was greatly influenced by the forces of familial consciousness and identity.

The primary force in Christie's development was her own family—a tightly knit middle-class unit dominated by strong women. The men are dim figures who died out early except for the prime male whose influence extended through two generations—Nathaniel Miller, Agatha Christie's paternal grandfather. He was an American from Massachusetts who worked his way up from office boy to partner in a New York City dry goods firm, later known as H.B. Clafin and Co. He married as his second wife an Englishwoman whom he met in Manchester, where the company had business connections. He and his second wife, Margaret Miller, became the guardians of her niece, Clarissa Margaret Boehmer. Their ward eventually married her step-cousin, Frederick Alvah Miller, Nathaniel Miller's son from his first marriage. In his will the elder Miller provided generously for his widow, his son, and also his ward. It was the money from his estate which became the source of this family's income.

The dominant head and ruler of this family was Mrs. Margaret Miller, the "Auntie-Grannie" of Agatha Christie who directed the financial and social well-being of her dependents for three generations and left a lasting impression on the affections and memory of her grateful granddaughter.

Mrs. Margaret Miller became the family matriarch. With her niece married to her step-son, Mrs. Miller had a triple role: aunt, guardian and mother-in-law to Agatha Christie's mother. From all descriptions she was a handsome woman who cut a figure like Queen Victoria—influential and enduring, retaining her power through ninety-two years of existence. She was one of ten children of a middle-class English family, a woman who outlived three husbands: "She had buried them in turn—one with tears—one with resignation—and one with decorum."[1]

In both *Unfinished Portrait* and the *Autobiography*, Christie speaks with delight of her visits to her grandmother's home, a comfortable townhouse at 99 Uxbridge Road in Ealing, then a small suburb of London. Here the young Agatha was spoiled by an indulgent "Auntie-Grannie." Grannie's home was filled with mementoes collected over the years—fine china, antiques, household necessities, remnants of fabric, as well as immense stores of food kept in a locked cabinet, a veritable treasure chest of sundries, sweets, hams, tinned goods and home-brewed liquor. The comfortable lifestyle is reflected in the family dinners on Sunday afternoon at Auntie Grannie's house—a joint of beef, the many courses, the special dessert served on the prized china dishes.

Mrs. Miller regularly entertained her younger sister, Mary Boehmer, who was the widowed mother of Agatha's own mother—known as "Granny B." This woman played a much less dominant role in Agatha's family. Because of compelling economic reasons she gave up her only daughter to be cared for by the "auntie-grannie" while striving to support the remaining four sons who lived on with her. A natural estrangement developed between this mother and her daughter, Clarissa. Yet the two sisters, Margaret and Mary, were close. Mary Boehmer and three of her sons were regular Sunday visitors at the elder sister's home.

Part of the routine of these women involved evaluating their house-keeping purchases. Frequently Mrs. Boehmer shopped for her sister. The store most frequented by the two sisters, the Army and Navy Stores, was a large department store where families of the military shopped. At that time Agatha's uncle, Mary Boehmer's son Harry, was also secretary of the Army and Navy Stores. Although Mary did most of the shopping, it was Margaret who was the spender, for Mary had to make ends meet on her widow's pension and even took in sewing to augment their income.

The Victorian belief in conspicuous consumption and the overly-laden dinner table, provided by a portly cook and served by maids, left its mark on the sizes and shapes of the two sisters. The young Agatha recalls that they had enormous bosoms and could barely reach each other to kiss. These happy, affluent domestic scenes of material blessing are set off by the pathetic degeneration of the physical grandmother in advanced old age, and the catalogue of unused, decayed and motheaten stores found in the old woman's drawers, cupboards and other hiding places. Among the most pathetic sequences which Christie describes, one involves the moving of Auntie-Grannie from this home in her old age. The vast cupboards had to be emptied—a herculean task. Many tears were shed over items that had to be discarded—now useless, but still important to the old, enfeebled woman.

For the young Agatha these visits to Ealing brought a taste of urban life. She took the train from Torquay to Victoria Station in London when she went on visits to Grannie in Ealing. From there, Grannie would take her to Victoria Station, then the two rode in a carriage on shopping and entertainment expeditions. Within her grandmother's house, Agatha received the pearls of wisdom that her worldly wise mentor freely dispensed—cautionary messages about how to deal with men, how to handle servants, how to avoid being cheated and abused. Amid the maxims, the old lady knitted endlessly, providing little garments for the progeny of her servants or waistcoats for some of the old gentlemen she frequently entertained. Christie reveals that Miss Marple had her genesis here with Auntie-Grannie. We can picture the "pink and white" old lady shrouded in a lace fichu filling her granddaughter's ears with wisdom of a lifetime.

Though age and the weakening of faculties took a sad toll on the ancient woman's spirit, mind and happiness, she was remembered as a powerful presence. She ruled her family like a queen, gathering her clan about her for rituals of feasting, visitation and recreation. She carefully nurtured the dwindling family fortune and passed it into the hands of Agatha Christie's mother. Above all, she taught and delighted her granddaughter with Victorian values, stories of her youth, concepts of will and evil; and she spoiled her young relative with visits to pantomimes, concerts, theaters and exciting shopping sprees. This grande dame fostered in her granddaughter a sense of family continuity and appreciation of Victorian ways, and an indelible memory of a remarkable woman who was a strong-willed character and a provider and nurturer.

The dominance of the females in the family was the natural result of the early demise of the males. No grandfather was living at the time of Agatha's birth, and her own father, Frederick Alvah Miller, died in 1901 when she was ten years old. From Christie's account in her *Autobiography* we learn that her father was brought up by his grandparents after his mother died and that he never prepared for a trade or a profession because he was the son of a rich man. He attended Vevey, a prep school in France, and apparently had the time and money for a leisurely existence. He never did a day's work in his life and lived the life of a "gentleman." When he married and the family eventually settled in Torquay, he spent his time at his club playing whist with his cronies. Agatha recalls his jovial singing and piano playing, and the many friends he entertained for dinner. She recalls accompanying him to the cricket matches on Saturday (he was the official scorer); and then on Sunday to the old Anglican church.

But the good life did not last; the family income was cut by declining investments. Plagued by money worries, Mr. Miller's health began to decline. In fact at the time of his death, he was in London searching for some added means of income. In her *Autobiography*, Christie states that the medical specialists consulted on her father's case could not agree on the nature of his illness. Though the death certificate indicates the cause of death as "complications from Bright's Disease," whether brought on directly by worry or hastened by it, the fact remains that Frederick Alvah Miller died suddenly at the age of fifty-five, leaving a widow and three children.

Agatha had two siblings—a sister, Margaret Frary Miller, who was eleven years older than she; and a brother, Louis Montant Miller, who was ten years older. Monty, as her brother was called, was something of a prodigal son. In fact, before publication of the *Autobiography* his name was never mentioned. One gathers that time may have softened Christie's attitude toward him, but that her judgment of him remained uncompromising: she considered him amoral, difficult, destructive but most charming. Monty had a troubled childhood. He attended Harrow, from whence he was "superannuated"—the exact reasons are not known. He eventually went into the army and served in East Africa, was wounded and came home critically ill. This scapegrace brother was handsome, clever and charming, capable of fascinating women with his wiles and then of fleecing those who fell in love with him. As in the past, the women in the family took care of him, particularly his elder sister who provided moral as well as financial support. His unreasonable demands on the household and servants, his outrageous behavior, and his destructive urges put a strain on the family and his harried mother.

Agatha and her sister ended up by buying him a cottage in Dartmoor just to get him out of the way—Mrs. Miller's health had been declining and Monty's escapades did not help. He lived in the Dartmoor cottage with a nurse-companion on funds provided by his family. Later, on a trip to France, he fell seriously ill and again the family had to come to his aid. Christie herself funded her brother's retirement to a small cottage in southern France with another admiring female companion-housekeeper to look after him. He died shortly thereafter and was buried in France. Christie is vague in her *Autobiography* as to the exact year of her brother's death, but it must have been sometime between 1926 and 1930. At that time Monty would have been in his mid-forties.

In character, Monty Miller resembled a type that Christie develops in her fiction—the handsome but irresponsible son who wastes the family fortune and honor and must be sent off into exile to an outpost such as Africa or New Zealand. Her brother may well have been the prototype of the prodigal son of her fiction.

Madge, as Agatha's older sister was called, appears to have been the most promising child in the family. And despite the differences in their ages, she and Agatha developed a life-long relationship. Madge grew up during the halcyon period of her parents' life when there was plenty of money, few worries and many advantages. She attended the Misses Lawrence's School (later to become Rodean College), went to Paris for additional study and then had her "coming out" in New York.

About nine months after her father's death, Madge married James Watts, a young man from Cheshire whose mother was a stepcousin of Frederick Alvah Miller. His mother, the former Annie Browne, was also a childhood friend of Agatha's mother who had been raised in Cheshire. Consequently, Madge married a man with close ties to her own family. The match was also a suitable one financially, for the Watts family owned a prosperous textile business in Manchester, had established itself as one of the county families, and possessed the ancient and magnificent Abney Hall.

Madge's influence on her younger sister strikes at the heart of Agatha's subsequent success as a writer of detective fiction. In the *Autobiography* Christie reveals that it was her sister who introduced her to Conan Doyle's work and to the works of other detective writers. The two sisters shared this interest long before Agatha began to write, and it was Madge who challenged her first detective novel by taunting her with, "I bet you can't write a detective story."[2] The sisters also played detective games with Madge as the schizoid character, the elder sister who could change voices at will and transform herself into a frightening and wicked character. From this evil spirit residing in the body of the good sister, Christie was to derive inspiration. A motif that Christie uses over and over again in her detective stories is *hidden identity*, particularly among sisters or close friends. Christie was to produce a portrait gallery of evil characters who disguise themselves—a motif used by Gaston Leroux in *The Perfume of the Woman in Black* and later by Christie herself in works like *A Holiday for Murder* and in *Funerals are Fatal.*

But the person who was most influential in Agatha's life was her mother, Clarissa Margaret Boehmer. As the ward of Auntie-Grannie and Nathaniel Miller, she had been brought up in Chesire with the advantages her own mother did not have the money to provide. Yet as Christie says in both *Unfinished Portrait* and the *Autobiography,* her mother resented being separated from her brothers and felt deprived of a mother's love. Perhaps this is why she was so possessive and protective of her own children. After the death of her husband when she found herself with only one child in the home—Agatha—she gave Agatha all her affection and attentions. Madge had married within a year of her father's death, for her mother felt she might become too emotionally dependent upon Madge if she remained at home much longer. Very likely, economic considerations were also a factor because Mrs. Miller could barely support herself let alone an older daughter accustomed to having money at her disposal. Consequently she had only Agatha, and upon this shy, sensitive child she lavished all her attention.

In some ways this mother-daughter relationship was symbiotic. Mrs. Miller became her daughter's companion as well as her tutor, preferring to educate Agatha at home rather than send her off to school. Economy may have been a consideration here again, but very likely the mother's strong attachment was as significant a factor. Mrs. Miller read to her daughter, encouraged her to write stories, and permitted her to indulge in girlish fantasies. According to the *Autobiography* Agatha felt that her mother was clairvoyant, for she had unusual powers of sensing danger and perceiving other people's thoughts. She experimented with various religions including some of the mystic Eastern beliefs. It is possible that some of her mother's dabbling in the occult may have influenced Christie's frequent use of seances, ouija boards and spiritualism in her works.

Stark reality produced one certainty. With Frederick Miller's death and the reality of a limited income to contend with, the family's lifestyle changed significantly. The expense of a large household was enormous: repairs were neglected, servants were released, fancy oversupplies of food were curtailed and Mrs. Miller began a long struggle to stave off the poverty she greatly feared. Their social life diminished, and as if drawing inward Mrs. Miller concentrated all efforts on bringing up her youngest daughter. *Unfinished Portrait* provides a rather touching account of this unusual mother-daughter relationship. They remained very close—separating only after Agatha's marriage to Archibald Christie, yet maintaining close contact. Mrs. Miller's health worsened progressively after Agatha's marriage; and she died in 1926 at Madge's home in Cheshire. It is understandable given the nature of their relationship that her mother's death would plunge Agatha into a severe depression and precipitate a crisis in her life.

What emerges from this profile of the family are the fine dominant female images and the dim, if not negative, male images, which were to become the primary prototypes of Christie's creative imagination. Christie knew and respected women, especially older women like her grandmother, mother and sister. In her fiction one can distinguish many memorable female characters much more clearly than the Christie male characters. She created an interesting and varied gallery of English types: the twittering spinster; the gossip; the domineering, strong-willed manipulator; the beautiful baby doll actress, lovely but stupid; the sweet, kindly grandmother; the healthy, outdoors horsey-type. She is particularly sensitive to mother-daughter relationships, though she creates plenty of other relationships: the professional woman; the lovely heiress pursued by her suitors. It is noteworthy that in Christie's work, there is not a single instance of a murder involving the killing of a mother by a daughter, or of a daughter by a mother. Yet sons murder mothers and fathers, and fathers murder sons.

II. The House Syndrome

Nurturance and security in Christie are associated with mothering, and the house itself and its environs become the material extension of that process. Christie reveals a life-long preoccupation with houses dating back to the prototype—her family home in Torquay. Not only does her actual life revolve about the acquisition and restoration of houses, but her fiction also focuses on houses. In fact, she specialized in crimes committed within the home. And often the description of the house bears great similarity to her childhood home.

Ashfield, as the Miller home was called, was located at 15 Barton Road on a hillside overlooking the town of Torquay and the bay. The house was large by today's standards; although not a mansion, it contained living rooms, a dining room, library, conservatory, several bedrooms, a nursery, schoolroom, servants quarters, kitchen and scullery. There were also several out-buildings on the property. It was a home that required servants—a cook, a parlor maid, a governess, a nurse and a gardener. The house itself was bordered with floral beds, and its back terrace led out into a spacious garden with numerous trees, shrubs, play areas, kitchen garden and back wall. The garden was an extension of the home, where parents could entertain their guests, relax in comfort with friends or children; it was a refuge for the child sent away by busy adults.

Above all, it was a well-cared for little Eden where a child could explore and find private and mysterious places to hide. It was a safe paradise where innocence could play out its fantasies, peopled with animated creatures and invented playmates. Christie retells some of her fondest memories of the garden and childhood in her works, especially in *Giant's Bread, Unfinished Portrait, Autobiography, Postern of Fate* and *Sleeping Murder.* One of her last detective stories, *Postern of Fate,* describes the restoration of an old house identical to Ashfield. The elderly heroine of the story discovers a child's pedal car in a run-down glass enclosure where discarded toys were stored. This sequence in the novel parallels Christie's nostalgic description of the same enclosure and the same toy car in her *Autobiography.*

In the *Autobiography* Christie also reveals her penchant for doll houses—an early sign of her preoccupation with houses as symbols of security and comfort. She describes how she redecorated her doll house using old wallpaper, how she added furnishings, and how the project grew so unmanageable that a huge cupboard had to be converted into an enormous doll house. This growing multiplication of domestic minutiae was a mild mania with the child and developed into a never-ending house syndrome. At one point, in fact, Christie owned eight houses. The mature Christie loved to look at houses; when she bought a house she lavished money and her own talents refurbishing it. Her life-long interest in houses and decoration was a hobby which made her an astute judge of real-estate.

The purchase of Greenway House in 1937 was the realization of a childhood dream. This choice property is situated on the River Dart, just south of Torquay. It was and still is one of the most distinguished homes in the Devon area. As a child, Agatha saw the house often from the deck of boats making the cruise up the river—it seemed then like a fairy castle with its white walls, its stunning green park, and its romantic appearance. Many years before, Agatha and her mother paid a social call to this elegant home and the child never forgot it.

Perhaps the most extreme indication of Christie's house mania is projected in *Come Tell Me How You Live* where she goes into great detail about the house she and her husband built in the desert during one of his archeological expeditions. Designed by an architect who accompanied the entourage to the dig, this house becomes an English woman's moorish castle—a home for a person who needed the security of a house, even in the desert.

A neighbor recalling the Miller home in Torquay says that the cluttered interior was filled with bric-a-brac, a veritable "curiosity shop."[3] However, references to china, furniture and objects of art indicate that excellent and tasteful examples of fine export china, Chinese screens, Chippendale and Hepplewhite furniture, etc., were owned and used; photographs of Christie's mother and "Auntie-Grannie" in their homes bears this out. Agatha comments that her father made some good investments in antique furniture, some of which her mother had to sell off in "hard times." Apparently Agatha's mother also had the acquisitive fever, collecting china and bibelots. Agatha herself was a collector and gradually moved from doll houses to real houses, from expensive papier-mache boxes to rare antiques.

Of all the memories connected with the house, Christie continued to dwell on the nursery. Memories of the nursery were to haunt this woman all her life. The wallpaper with its mauve irises, the bookshelves lining the walls filled with old classics, the window overlooking the sea—all these components are regenerated time and time again both in her fiction and her *Autobiography*. She recalls the night nursery at the top of the house—the quiet little room she shared with "nursie," her governess; then there was the big day nursery on the lower floor where she had space to grow and spend time by herself. The imprinting of the nursery reflects a womb motif, the center for intensive mothering, an area associated with "nursie" who though quite elderly still managed to carry out her functions with understanding and expertise. To Agatha the nursery represented complete protection, the Edenic refuge protecting the child from both the adult world of worry and the world of knowledge of good and evil. All her life, Agatha was to be haunted by the loss of Edenic innocence and happiness, order, comfort and lavish love—feelings for which she yearned all her life.

Thus, Paradise for Christie was the home, the garden, the nursery, an Eden where innocence and child-like simplicity prevailed. It was a child's world where nurturance and security were assured. As she completed the *Autobiography* she expressed fondest memories of that first home: "I go back to that always in my mind, Ashfield."[4]

III. The Recurring Country Village

The total environment of the Devon countryside with its beauty and isolation became the prototype for the towns and villages Christie herself preferred and chose to write about. Although many charming villages dot the map of Christie's fiction, they are quite similar: for the town of Torquay makes its appearance as a prototypical force over and over again in her works.

During Agatha Miller's girlhood, Torquay was a well-made seaside resort community of some 53,000 residents and numbers of vacationers from all parts of the world—for it was accepted as the Riviera of the British Isles. The lower town consisted of the seaside resort area with its hotels, town hall, theatre and public buildings. Above this area rose the High Street leading to the hillsides and cliff tops, known as torres, where the residents lived. This section of town, removed from the resort area, became an enclave for middle-class families who inhabited the large homes attended by ranks of servants. These families lived a comfortable life regulated by the decorum of class and the light pace of a vacationer's retreat. Visitors from Britain's cities came here to relax and enjoy the sunshine, the beaches and the palm trees. Americans came too—this is how the Millers first discovered Torquay as a vacation spot where both their British and American friends gathered.

Although the routine life of a resident usually involved visitations (snobbery decreed only if cards were first sent and accepted), charity bazaars, elaborate garden teas and trips to the theatre, large parties were also part of the scene. The writer Eden Phillpotts and his wife, who lived quite close to the Millers, gave a yearly bash for around 250 people—a splendid, catered affair to which residents as well as large numbers of literary celebrities were invited. The Phillpotts' home was a gathering place for the literati of the day—Conan Doyle, E.C. Bentley, Rudyard Kipling, Thomas Hardy and Arnold Bennett were some of the guests. In her *Autobiography* Christie says her mother spoke of having had Rudyard Kipling and Henry James to tea (though not at the same time). This occurred early in her life and undoubtedly at the time when her father was still alive.

Apparently her father had many friends and acquaintances who dropped in and out of Torquay during the season, and naturally the Millers would have entertained them. One did things in the proper way—one dressed even for ordinary dinners. A typical dinner for ten (always worked out between Mrs. Miller and the cook) is described in the *Autobiography*: this "began with a thick or clear soup, then boiled turbot, or filets of sole. After that came a sorbet. Saddle of mutton followed. Then rather unexpectedly, lobster mayonaise. Pouding diplomatique and charlotte russe were the sweets and then dessert."[5] Quiet elegance and conspicuous abundance seem to have set the tone.

The social life of a child was more limited, for the child's world was carefully separate from that of the adults. The child did not feed at the family table but ate her meals in the nursery with "Nursie." Spatially the child's room was as far removed as possible from the drawing and dining rooms. The child was circumscribed by the rules of class—a child could not interact with another child unless their parents exchanged cards. When holiday parties were given for the children, the young people were expected to be mannerly, if not friendly toward each other. Agatha Miller attended the parties and also the dancing classes in the studio above the confectioner's shop on Fleet Street. She also learned piano. Interestingly, Agatha Miller like most of the children walked to the parties and dancing classes, for only the very wealthy maintained a carriage and driver. Even when they went to town to the beaches, the fairs and the theatre, they walked.

One of the most pleasant activities for the Miller children was bathing at the beach above Babbacombe Bay (in those days one area was reserved for males and another for females). Christie developed an early love for swimming, although she recalls a time when she almost met her death by drowning and had to be rescued by the guard who flew out swiftly in his rescue boat to pluck both her and her nephew out of the water. Death by drowning was to work its way into her fiction. In all her travels, she gravitates to the attractions of the beach. One of her happiest experiences occurred on her world tour with Archie—they went surf riding each day in Hawaii. Some of the most exciting episodes in her stories deal with dramas enacted on the sun-drenched seashore such as in *The Companion, Problem at Pollensa Bay* and *The Bloodstained Pavement.*

As the youngest child in the family, Agatha was left to her own devices for amusement, and developed a set of imaginary games and playmates who romped around the garden or invaded the secret places in her home. A favorite fantasy playmate was the maternal Mrs. Green with her hundred children. This nurturing figure reappears with a sex change as part of little Vernon's fantasy visitors in *Giant's Bread.*

Although it was not customary for the families of the gentry to shop downtown in Torquay, Agatha saw the shopkeepers' boys, assistants and tradesmen who took orders from the cook and the housekeeper. Her governess also took her for long walks into both the town and into the countryside, where the child marvelled at the beauty of the flowers. And the youngster spent time with the servants listening to their conversations and enjoying little treats bestowed on her by the family cook. She observed the interaction of the servants, their routines, their likes and dislikes, their expressions—and sometimes overheard private conversations of a sordid kind. Secluded as her life was intended to be, the young Agatha still had an interest in the routine of life in her home and in the town—she was an inveterate observer even though she was shy and rarely voiced what she had seen or heard.

Her receptive mind was absorbing the diurnal life about her: the shifting environment, actions of people, facial expressions and especially their dialogue. At an early age indeed she became imbued with the social aspirations of her family and class, the ideals, the fears and the growing awareness of the force of evil: one did not play with working class children; one never insulted a servant; one did not carry tales or scandal; one played fair. The intensely religious "Nursie" inspired in the child a fear of even seeming to disrespect the Lord's Commandments. From the righteous lips of "Nursie," Agatha garnered the first but indelible traces of Calvinistic moral convictions.

IV. Money and Status

Motives for murder are legion in Agatha Christie's fiction. When evil forces its way to the surface, one notes that money or protection is the driving force. More blood is shed to gain property or title than for any other motive. And Christie's upbringing demonstrates that these are the values she learned early in the home setting—the validity, unity and life of the family depends mainly on the acquisition and protection of money and status. Her father's life and happiness may have been destroyed by financial reverses, aunties and grannies constantly lectured on the perils of poverty, and Agatha saw personally the toll that shrinking funds had on the health of her mother. After Agatha's marriage to the handsome but inpecunious Archie, their early years in a London flat were marred by lack of money and stringent economies that had to be enacted. The force that kept one alive was money and plenty of it. Money later became the major motivation for the writing of Agatha Christie, as she freely admits in her autobiography. When the first monetary rewards from her writing began to flow in steadily, the first purchases made by the Christies were a home, an automobile and a fur coat for Agatha—all effective status symbols.

The place of the Miller family in late Victorian society was determined by the money Nathaniel Miller, Agatha's paternal grandfather, accumulated in trade. This American literally bought upper middle-class status for his English wife and her family. But the fear of returning to the poverty the family once knew haunted its survivors. Loss of income did become a reality in Frederick Alvah Miller's lifetime and may, in fact, have precipitated his death. In her *Autobiography*, Christie discusses the financial reverses that radically changed her family's lifestyle. She implies that shares in the business with which her grandfather had been connected lost their value and that other investments may have been mismanaged by his executors.

A history of the firm H.B. Claflin & Company, a New York City dry goods establishment located on lower Broadway, indicates that after the Civil War the company suffered great losses from their Southern creditors; then the United States tax structure changed, greatly reducing profits to the company. Profits never reached the heights of success realized before 1860; ultimately, the company folded in the stock market crash of 1927. But obviously if the elder Miller's investments had been managed shrewdly, his fortune could have increased. Christie hints that mismanagement, fraud and sheer waste were to blame.

Consequently, in those years just prior to his death Frederick Alvah Miller and his family had to economize. They rented out their home in Torquay for a profit and moved into a hotel in southern France for the season, finding it cheaper to live away from home. After her father's death when her mother found out just how little money she had, Agatha recalls a drastic change in the household. Most of the household help was dismissed; there were no more lavish dinner parties; and every penny had to be counted. It is likely that lack of money may have been a reason for not sending Agatha to one of the better schools. Again when it was time for her "coming out," her mother found it less expensive to spend the season in Cairo than in London. Christie remembers how one of her evening gowns was made from fabric salvaged from among Auntie-Grannie's trunks.

Amid the perils of declining fortune, however, the compulsion to retain her position and ensure that of her youngest daughter obviously cost Mrs. Miller some money— for fine clothes and travel were luxuries the family could ill afford. But these were investments in the marriage game, the reward to be a suitably wealthy husband for young Agatha. Ironically the costly "coming out" process did not pay off in the snaring of a wealthy husband. Instead of aligning herself in an affair with a well-placed and wealthy man, Agatha chose to marry a young soldier who had no money. This marriage to Archibald Christie, an officer in the flying corps, meant more scraping for funds. The Christies' first flat in London was modest. Agatha speaks of receiving financial help from her mother and also from Auntie-Grannie who could be counted on to send a five pound note through the mail (half at a time to avoid theft). During this time both the need for money and the desire to write started her on a career. Her first publisher, John Lane, taking advantage of her inexperience, actually bilked her out of money she felt she deserved by having her sign a contract limiting her earnings. She neither forgot nor forgave this painful lesson.

Speaking through one of her own characters, Mrs. Ariadne Oliver, Christie comments openly on the fact that money continued to motivate her writing. And although she was known to laugh about the overdrafts on her bank accounts, she must have developed some skill in managing her fortune. Considering the fact that in a lean year Christie must have earned well over half a million dollars, she was not an ostentatious spender. She also had the financial acumen to incorporate her earnings in Agatha Christie Limited. A lingering mystery the public and British tax collectors have yet to fathom is what she did with all the money she made. Her estate was so minimal that the Crown's portion was surprisingly small. But given her background and her orientation toward money, even an amateur detective should not be surprised that Christie had found some way to keep as much of her wealth as possible in the family.

During her lifetime, the most obvious use for her money proved to be property—at one time she owned eight houses. She respected property, loved old homes and enjoyed restoring them. And she collected furnishings and art for her houses. Greenway House, the Devon country home she acquired in 1939, has since her death become a repository for Christie memorabilia—a trust which now is open to the public on a limited basis.

The urge for status and a recognized place in the power structure of the community was strong in the Miller and Christie families. Agatha was made aware during her childhood of the differences between classes of people. The

Millers fought hard to get a toe-hold in the upper middle class
society of Torquay, and were threatened by the prospect of
being considered *déclassée*. She speaks of her father's pride in
making a large monetary contribution in her name to the
building of a new church for Tor Mohun parish—thus
conferring upon his infant daughter the status of founder.
While the young Agatha may have taken the rewards and
prerequisites of wealth and class for granted, she was to learn
in a bitter way that when money became scarce the middle-
class family no longer enjoyed the same social position. Celia
and Dermot (characters in *Unfinished Portrait*) living on
reduced income in a small London flat, learn too well that
sharp economies must be made, visitations cut out, clothes
buying stopped and entertainments and social activities
stopped. Poverty destroys the material means to keep up with
the money life and pleasures of wealthy friends.

Agatha recalls fantasizing as a child about becoming a
lady: "I wanted above everything in the world, to be the Lady
Agatha one day." She was quickly taught that to be a lady, one
must "be born it."[6] Ironically, she was to *earn* that title twice
through Royal Honor, once as the wife of Sir Max and again as
the celebrated author, Lady Agatha Christie. But as with all
honorary titles, she could not pass it down to her progeny, for
honor is never substituted for birthright. Still, good child of the
Victorian mode that she was, Christie defended the system. Of
snobbery she says: "On the whole I think the snobbery of my
childhood, the snobbery of birth that is, is more palatable than
the other snobberies: the snobbery of wealth and today's
intellectual snobbery."[27]

V. The Marriage Game

The best conduit for the continuum of wealth, family
integrity, class and snobbism in the Victorian-oriented family
was the "proper" marriage. Inpecunious noblemen or prodigal
sons of debilitated middle-class families could recoup financial
stability through marriage with the daughter of wealth.
Conversely, the gifted, trained, beautiful daughter of a well-
placed but impoverished family could align herself to a
wealthy suitor and thus vastly improve the prospects of all.

What Jane Austen did with the marriage game on the grand scale in her domestic novels, Agatha Christie was to do on a lesser scale—portray the marriage-brokerage game as a life and death struggle—in her romances and detective novels.

"And they lived happily ever after"—or so it seems in most of Christie's fiction. Match-making is a persistent motif in her work, for no marriageable character gets off without finding the "right" mate. Christie herself was committed to the traditional roles for men and women, to marriage and the family. Admittedly, she was not a feminist. With a wry laugh, she dismisses the "gains" of the "so-called" modern liberation movements which permit women to work as hard as men.

As a young child Agatha had a tendency to idealize and romanticize human relationships—especially those of family and the marriage bond. A home-body from girlhood, Christie pursued the protected kind of relationship normally found then in marriage. In fact, for young women who had grown up during those late Victorian years, marriage was the culmination of all their fantasies as well as the very real means to a lifetime of security.

The total impact of Agatha Christie's environment tended to foster marriage as the end toward which all parental effort was directed. From Auntie-Grannie, to mother and elder sister—the message was consistent—a good match ensures the future. Agatha's sister, Madge, had married well. James Watts was almost family, and he had the added advantage of being the heir to the Watts' fortune.

Mrs. Miller's attention, efforts and wiles were all directed to the marriage-game wherein she hoped to help her inexperienced daughter Agatha find and select a suitable mate. After Agatha had spent over a year in finishing school in Paris and had had a coming-out in Cairo, Mrs. Miller had fond hopes that her youngest daughter would marry at least as well as her sister had. But when the popular and well-courted Agatha finally chose from several suitors, she picked a stranger and a man without money. We know from accounts in both *Unfinished Portrait* and the *Autobiography* that Mrs. Miller did not approve of Archibald Christie. He was a "stranger" to a family that had found success in making matches within a known circle. She voiced concern that this young man would not take care of her daughter (and, of course, time proved her to be right).

The suitor selected by Agatha was a handsome, energetic and most ambitious young man. "Archie" Christie, an officer in the military, came from an unprepossessing background—an Irish mother and a British father who had made a career in the military and had seen service in India. The fact that "Archie" had no money of his own almost prevented the match; and at one point, when Agatha and he took stock of their incomes, they almost called the marriage off. But Agatha, very much the romantic and strongly under the influence of her lover, eloped with Christie in 1914 on Christmas Eve.

Her expectations and disappointments in this marriage are candidly set forth in the marital struggles of Celia and Dermot in *Unfinished Portrait*. We learn about the difficult financial adjustments the young couple had to make and the stresses of post-war society. But, most of all, we discover that Agatha suffered great loneliness, as she became more and more alienated from her husband, who was preoccupied with his own affairs. As a result, she reverted to childhood habits of slipping into her fantasy world for company; her imaginary companions ultimately developed into characters in her stories. Thus, she began to write as an outlet for her fantasies, as a compensation for partial rejection by her husband, but when surprisingly her books began to sell, she wrote to augment the family income.

Lifelong habits were too strong to break, for whenever Agatha had problems, she went to her mother for advice and consolation. Preoccupied with job advancement and the fulfillment of personal goals, Archibald Christie was not one to dwell on his wife's needs; so in a sense, Agatha remained strongly dependent upon her mother for emotional support. Consequently, when Mrs. Miller died in 1926, Agatha went into a severe depression. She was away from her husband for periods of time as she attempted to sort out her mother's affairs at Torquay. Disconsolate and alone, her mental health deteriorated. Depressed by the death of her strongest support, isolated by her grief, weakened by ill health and overwork, Agatha suffered a breakdown.

Her world totally collapsed a few months later when

Archibald Christie demanded a divorce so he could be free to marry the young Miss Nancy Neele. Agatha was taken completely by surprise, never suspecting that her husband would do such a thing to *her*! Her reactions ranged from disbelief to guilt, for she felt that she herself was to blame for breaking one of the "marriage rules" reiterated time and time again by both her mother and Auntie-Grannie: never leave your husband alone; never give him time and opportunity for other women. Her guilt increased as she considered the effects a divorce might have on her eight year old daughter.

During this period Agatha suffered untold grief and frequent periods of disorientation. *Unfinished Portrait* recounts the depths of the strain on her psyche. (Her second husband, Sir Max Mallowan, says in his *Memoirs* that the details of the break-up of her first marriage are realized quite well in *Unfinished Portrait*.)[8] The very fact that Christie avoided any reference in her *Autobiography* to the crises that ensued is itself telling. A vulnerable person who embarrassed easily even in her late years, she scrupulously avoided any mention of the events of December 1926. At this time she was coping with the loss of her mother, and then she had to deal with rejection by her husband. Suddenly, bereft of all her emotional supports she found herself alone and desperate.

A strange scenario, very much like one of her own mystery plots, was enacted before the public eye. Set in motion, either consciously or unconsciously by Agatha herself, a series of events occurred which might have led to the arrest of Colonel Christie for murder—the murder of his wife!

On the surface, the Christies were the picture of happy married life. Archie's continued success in the "City" and Agatha's royalties from her books gave both of them a measure of affluence and freedom to develop their individual interests. The Christies had acquired a palatial home called "Styles" in honor of her first book. Their prosperity brought in its train servants, automobiles, a secretary for Agatha and new friends. Then on December 5, 1926, Archibald Christie went off to spend the weekend in Godalming at Hurtmore Cottage, the home of Mr. and Mrs. James; among the other houseguests was Nancy Neele, the woman he planned to marry. It is possible that before his departure a terrible argument broke out between

Archie and Agatha over his decision to marry Nancy Neele. That evening Agatha Christie left Styles carrying a small bag and drove off alone in her bottle-nosed grey Morris.

The next morning her car was found abandoned on the edge of a cliff overlooking a pool. For two days police searched for her, even dragging the pool for her body, yet she was nowhere to be found. Finally on December 7 word reached the press that the famous mystery writer had vanished. The *Daily Mail* offered a £100 reward for information leading to her whereabouts. An investigation revealed that Mrs. Christie, before leaving home, had left three letters: one to her brother-in-law, Campbell Christie, saying that she was not well and was going to a spa in Yorkshire; another to her secretary, Miss Fisher; and a third to her husband. The contents of the second and third letters were never revealed, but the letter to Colonel Christie was "sealed" by the police—apparently, this letter disclosed her reasons for leaving home, and according to the press, placed her husband in a highly suspicious light.

Colonel Christie was further implicated in his wife's disappearance when her secretary acknowledged that she telephoned him at Hurtmore Cottage to tell him of Mrs. Christie's departure. In a recent article on the case, Ritchie Calder, who was a cub reporter at the time, says that at the cottage "a dinner party was in progress. This was more than just an assignation; it was what the household described as an 'engagement' party for Colonel Christie and Miss Neele. He was called from the table, took the call, made abrupt apologies and drove off in his car."[9] Police then checked the distance between where Mrs. Christie's car was found abandoned and empty and the weekend cottage and decided that the two could have met. The inference here is that Colonel Christie was suspected of foul play.

Fortunately Mrs. Christie was discovered alive and well nine days later at the Harrowgate Hydro, a Yorkshire spa. She was said to be suffering from amnesia, having registered at the spa under another name. But the bizarre touch was the fact that she was registered as Mrs. *Neele*, the surname of the "other woman." A *New York Times* correspondent interviewed the father of Nancy Neele who expressed consternation over the involvement of his daughter: "I cannot hazard any theory why Mrs. Christie used my family's name.... My daughter, Nancy, is naturally upset about it and so are we all. There is not the slightest reason for associating Nancy with the disappearance of Mrs. Christie."[10] But of course the public *did* associate the Neele name with Agatha's disappearance as the press focused on the nature of Miss Neele's relationship with Colonel Christie.

After Colonel Christie and the police had found Agatha at the Harrowgate Spa she was taken to her sister's home, Abney Hall, in Cheshire. Madge and Jimmy Watts came to her rescue, firmly closing the gates of their estate as the family went into seclusion. A lecturer in neurology, Dr. Donald Core of Manchester University, was called in to see Agatha and issued the following statement:

After careful examination of Mrs. Christie this afternoon, we have formed the opinion that she is suffering from an unquestionably genuine loss of memory, and that for her future welfare she should be spared anxiety and excitement.[11]

But the public was not satisfied with what seemed a rather simple explanation. A great uproar broke out over the disappearing and reappearing act of Agatha Christie. A widespread rumor implying that this disappearance was a publicity stunt to tout Agatha's latest detective novel aroused the ire of many Britishers who voiced their indignation at this supposed hoax by posting letters to the newspapers. In fact, some taxpayers invoking their rights pressed for damages against Christie for wasting £1000 of their money. The *Westminster Gazette* even published the divergent opinion of two leading medical specialists who discredited the loss of memory theory:

Whatever the cause of Mrs. Christie's extraordinary behavior, it was not loss of memory.... A person who has lost his or her memory may lose all recollection of identity... but he or she would be in such a state of distress that it would be apparent to everybody and they would not calmly manufacture a new identity, as Mrs. Christie did with such completeness.[12]

Strange facts concerning Mrs. Christie's behavior at the spa tended to cast doubt on the loss of memory theory. Guests observed that she had a great deal of money at her disposal—

this seemed to indicate some rational planning. She was wearing new clothes, including evening dresses and accessories. Then she appeared to be at ease, dancing and singing—even playing the piano and singing along with the band on occasion during the evening. One wonders here if the "shy" Christie under normal circumstances would have been so gregarious. The clincher, however, was Mrs. Christie's use of the Neele name, for as Calder points out, "the touch was freakish but it could not be coincidence."[13]

What really happened? During the course of her disappearance, various people offered theories but Edgar Wallace's is the most plausible. He contended that her action was "a typical case of 'mental reprisal' on somebody who has hurt her."[14] Wallace believed that Mrs. Christie had suffered an "hysterical breakdown." Hysteria is a likely diagnosis; given the circumstances Mrs. Christie may well have desired subconsciously either to become the woman whom her husband preferred or to punish him for his rejection of her. Whether brought on by amnesia, hysteria, or rational intent the disappearance produced the *same effect*—to focus on Colonel Christie and the woman with whom he was involved, and to place on the front page of just about every newspaper in England and abroad the name of the woman.

Another dimension of the issue is developed in *Unfinished Portrait*. The heroine of this autobiographical work is most disturbed when her husband pushed for divorce under the condition that the name of the other woman never be mentioned. He asks his wife to divorce him using the usual evidence—a trumped up case of infidelity in a sordid hotel using a paid model to represent the unnamed woman. The name of the real woman is never to be dragged through the mud. The heroine rejects this plan as dishonest, contending that real lovers should be open in their profession of devotion to each other. In reality, though not in the romance, Agatha Christie brought the woman's name to the attention of the whole world.

Now we come to a most bizarre and sinister explanation of the disappearance: foul play or threats of foul play. A second dimension is the suggestion in *Unfinished Portrait* that the husband may be slowly driving his wife crazy, and that at one point he gives tacit approval to his wife's potential suicide. At the point of distraction, she asks him what she should do—a look on his part is enough to reinforce the concept of suicide. Did Agatha Christie herself plan to commit suicide and then when faced with the reality change her mind? Or did her fertile imagination and overstimulated creative brain suggest the plan of a faked suicide to look like murder? This latter concept was already deeply imbedded in the consciousness of Agatha Christie, and it was to become an idée fixe in later years as one of the dominant motifs running through her detective stories. The implications of this theory are grim: did Archie try to drive his wife to the verge of suicide and thus free himself for his lover? Did Agatha, pushed into a desperate corner in the life and death struggle with her cruel husband, fight back with her cunning plan of revenge—a faked suicide made to look like murder?

These theories are possible. Agatha may very well have acted out her fantasies in any number of ways, particularly with those methods she knew best—careful plotting of situation and character in a potential murder mystery. A shy woman who was no match vocally for her husband, she used this incident as her way of communicating with him—whether she was in complete control of her faculties or whether in fact she was suffering from hysteria.

Although Agatha Christie never disappeared again, she continued to explore the concept of hidden or exchanged identity in her fiction. Characters in her stories and novels repeatedly assume other identities; disguises are employed as cover-ups in her mystery stories. The trauma of personal amnesia was sufficiently subdued for Agatha to use the loss of memory idea successfully in her fiction. (Much earlier she had used the real and faked amnesia as a motif in *The Secret Adversary.*) In *Giant's Bread,* published in 1930 under the pseudonym of Mary Westmacott, the main character suffers from the only genuine case of memory loss in her fiction; his amnesia is brought on by the double effect of an accident and the rejection of a loved one. The startling parallels between this case and the author's own memory lapse can only be hypothesized. One can presume, however, that the issue was still very much with her in 1930.

Archibald Christie and Agatha Miller Christie were divorced in 1928. He married Nancy Neele two weeks later. During the years following the disappearance incident and the divorce, Agatha had to adjust to the reality of failure. The marriage game had been played, and she had lost. Although she made an adjustment which eventually enabled her to enter another match, it was not without regret. Throughout her *Autobiography* she laments her loss, even conjuring up what might have been if she had not been so remiss. She married again in 1930, this time choosing a younger man.

VI. The Second Spring

The second spring marked by her marriage to Max E.L. Mallowan, a young archeologist, put her back into the marriage game. This time she followed the rules, accompanying her husband on his expeditions instead of leaving him alone for any extended periods. With a husband and a home, life was now complete again. Agatha went on to write some of her best work during this prime period of the 30s. This time she had a supportive mate who read her work, criticized it and encouraged her.

During that forty-five year period of her second marriage, she found support in her husband. Speaking of their marriage in his *Memoirs*, Mallowan says: "Few men know what it is to live in harmony beside an imaginative, creative mind which inspires life with zest."[15] When Agatha first met her second husband in 1930, she was travelling alone on her way to Baghdad. From there she travelled to Ur to visit Leonard Wooley and his wife, who had invited her to see their dig. She returned for a second visit the following year; this time she met one of Wooley's assistants, Max Mallowan; they fell in love and were married that year.

Yet this marriage, in some respects, seemed an unlikely match: Agatha was sixteen years older than Max and was still recuperating from the crisis of the divorce. Even Mallowan acknowledges that the divorce was an experience in which "deep scars left marks that never wholly disappeared."[16]

Although she continued to suffer pangs of guilt over the failure of that first marriage, Agatha managed to deal with it in her own way. In his *Memoirs*, Max Mallowan says that in 1944 when Archibald Christie's second wife died, Agatha wrote him a sincere note of consolation. He was touched by it and said that he hoped she had not begrudged him those sixteen years with Nancy Neele.[17] That very same year Agatha wrote what she claimed was the work which gave her the greatest satisfaction, *Absent in the Spring*—a romance published under the Westmacott pseudonym. This novel focuses on the pain and defeat that a middle-aged woman suffers when she realizes that her husband really loved another woman more than he loved her, that he cherished the memory of that dead woman; and that though he had remained her husband, their marriage was a failure. What Agatha Christie seems to be doing here is assuring herself that her own divorce was the best course. The heroine of the novel could well be a projection of self, triggered by Nancy Neele Christie's demise, in which she imagined what might have happened had she convinced Archie *not* to pursue the divorce. She could be projecting how she might have felt if she had to face the fact that she was not really loved. Very possibly this work, like *Unfinished Portrait*, enabled Christie to "write out" that painful period in her life in the form of a literary catharsis.

For Agatha, marriage to Max Mallowan was a "second spring" because she was able to rebuild her life with a person who complemented her in many ways. She was the romantic; he was the realist, with scientific training. And marriage to an archeologist provided opportunity for travel and for collecting—two of Agatha's penchants. She traveled with him to the Middle-east on all of his expeditions and made herself useful by photographing and cleaning their finds. He read all of her novels, offering suggestions freely. And she created for both of them a comfortable physical world—redecorating and then maintaining a commodious abode. Her novels reflect the same kind of preoccupation with reconstructing worlds, complete with her own setting, characters and social situations.

A backward glance at the major forces operating in Agatha Christie's personal life reveals that those in the beginning were the most important. Her personality, character and interests were formed in childhood. She became a romantic—sensitive and vulnerable emotionally, yet stalwart in her Victorian values. The women, especially in her childhood and developing years—nurses, her mother, auntie-grannie, her elder sister—each contributed to her nurturance. She grew up perceiving herself as a person who needed to be taken care of. The environment of the home and of the small town tended to reinforce totally what she learned from the people in her life.

Although her character was formed by the time she met Archibald Christie, this relationship affected her developing view of men and marriage. And the fact that a sensitive creature like Agatha could enter into a second marriage after defeat is a testament to those values she learned in girlhood— the need for home and husband, the need to assume the adjunct role for a strong man. The fortuitous marriage to Max Mallowan created a positive atmosphere in which to write— an atmosphere where discipline and creativity were respected. Of Agatha Christie, one might say, that she never really left her childhood home; for in her fiction she is still there rearranging it, redecorating and breathing life into those memorable people who are reincarnated in her stories.

Chapter II
From Fairy Tales to Detective Fiction

Fantasy had always been part of Agatha Christie's life. As a young girl playing alone in the environs of the large family home in Torquay, she had a host of imaginary friends who enjoyed daily adventures. Christie herself felt that this aspect of her growing years was so memorable that she spends chapters describing these adventures in her *Autobiography* and in two of her romances, *Unfinished Portrait* and *Giant's Bread*. Her fantasies were encouraged by her mother and her older sister who indulged in her games and introduced her to the vast world of fiction. Agatha's unusual powers of imagination coupled with a basic personal shyness led her to pursue creative writing where she found a natural outlet for her fantasies.

But why did Agatha Christie write detective fiction? Two highly significant determinants were operating in the early twentieth century when she began writing. First, detective fiction had become increasingly popular and acceptable among the middle class reading public, and Conan Doyle's Sherlock Holmes was making literary history. Secondly, those staunch Victorian values Agatha had absorbed so completely from her family provided that structure needed for creating fictive worlds in which the forces of good and evil are so clearly distinguished.

The delights of childhood are recurring subjects in the Christie canon; they are especially fleshed out in *Unfinished Portrait, Giant's Bread* and the *Autobiography*. In each of these works the child's world is far more exciting than the "real" world outside the confines of home and garden. The child plays with a hoop which can become almost anything; the child travels to the ends of the earth in a toy cart or on an imaginary railroad complete with handmade timetables and assigned stops. Imaginary children people the little empire with an imaginary mother, Mrs. Green, who cares for each of them. Such was Christie's little world, obviously a secure and private place.

One of the most charming vignettes in the *Autobiography* is a typical scene with Mrs. Miller reading Dickens aloud to her daughter Agatha, then nodding with sleep and picking up again to finish reading. Actually, Agatha came from a family of women readers—her mother, grandmother and sister not only read for their own pleasure but also read aloud to one another. A strong oral tradition prevailed. "Auntie Grannie" was never without an appropriate cautionary tale to admonish her youngest grandchild. Agatha's mother, Clarisssa, appears to have been a rather gifted storyteller who could spin a yarn at a moment's notice. Agatha recalls one exciting story, "The Case of the Missing Candle," which remained unfinished because her mother was interrupted in telling the story. Her elder sister, Madge, was a raconteur in her own right—a marvelous maker of tales, later to publish a few stories for the periodical market.

Agatha was an avid reader, having taught herself to read by the time she was five years old. She loved fairy tales and romances. In the *Autobiography* she speaks nostalgically of reading the *Yellow Fairy Book* and the *Blue Fairy Book*, two of the several edited by Andrew Lang in the 1890s. Actually, Agatha had an enviable library for a young girl—many books she received as gifts and others were inherited from her older brother and sister. In her autumn years as she was writing *Postern of Fate*, Christie wove into this mystery story a catalogue of the children's books that could have been found in her own library at Ashfield. (This novel contains a lively commentary on the values of children's literature; it really is an apogee to the delights of reading.)

The fairy tale, a staple of Christie's nursery library, attracted Agatha's imagination with its mysterious adventures, strange people and creatures and its marvelous story-telling techniques packed with action, wonders and rigid simplistic morality. The fairy tale provided a hero or heroine setting out through fantastic realms on a quest involving struggle, tests, dangers and eventual success over evil antagonists (the witch, the evil genius, a monster, despotic stepmother, a giant). Within the pages of the fairy tales, young Agatha found the war of good and evil; supernatural spirits disguised as humans; the ability of some beings to change themselves into any shape at will; the gruesome catalogue of violence, mutilations and deaths—all related in an objective, cold-blooded manner devoid of emotional involvement on the part of the reader. Here, Christie found the theme of disguise in the shape-shiftings and transformations; here, she found the puzzle in embryo; here, also, she found the success story with its materialistic victories—the evil vanquished, a princess rescued, a treasure secured, a kingdom obtained, a villain destroyed. Within those fairy tales relating the exploits of a hero unravelling a set of riddles or performing a series of impossible tasks, Agatha found the seed of early detection or riddle solving—to be brought to a high peak of development in the exploits of her sleuths.

Her interest in books was reinforced by the family's encouragement of reading aloud and acting out selections from fiction. Then too the opportunity to attend the theatre as well as to see the masterful pantomime artists of the day gave the developing Agatha some insight into dialogue and mannerisms. Later as she engaged in prolific periods of writing, she *talked* out her books—listening to how the story would sound as much as to how it would read.

During the period between 1900 and 1920 when Agatha was consuming a steady diet of fiction, she had the opportunity to peruse the classics as well as current publications. In 1906 the Carnegie Public Library opened in Torquay, providing the populace with a vast collection of books. Private libraries such as Boots and W.H. Smith catered to the tastes of the enlarging circle of middleclass readers. And, of course, secondhand book stores abounded, filling the needs of those who wanted to acquire books cheaply. But perhaps the greatest impact on the national reading level was the increasing success of periodicals like the *Strand* and *Punch* in satisfying the tastes of the day for both novels and short fiction. These magazines were consumed by the masses of middle class readers, especially women, who had the time and interest to absorb the plethora of romance and detective fiction on the market.

In her *Autobiography* Christie recalls specific works that

she enjoyed, although she is understandably vague as to the exact time period for individual selections. She remembers her sister Madge recounting the *Leavenworth Case*, published by Anna Katharine Green in 1878, to her when she was only eight years old. Other classics of detective fiction which she shared with her sister include *The Mystery of the Yellow Room* by Gaston Leroux and the Arsene Lupin stories of Maurice Leblanc, both published in 1907. She also enjoyed the Paul Beck stories by M. McDonnell Bodkin (1898). Again, it was her sister Madge who introduced her to the "Master," Arthur Conan Doyle in the Sherlock Holmes saga. Detective fiction was becoming increasingly popular and prolific by the turn of the century. Julian Symons believes that "what crime literature offered to its readers for half a century from 1890 onward was a reassuring world in which those who tried to disturb the established order were always discovered and punished.... Behind the conscious Victorian and Edwardian adherence to a firmly fixed hierarchical society, there lay a deep vein of unease about the possible violent overturn of that society, especially by anarchists."[1] Consequently, mystery fiction or crime literature fulfilled a need and claimed an enormous audience. Writers were quite literally drawn to the genre. The *Book Review Digest* of 1918 reveals the vast number of books and authors writing detective fiction just prior to Agatha Christie's first publication.

Looking back almost one hundred years to the beginnings of detective fiction, to the works of major writers who shaped the genre, we can see how Christie was influenced by her reading. By 1915 when she began writing *The Mysterious Affair at Styles*, Christie had consumed scores of detective stories. Impressions gleaned from her voracious reading were eventually to coalesce into the famed Christie concept and method of detective fiction. It was from these early writers of the genre that Christie was to derive her greatest inspiration: Poe, Gaboriau, Dickens, Collins, Green, Rinehart, Doyle, Leroux and Chesterton. Admittedly, Doyle was the "master," yet Christie was influenced by the others as well.

Edgar Allan Poe, the undisputed Father of the Detective Story, influenced all of his successors—including Agatha Christie. Poe introduced the basic features of the detective story: the character and method of the amateur sleuth, the concept of the sleuth's companion, the puzzle and the specific devices and motifs which were to become conventions of the genre. Whether Christie was influenced directly by the works of Poe or indirectly by his heirs, the parallels between her work and that of Poe are significant.

First, Poe established the character of the armchair detective. His Chevalier Auguste Dupin was able to solve inscrutable problems through his application of deductive reasoning and expert intuition. By developing Dupin through several stories including "The Murders in the Rue Morgue" (1841), "The Mystery of Marie Roget" (1842) and "The Purloined Letter" (1844), Poe created a recognizable and memorable character. Dupin became the prototype for the brilliant sleuth who contrasts sharply in his intellectual ability with the inept official police. Like Dupin, Christie's long-lived Hercule Poirot is gifted with astute powers of observation and deduction, and though a Belgian he is often mistaken for a Frenchman. His "little grey cells" are still his most outstanding features, even though he is developed in greater physical detail than Dupin.

Poe also bequeathed into the genre the companion to the sleuth who serves as a sounding board, a foil and a narrator. Later to be known as the "Watson" figure after Sherlock Holmes' assistant, this companion had his genesis with Poe. Through the years this character became a mere stooge, a foil who was usually clumsy and inadequate—thus setting off the brilliance and effectiveness of the master sleuth. We see a parallel here with Christie's master detective, Hercule Poirot, and the friend who assisted him on many of his cases, Captain Hastings. Although at times Hastings appears terribly average in ability, he is not a mere stooge; for Christie strives to create a humanizing background and a family life for Hastings that is quite separate from Poirot.

The convention of the confrontation scene in which the successful sleuth presents a resumé of the crime in the presence of all those involved—his companion, the police, all the suspects, and the murderer—also comes from Poe. This method, which had worked so successfully for Dupin, later became Hercule Poirot's finesse. Poirot's flair for the dramatic distinguishes his performance from that of his predecessor, however. His reenactment of the crime points to a most likely suspect, but then he cleverly reverses himself to reveal the true murderer—often someone who appears beyond reproach.

In addition, Poe was responsible for the creation of certain motifs which have since become conventions in the field of detective fiction. Foremost among them is the locked room motif—the concept of a murder victim in a closed room which has been locked from within. Christie used this device numerous times, but notably in her first novel, *The Mysterious Affair at Styles*. Another device which Poe used successfully and which became a favorite of Christie's is the use of the village setting. Typically, the entire community becomes enmeshed in the nefarious deed committed in the vicinity involving one of their well-known neighbors. In fact, the village is the most frequently used setting in the Christie canon. One other device for which Poe became famous in "The Purloined Letter" is the concealing of an important document in an obvious place in a disguised form. Christie used this device in her first novel when the murderer conceals evidence disguised as a fireplace spill (a paper whisp used for starting the fire). A humorous variation of the same device is found in Christie's "The Affair of the Christmas Pudding."

Of all the contributions Poe made to the form of the detective story, perhaps his greatest was in the construction of the basic puzzle. The quest for the perfect puzzle fueled Christie's imagination too and eventually won for her distinction as a designer of mystery puzzles. Both Poe and Christie had an affinity for the unravelling of conundrums; they were attracted by mottoes or cryptic messages which could be used for locating treasures, clues and vital documents. Since the puzzle is actually the very heart of the detective story, it is the single factor which has remained constant in the continued development of the genre.

Poe's legacy was passed on by Emile Gaboriau who produced ten novels over a period of eight years (1865-1873), each developing the sleuth in greater detail and deepening Poe's suggestive Parisian scene into fully developed backgrounds. Gaboriau not only developed the character and skills of the detective hero in his police novels ("romans policiers"), but he also heightened the rivalry between corrupt officialdom and the honest sleuth.

Unlike Poe, who stressed the crime itself, Gaboriau focused entirely on the gyrations of the sleuth. Gaboriau begins with a gruesome murder; then the detective is introduced and the puzzle presented. The procedure is similar to the one used by Christie, who, like Gaboriau, preferred the scope of the novel to the more limiting short story form.

Maps and diagrams of the murder scene are Gaboriau's trademark. Setting in motion a new trend as a master of detectival devices, his master sleuth makes casts of suspect's footprints in melting snow by quickly scraping plaster off walls and mixing this with water to take instant impressions. He correctly obtains the time of murder despite tampered clocks with altered hands. Following Gaboriau's lead, other writers adapted his "scientific" techiques to their own works, Christie among them. We have seen repeated evidence of her preference for maps and diagrams in her works. Although Christie's detectives never made any plaster casts, there are instances where Poirot uses scientific means to trace evidence. And Christie also experimented in her novels with tricks involving the alteration of time; the most memorable is *The Clocks* where the cunning criminal uses many clocks set at different hours as an elaborate smoke-screen to confuse investigators.

As the master of disguise, Gaboriau's detective is capable of infiltrating even a closed environment. Though Conan Doyle was to pick up this characteristic, Christie used it to lesser degree. Upon occasion Hercule Poirot disguises himself, but in a Christie story it is usually the murderer rather than the detective who assumes a disguise. Both Gaboriau and Christie characters masquerade under false pretenses. They assume identities of others completely, or they function under temporary disguise for either deception or self-protection. Thus it becomes the task of the master sleuth to smoke out the disguise and blow the cover of the deceiver.

Meticulous trial scenes with expert dialogue and dramatic questioning are distinctive features of Gaboriau's novels. Through his own experience as a reporter covering the courts, Gaboriau translated into fiction well-realized courtroom scenes. Aside from her famous story "Witness for the Prosecution," Christie did not dwell on the courtroom scene. She chose instead the local inquest, a less formal setting requiring less knowledge of the intricacies of the law.

Christie was more like Gaboriau in positioning crime in a domestic locale—in embroiled family scandals and legacy hunting, often relating the sins of the father on to the present generation. She too chose well-placed families—though not as exclusively as did Gaboriau.

Of his various contributions to the development of the genre, Gaboriau's treatment of the master sleuth as an honest professional was to have the greatest impact on those who succeeded him in France. In England, Charles Dickens, who had a life-long interest in crime and police work, had already created the detective in *Bleak House* (1853) who is considered the first fictional English detective—Inspector Bucket.

Charles Dickens was fascinated by the work of the newly formed London police force. He visited the police, interviewed them for material to publish in his magazine *Household Words* and honored them by praising their work. In particular, Dickens became interested in Inspector Field, a member of the detective force affiliated with Scotland Yard. This real detective became the model for Dickens' fictional sleuth, Inspector Bucket, who made his appearance in fourteen of sixty-five chapters in *Bleak House*. Bucket is thoroughly British in his values—solid, hard working and persevering.

Agatha Christie was fascinated by *Bleak House*. Doubtless it left an enduring impression on her as a young reader. Aside from the positive attitude toward the police which Christie shared with Dickens, she also derived two important devices from him: use of the Least Likely Person ploy and the confrontation drama. The use of the Least Likely Person to commit the crime appears so often in Christie's works that eventually it became *her* trademark. Springing from Poe's meticulous resumé of the crime, Dickens' summation was dramatized to provide excitement and to sustain the mystery until the final hour. Bucket, and also Christie's Poirot, are seen assembling implicated personae together in one room, then slowly, by revealing the sequence of events in the correct light, they unveil the identity of the murderer.

From Dickens, Christie may also have gained some insight into developing a female assistant to the sleuth. Inspector Bucket does not employ the traditional companion, but he has a resourceful companion in his wife. Mrs. Bucket shares her husband's professional life and is herself adept at shadowing suspects, picking up clues, and retrieving vital evidence. Many of Christie's amateur sleuths are couples, a clever girl and a young man, who work together to unravel the puzzle. Poirot is also fond of attaching himself to an impressionable young woman who will act as his helper; he works as well with Mrs. Ariadne Oliver, a middle-aged writer of detective fiction who likes to try her hand at the *real* thing. With the creation of the husband and wife detective team, Tommy and Tuppence Beresford, Christie gave equal prowess to both her male and female amateur sleuths.

The major difference between Dickens and Gaboriau is, primarily, in the image of the police. The scorn the "romans policiers" projected for the official French police contrasts sharply with the low key praise of the police in Dickens' work, for, as we indicated earlier, Dickens admired the London police. Although Agatha Christie was selective in the members of the police force that she chose to admire—usually those from the "upper ranks," she is not highly critical of those who are either slow-moving or lower-class. Her Inspector Battle of the CID is, in fact, very much like his ancestor, Inspector Bucket.

The tradition of the "honest professional" detective lives on in Wilkie Collins' *The Moonstone* (1868). His Sergeant Cuff is drawn on low-keyed lines. Like Bucket, he spurns all melodramatic poses, emerging as a - believable character. Cuff's forte is his passion for collecting evidence and leaving no stone unturned; he is a stalker—a human bloodhound. Upon entering the scene of the crime, his method involves interviewing the entire household from family, to guests, to servants in his quest for evidence. This was to become the standard procedure of Christie's detectives as well.

The action is expertly developed around a central puzzle in Collins' work. As Sergeant Cuff works on the suspects one by one, the pieces of the puzzle are shifted around—teasing the reader with flashes of suspicion here and there as suspects are relentlessly examined. This process was subsequently adopted by Christie's Poirot. A variant of the same process involves burdening the detective with differing accounts of the same events by different suspects. In this kind of situation both Sergeant Cuff and Hercule Poirot manage to cut through the veneer of deception to reveal the truth.

Besides shaping the plot and the concept of the detective, *The Moonstone* provided the basic motif of the theft of the precious jewel. Collins' heirs breathed new life into the motif in their own fiction. Whether directly from Collins or from Doyle (who followed him), Agatha Christie used the loss of a stolen ruby as the basis for her story "The Christmas Pudding."

Another feature generated from *The Moonstone* also appealed to Christie—the milieu of the upper class home with its mid-Victorian opulence. Dickens had used this setting successfully, then Collins and his successors developed the closed social circle of the country home with its servants, its ambience and its pastoral setting. For Christie, the home—especially the country home—was the ideal place for a murder!

From the first female writer of detective stories, Anna Katharine Green, came reinforcement for many of the devices employed by predecessors as well as a unique legacy of the female mystique in detective fiction. Agatha Christie acknowledged positive impressions of Green's *The Leavenworth Case* (1878)[2] a well plotted detective story featuring two sisters and a persistent detective who attempts to discover if one of the two women is a murderer. Although Christie praised the characterization in the novel, the influence of Green was probably significant in several other respects.

Anna Katharine Green, like Agatha Christie, was from a well-to-do and socially prominent family; as the daughter of a New York criminal lawyer, she was in a position to know about crime. Her fictional presentation bears some similarity to the Poe-Gaboriau tradition. She shared their obsession with crime in high society, the kind that is plotted with intricate detail and with great emphasis placed on the role of the detective.

By providing more female characters with a feminine point of view and psychology, Green set the precedent in detective fiction for those female writers who followed. Along with credible women characters, Green developed two female amateur sleuths—Miss Violet Strange and Miss Amelia Butterworth. These prototypes may well have influenced Mary Roberts Rinehart's female snoops and also contributed to the development of Christie's Miss Jane Marple.

Another achievement of Green's was her development of the master sleuth, Mr. Gryce, who appears in a series of novels. This American policeman bears characteristics of his British counterparts, Dickens' Inspector Bucket and Collins' Sergeant Cuff. A middle-class, honest professional, Mr. Gryce has a sharp eye for clues, great insight into human nature and a dogged determination. Christie's Inspector Battle moves within the same tradition.

In Green's novels, Christie would have encountered several of the more refined conventions of the genre: the Most Likely and the Least Likely Suspect ploys; the highly complex puzzle and its solution; the brilliant sleuthing and deductions of a master detective; the sleuth's use of assistants; disguises and mistaken identity; a highly charged courtroom scene; the sketch of the murder scene; the side-stepping of red herrings by the wily sleuth; and the shifting of suspicion from one suspect to another.

Christie's love of the country estate milieu as a favorite staging for her murders follows traditions set forth by both Miss Green and Mary Roberts Rinehart. Rinehart also portrayed the socialite world and its interlocking relationships. In *The Circular Staircase* (1908), a spinster's holiday in a rented country house turns into an experience of terror, murder and detection. The world of the rich, the country club, and leisure class ambience is minutely portrayed as Miss Rachel Innes attempts to discover the truth of various mysteries while she wages a secretive campaign to withhold evidence from the official detective. As a matter of fact, the meddling of this spinster brings her close to death when she becomes accidentally imprisoned in the secret chamber with the murderer.

Mary Roberts Rinehart's spinsters are modern incarnations of Miss Green's earlier Amelia Butterworth, that rich, highly placed spinster of inquisitive and forceful will. Christie follows the tradition of using a strong female brush to paint the environment of her spinsters and their lifestyle. The living habits, housekeeping duties and social functions of both Misses Innes and Butterworth are minutely delineated in the roomy, richly appointed habitats of both women. Whether prying into the affairs of others, playing games with the detectives, battling with maids and servants or jockeying young lovers into marriages, these patterns will appear again and again in the Christie canon.

The greatest literary influence upon Christie's detective fiction, however, was Arthur Conan Doyle's stories of the adventures of Sherlock Holmes. Captivated from girlhood by her older sister's recitations of the stories, Christie became an avid reader who pursued Holmes and his adventures with a passion. But she did more than simply enjoy Doyle's work; she absorbed ideas and methods which eventually shaped her own style of writing.

The world's most famous detective, Sherlock Holmes first appeared in 1887 in *A Study in Scarlet*, but it was not until Doyle began writing for the magazine market in the 1890s that his hero became famous. So completely did Holmes capture the imagination of readers that when Doyle attempted to "kill" him off, an outraged public forced Doyle to reclaim him. Then, for almost forty years Holmes and his adventures continued to fire the imagination of a massive reading public. Why? Essentially, Doyle humanized his detective to the point people began to think of him as a real person, and he presented his hero's adventures in a highly readable form.

In Doyle's detective stories, Christie had excellent models. Doyle blended the basic elements of character, setting and plot into a fascinating unity. But Christie was especially influenced by Doyle's conception of the detective and his assistant, by the racy style of the stories and by certain recurring motifs which were later to appear in her own stories.

The major innovation of the Holmes' saga was the creation of the highly intelligent and eccentric yet *human* figure of the master-sleuth himself. Possibly the characterization was so successful because Doyle had real life models. Doyle developed Holmes from two role models: Dr. Joseph Bell, who was his surgeon-teacher at the Edinburgh Infirmary and Doyle himself, who as a trained physician shared the method of observation and thought used by his fictional hero. To a degree, Doyle's conception of his sleuth was influenced also by Poe's Auguste Dupin who was a private investigator with a similar method, for both Holmes and Dupin share the Cartesian mind and the all-seeing eye.

But Holmes is much more human than Dupin. In spite of his elegant bearing and social graces, Holmes is not an aristocrat: his ancestors were country squires. On his mother's side, he was related to the great French artists, the Vernets. Even so, his background and his tastes were bourgeois. He was just as much at home in a Limehouse opium den as in a reception room of a palace. Consequently, readers could identify with Holmes who, though not their intellectual equal, was at least socially within their range of association.

The reader's awe for this brilliant man is also tempered by his sociability, and his foibles and eccentricities. Holmes' bachelor quarters at 221 B Baker Street served as a humble but cozy social center for clients, Inspectors from Scotland Yard, the Baker Street Irregulars (his reformed vigilante crew), not to mention the ubiquitous Mrs. Hudson, his housekeeper. Social but erratic, Holmes succumbed to fits of depression and cocaine addiction. And he was incredibly untidy: he frequently practiced shooting his revolver indoors and conducted various scientific experiments in the drawing room. All this made Holmes that much more human to his readers, who accepted him even *more* because of his faults.

Still Holmes was a genius. All his life he absorbed data from his laboratory experiments, his research into various aspects of crime, and his complete immersion in criminological matters. He was a walking encyclopedia of the history of crime, of criminals and their methods and of the skills required for successful crime prevention. He studied British law, yet he was also interested in geology, anatomy, horses, boxing, exotic flora and fauna, and the snakes of India among other subjects.

We can see some obvious parallels between Holmes and Hercule Poirot. Although Poirot's background is vague, he presents himself as a foreigner—a Belgian, with an illustrious past as the head of the Belgian police force. He is brilliant, like Holmes, and yet he too has many eccentricities. Though the reader may not identify personally with Poirot, his eccentricities permit the reader to laugh at him occasionally but to respect him always without being awed by his superiority. The humanizing touches—his love of hot chocolate, his absurd neatness, his physical ailments—all help to make him a more credible character. These humanizing devices Christie may well have learned from the master, Conan Doyle.

Other parallels abound between Holmes and Poirot. They both served a variety of clients. Holmes numbered among his clients dukes, duchesses, heads of royal houses, government leaders and Vatican officials. His cases were both public crimes of great importance and private cases. Holmes' services often reached the height of patriotism as when he restored the ancient crown of England in "The Musgrave Ritual" or recovered stolen naval documents. Poirot also performs in both the public and private sectors. Though he takes cases from lower class plaintiffs (as in "The Case of the Clapham Cook"), he prefers to serve the higher echelons of society and government. He not only foils spies who steal secret military documents but also solves the kidnapping of the British Prime Minister.

Holmes responded to praise and he readily accepted honors: he received a diamond ring from the reigning house of Holland; he was presented with a snuff box of old gold from the King of Bohemia; he was honored with the Legion of Honor from France; and Queen Victoria herself presented Holmes with an emerald stick-pin. As a rule, Holmes is too intellectual to be moved by praise or flattery; he scorns applause. Poirot appreciates praise and searches for it with comic conceit. Proud of his reputation, he is chagrined when people do not recognize his name. Proud also of honors received, he readily acknowledges his work done for royalty and foreign governments. His vain concern for appearance, health and reputation is pervasive.

Both Holmes and Poirot have an inside connection with Scotland Yard. The private investigator also listens to appeals from inspectors who seek help in solving difficult crimes. (Inspector Lestrade of Scotland Yard, who often works with Holmes, is a sallow rat-faced man whose garments are untidy and disarranged. Lestrade may well be the model for Christie's Inspector Japp.) Both Holmes and Poirot take a humorous, condescending air toward the inferior talents of their public colleagues, yet they do offer help, do solve the cases, and seldom take personal credit for the solutions. As a result, both Holmes and Poirot have ready access to the files, the laboratories, services and man-power of Scotland Yard's elaborate machinery. Though the sleuth can pin-point and corner the killer, the arrest must be made by the official arm; hence the usual combination of private and public detectives and police tightening the net around the criminals at the end of the stories. Holmes, in "The Three Garredibs," while searching through the "rogues gallery" to spot a criminal face, commends the Yard for its thoroughness and its resources but faults its lack of imagination and intuition. These are Poirot's feelings—exactly.

As private investigators, both Holmes and Poirot accept fees. They often take cases with no payment and sometimes expend their own funds to see that justice is obtained. It is a matter of record that Holmes sometimes asked for a fixed fee, no fee at all, or an exorbitant fee, as in the case of "The Priory School" where the Baker Street sleuth accepted a check for six thousand pounds from the Duke of Holderness. In fact, Holmes amassed such a large fortune from services rendered to the Royal Family of Scandinavia and the French Republic that these "alone would enable him to retire from practice altogether if he so wished." Poirot waxes so wealthy from fees charged that even as early as the period of *The Blue Train* he thinks of retirement. (Inspector Japp is amazed at the monetary success Poirot has made of the detective business.) A variety of motives spur the other Christie sleuths to snuff out crimes: Parker Pyne charges fees regularly as befits his shingle; Ariadne Oliver involves herself in various cases to oblige frantic friends and thus obtains further grist for her own creative mill.

The showman in Holmes could not resist theatrical effects and dramatic stagings, favored surprise effects to cap his cases and startle his clients, Watson, or the police. He hired actors to play out the drama outside Briony Lodge in the case of Irene Adler so that he could enter Irene's rooms as a wounded clergyman and discover the hiding place of the much sought-after photograph involving the King of Bohemia. He served up

the missing naval treaty under cover for breakfast to the
luckless client who had lost it, his honor, and his health in the
process. Poirot also has his theatrics and sensational effects.
In "The Harlequin Murders" Poirot hires an ensemble of actors
to enact through costumes and movements the events of the
murder at the costume ball. All of the staged confrontations at
the end of his cases are likewise theatrical productions with
Poirot enacting the role of impressario and magician
producing startling effects for his audience.

Holmes, as moral superman, could and did break the law to
obtain evidence in his cases: he had a complete house-breaking
kit for burgling the home of Charles Augustus Milverton in an
attempt to recover stolen love letters. He went beyond the limits
when he attempted to break and enter homes and even banks
as in "The Case of the Stockbroker's Clerk" and "The Case of
the Three Gables." Holmes could prevaricate, misrepresent
and conceal information from clients, suspects and police
when it suited his purpose. He could don a disguise, make love
and promise marriage to an unsuspecting maid just to squeeze
information out of the woman. In some adventures Holmes
even permitted death to occur when he could have prevented it.
He admitted he was responsible for the death of Dr. Grimesby
Roylott in "The Speckled Band." In another instance Holmes'
anger is so aroused at villainy that he deliberately shoots to
kill.

Christie also endows Poirot with extra-legal activities in
pursuance of justice, much to the horror of Captain Hastings
who frowns on lies, house-breaking, listening at doors, opening
other people's mail, to gain evidence or shake confessions out
of suspects. Poirot, when necessary, can enter rooms and
homes with subterfuge, lies and special pass keys. He is not
above hiring second-story men to burgle residences and
retrieve stolen or incriminating evidence. Poirot can readily
wink at the law, which ties the hands of the official police but
permits the private investigator a wide area of license. The
Belgian sleuth thinks nothing of hiring actors and staging
phony scenes to force confessions from murderers as was done
in *Cards on the Table.*

In rare instances, Holmes acted as judge and jury and let
the criminal go scot free. His compassion and conscience were

more on the side of the justified manslaughterer than on the victim and the law. He had compassion for James Ryder, the attendant at the Hotel Cosmopolitan who stole Lady Morcar's Blue Carbuncle, but was crushed with remorse at the realization of the cost of his crime. Holmes likewise allows the victim of Charles Augustus Milverton to shoot him dead and escape the consequences. Her act of judicial vengeance is justified by the tragedy brought down upon the woman and her husband by the vicious blackmailer. Thus, Holmes allows this victim to act as private executioner. As he admitted in "The Three Gables," Holmes could "compound a felony." The key to the murder of cruel Sir Eustace Brakenstall in "The Abbey Grange" is the defense of the terrorized wife by a male admirer, Captain Jack Crocker. When Holmes discovered that the tyrant was killed during his brutal attack on his wife by the friend, he helped to get the man off. Holmes justified his action by saying: "I had rather play tricks with the law of England... than with my own conscience."

Christie likewise permits some criminals to get away with their deeds: sometimes Poirot, as in "The Box of Chocolates," permits a correctly-motivated mother to escape the law after poisoning her homicidal son. In several other stories, such as "Witness for the Prosecution" and "Accident," the killers escape. Christie permits members of families to act as executioners of the bad seed in their midst—thus the lovely but homicidal movie star in *The Mirror Crack'd* is put to eternal sleep by her compassionate husband with the tacit approval of Miss Jane Marple. The murderer in the Christie story or novel may be permitted to exit gracefully through the unwritten code: escape from disgrace and the gallows by suicide, through poison, a process approved of and supported in many instances by Poirot himself. Consequently various killers are never brought to trial, having taken their own lives with assistance from the sleuth. Such was the quietus offered to the murderers in *The Murder of Roger Ackroyd* and *Peril at End House*.

Various incidental parallels abound between Doyle and Christie: Holmes began his residence in London in 1874 in Montague Street, near the British Museum. It was later that he moved to the famous 221 B Baker Street address. Poirot also lived at only two separate addresses in London. When Doyle tired of Holmes in 1893 he killed him off in the struggle with Moriarty. Public clamor, pressure from publishers and own interest prompted Doyle to resurrect Holmes, which he did in October 1903 in "The Empty House." Later in December 1904 we find that Holmes has retired to a farm on Sussex Downs to devote his last years to rest, bee-keeping and to write his book. Christie early in her career also destroys and resurrects Poirot. This sleuth in *The Big Four* pretends to die so that he may better work against his enemies: he returns disguised as his brother Achilles. Only at the end of this novel does the reader realize that both Christie and Poirot have "tricked" the reader.

The enduring charm of the Holmes stories stems from the well-sketched portrait of Dr. Watson. He is fully developed as an engaging character, fond of his comfort but a bit dull, and certainly not up to the intellectual measure of his companion. Yet this friend is a respectable, long-time sufferer from the jibes of his companion; he answers numerous calls on his intellectual powers (where he fails), and calls on his physical resources and his trusty revolver (where he succeeds). This friend is not only the chronicler of the master-sleuth and his exploits, but becomes himself a participant in most of the adventures. He serves admirably as a Boswell—for he translates for the reader—the detective's history, his appearance, his personality, his techniques and his adventures.

Dr. Watson is intimately involved in most of the cases of the sixty tales, in the housekeeping of 221 B Baker Street, in the action of the stories. Above all, Watson is deeply involved in the telling of the stories: for he selects the tales, changes names, dates and maintains a particular point of view, tone and deference. This is most unlike Captain Hastings who drifts in and out of the Poirot tales, who has little influence on action or results and who, as author, does not function in as important a role as Dr. Watson does. In fact, at one point Christie ships the unwieldly Hastings off to Argentina to get him out of the way.

Watson served many purposes in the Holmes' stories. He was primarily a contrast personality, a foil—to reflect the highlights of his companion's brilliant intellect and his methods. In addition, someone had to occupy the role of "dummy" in the dialectic that Holmes employed. He needed a "patsy" on whom to practice his theories. Also, the Dr. Watson figure provided a ready arsenal of false theories and false impressions—to demonstrate the wrong method—in contrast to the master-sleuth's right method. Thus, we see Watson picking up worthless clues, chasing red herrings and making wrong inferences because, though he is a doctor, he lacks the intuitive skills of Holmes. Watson serves to complicate the action of each story because his comments and observations merely confuse the issue for the reader; as a result, problems remain since Watson's comments do not serve to clarify them. In a sense, Watson becomes a scapegoat, for he is the butt of jokes. Even when the right path opens up, he fails to travel on it. The constant failures of Watson merely point up the impressiveness of Holmes' successes.

Watson also serves as the confidant who through constant dialogue opens up the mind of Holmes and keeps a running commentary on the story; he serves also as a chorus in that he often explains what is happening to the reader. Thus, the reader finds Watson's explanations and comments most clear. Furthermore, since Holmes seldom reveals his own evolving thought patterns until the end, it is necessary that the reader have an interpreter or translator of the master-sleuth. The function of the Boswell-Watson narrator is to universalize the hero so that the average reader will grasp the essentials, yet the interpreter must be both parochial and simplistic in his explanations so as to achieve maximum understanding and sympathy for the sleuth.

Of all the assistants to the sleuth that Christie employs, Captain Hastings is most like Dr. Watson. Hastings is developed, like Watson, as a credible person—he has an honorable war record and a successful courtship and marriage to his credit. So aware of the need for his friend to have a life of his own, Poirot even engineers the romance and sends him off with a wife to a ranch in Argentina. Hastings departs after *The Murder on the Links* in 1923, but returns conveniently for occasional visits and adventures with Poirot. However, he is not Poirot's only companion or assistant; Poirot often chooses young people on the scene to help him solve puzzles. In other respects, Hastings fulfills all the Watson-like functions—

serving as narrator, acting as foil, becoming the reader's substitute on the scene.

Christie's preference for a variety of helpers may well have sprung from Doyle's use of secondary assistants. In most of his cases Holmes draws upon a contingent of helpers who operate along with Watson; these include Holmes' brother, Mycroft; the Baker Street Irregulars; and even Porlock, one of his adversary's trusted henchmen. Poirot often pays special agents to secure vital information for him, though he frequently works without the typical Watson-figure. Miss Marple, notably, has no particular companion, but relies instead upon a host of acquaintances or paid assistants such as Lucy Eyelesbarrow, the young mathematician who accepts the challenge in *What Mrs. McGillicuddy Saw* (1957). By varying the sleuth's assistants, Christie avoided the potential boredom which might have developed by presenting a gallery of fresh characters to breathe new life into her stories.

The public's infatuation with Holmes and his cases came also from the marvellous structure of the tales themselves which are rightly masterpieces of the story-telling art. The plots are fast-moving, tightly-structured and contain a surprising number of bizarre and exotic incidents. The stories are replete with ordinary settings, yet a varied gallery of curious characters flows through the action, with their startling personalities, peculiarities and attendant strange happenings—all the more bizarre because they evolve in commonplace settings. That Christie was attracted by these features is evident from her use of "The Blue Carbuncle" as a basis for her "The Theft of the Royal Ruby" and from the use of similar elements in her pastiche of the Sherlockian canon in *Partners in Crime*.

In the Holmes stories, incidents are clever and shocking; for example, the amazing means for murder; the peculiar motives; the cunning red-herrings; and the surprise confrontations and explanations. Above all, the reader is constantly alert to the movements and thoughts of the master-sleuth in action gathering themselves, as the sleuth works his way through problem puzzles and effects the *dénouement*. The prime vehicle for moving the reader through the scaffolding of the stories is the simple language developed not in descriptive passages but in intelligent dialogue.

Dialogue is the key to Christie's success as a distinctively readable author. The burden of the plot is carried entirely by the conversation of the characters. This important trait may have been either learned from or reinforced by Doyle's style, for both Doyle and Christie were natural storytellers who knew how to spin a yarn. Although Christie's work has none of the masculine tone and bizarre surprise of Doyle's, she had an ear for dialect and phrasing as well as a feeling for conversation.

Christie loved Doyle's stories, learned much about writing from a study of them, and used her knowledge to advantage in structuring her own stories. She reveals her indebtedness to the tone, atmosphere, milieu, personae and motifs which she borrowed from Doyle. Her admiration is tinged with humor and she can playfully poke fun at Holmes, his methods and the idolatry practiced by his admirers. Poirot often humorously repeats distortions of famous Holmes' sayings. In unravelling the "Case of the Missing Lady," a charming spoof on Doyle's story of the disappearance of Lady Francis Carfax, Christie's Tommy Beresford attempts to find the missing Hermione Crane, feared abducted for her fortune. Using Sherlockian methods, Tommy traces the woman to a sinister-like nursing home and discovers that the woman is at a weight-reducing clinic. In the novel *Hickory Dickory Death* Christie makes a playful dig at the Holmes cult in referring to the Baker Street Societies: "Grown men being so silly! But there that's men all over. Like the model railways they go on playing with. I can't say I've ever had time to read any of the stories. When I do get time for reading which isn't often, I prefer an improving book."[3]

A dominant and curious theme found in the detective stories of both Doyle and Christie is that of "a murder passed off as a suicide" and its correlative "a suicide passed off as a murder"; both variations are tied to the revenge motif. This revenge motif was a strong one in the Doyle stories, appearing in "The Five Orange Pips," "The Case of Black Peter," "The Adventures of the Devil's Foot," "The Gloria Scott," and The Sign of Four." Of particular interest is the theme of a murder made to appear as a natural death due to "supernatural means." A variation of this theme occurs in "The Adventures of the Devil's Foot." Christie's most elaborate treatment of this theme occurs in her novel *The Pale Horse*. Coupled with it is the suicide which appears as a murder. The manic desire for revenge, the attempt to implicate an innocent person in a trumped-up murder charge is also used by Doyle in the story "The Norwich Builder" wherein the vengeful, rejected suitor years later takes out his revenge upon the woman by framing her son for his staged murder (using a burning barn to cover the evidence of corpus delicti). This diabolical villain, hiding low, having spread much incriminating evidence anxiously waits for the arrest, trial and execution of the innocent man. He is literally smoked out of his lair and plot. Variations of this theme found their way into Christie stories, especially "Murder in the Mews" and "The Market Basing Mystery" where victims of blackmailers commit suicide but outraged friends or servants manipulate evidence to turn suicide into murder and implicate through planted clues a blackmailer who drove the victim to death.

Christie's obsession with hidden identity, with impersonation and disguise may also have been influenced by Holmes, the master of disguise, whose various adversaries likewise used disguise or operated under hidden identities such as the clerk in "The Red-Headed League," the villain in "The Hound of the Baskervilles" and the beggar in "The Man with the Twisted Lip." Holmes himself used deception and disguise to delude his enemies. He at different times assumes the guise of an old woman, an old sailor, a groom, a nonconformist clergyman and even an Italian priest. So excellent is Holmes in these roles that he easily fools Athelney Jones and Watson himself. Holmes not only changed his costume but his manner, his stance and his expression. Legend has it that Holmes had five different hideouts in London; he moved about secretly in his private war with criminals and needed private lairs in which he could change his disguise, clothes and kits. The uses of disguise seems to be a heritage from various shape-shiftings of Lecoq, just as the method of deduction seems to be influenced by Gaboriau.

Seldom do Jane Marple and Hercule Poirot resort to disguise, though Tommy and Tuppence practice extensive deceptions and role playing in works such as *The Partners in*

Crime and *N or M*. Poirot sneers at disguise and refuses to stoop to such methods; yet he is all too ready to dissemble and misrepresent himself and intentions when he sets out to garner answers to questions. A rare exception to physical disguise by Hercule Poirot occurs in the gigantic hoax in *The Big Four*, wherein he plots his supposed death and the appearance of a nonexistent brother Achilles (actually Poirot without mustaches). Yet in almost every Christie story one or more cases of disguise or impersonation occur—but among murder suspects and the villains rather than the sleuth.

Many were the influences, general and specific, transmitted from Doyle to Christie as the concept of the private investigator and his Watson are the direct inspiration for her Poirot-Hastings duo. Both Doyle and Christie were attracted by the charms of the Victorian period; thus the milieu of the stories, especially the love of the English countryside, is a reflection of the Holmes' environment. Likewise, both authors concentrate their attention on a particular level of English life; they make use of similar social lifestyles and the accompanying social types are presented in an interesting and realistic way.

The structure of the Holmes' stories, with their rapid movements and suspenseful surprises, and their abrupt turns of direction, also appealed to Christie. She was impressed not only by the kinds of crimes and the development of certain motifs but also by the curious and clever concept of the problem-puzzle solved by Sherlock Holmes. A great deal of Christie's art of characterization in her detective works may have been influenced by Doyle's successful example; in particular the major element for Christie is the expert and ingenious use of ordinary language and dialogue as the magnet to draw the reader's attention along the story line. The obvious prototype for this use of language was Conan Doyle.

In *Partners in Crime* (1929), a volume of short stories, Christie casts her young detective duo in a series of varied roles burlesquing the detective heroes and heroines of detective fiction.[4] This work is especially useful because it verifies Christie's deep familiarity with the works of her predecessors and contemporaries. She knew the authors' styles and methods so well that she was able to parody them brilliantly as vehicles for her own young amateur detectives, Tommy and Tuppence Beresford. Tommy and Tuppence have set themselves up as consulting detectives, and Tommy has bought a whole set of detective novels and stories by the leading masters of the art. He plans to experiment with different styles and compare results. In "The Affair of the Pink Pearl," Tommy imitates the great Thorndyke while Tuppence serves as Polton. Other stories find Tommy and Tuppence enacting the roles of McCarthy and Riordan, Sherlock Holmes, Thornley Colton "the blind Problemist," Father Brown and one of the police detectives of Edgar Wallace. In "The Sunningdale Mystery" Christie has her fun with Baroness Orczy's Old Man in the Corner; the "House of Lurking Death" emerges as a wonderful spoof on A.E.W. Mason's Hanaud; "The Unbreakable Alibi" is an effective parody of Inspector French (Freeman Wills Crofts); and the "Ambassador's Boots" is a pastiche satirizing Reggie Fortune. Christie's humor is so well balanced that she is capable of self-parody. Thus even her Hercule Poirot comes in for a ribbing in "The Man Who was 16." It is the concluding story in this series, and Tommy chooses the role-playing carefully for it fits in with the tradition of the retiring sleuth: "This is our last case. When they have laid the super spy by the heels, the great detectives intend to retire and take to bee-keeping or vegetable marrow growing."[5]

Christie's lifelong obsession with hidden identities and impersonation was fed by the theme of the Least Likely Suspect in the history of detective fiction—especially the theme of the detective crossing the line into the field of criminality. Holmes admitted at one point that he could become the world's greatest criminal, if he put his mind to it; even Poirot admitted that, if necessary, he could commit the perfect murder—and so he does in *Curtain!* A variation of this concept is found in the stories of Baroness Orczy depicting the exploits of *The Old Man in the Corner* (1901). He is the embodiment of the "armchair detective" playing with his knotted string in the corner of the ABC tea shop. Over snacks and the hubbub of the tea shop, Miss Polly, a reporter, discusses recent cases with him, and she discovers to her surprise that The Old Man correctly solves the crimes just through thought and clues from newspapers.

This tea shop detective empathizes deeply and curiously with the mentality of the criminals he examines; he has admiration for them, and admits that they would have committed perfect crimes, except for *his* uncovering their guilt. A most curious twist occurs in the last tale when strong inplication leads the reader to suspect that perhaps the culprit of the last crime analyzed for Miss Polly was committed by the Old Man in the Corner himself.

One of the amazing pastiches found in *The Partners of Crime* is the brilliant parody of G.K. Chesterton in the story "The Man in the Mist" which presents Tommy hard on the track of a gambling Countess while he is disguised in the garb of a Roman Catholic priest. Christie recaptures the atmosphere, the nebulous air, the frisson of terror associated with G.K. Chesterton. Christie's tale of the murder of Gilda Glen in the White House by the cemetery and the startling vision of the policeman in the mist rivals some of the stories by Chesterton. The handling of Tommy's deductions fits easily into the mold of the Father Brown original.

The strange-looking Father Brown presents a shabby disordered appearance; he casts a disheveled impression with chubby face, stocky body, clumsy hands, clerical suit of black rumpled and shapeless, forever dropping umbrella and brown paper parcels, and darting, flitting and zooming off in all directions with enormous, surprising bursts of vitality. The appearance of this detective is so disarming, especially in the crisis of the chase, that the brilliant deductions come as a complete surprise. For this detective does not chase footprints, clues, physical manifestations as a corpus to be trapped and sent to prison (though he does plenty of clue gathering and observing); instead, Father Brown approaches the criminal not the crime, for he regards the criminal as a fallen soul to be trapped in Saint Peter's net and converted from sin to good, from a life of crime to redemption, from punishment to grace. His approach to crime is metaphysical: the saving of souls not the destruction of men's bodies. Hence his method is intuitional. For Father Brown must know the motives of the criminal's act, the character of the criminal, the psychology of behavior, and the potential for salvation.

Father Brown works out his redemption drama with two

major pawns. Flambeau is the rogue-hero, the gentleman-cracksman endowed with gifts of intelligence, courage, marvellous athletic physique—excellent qualities for a super-thief. The mental agility and sense of humor belie the sensitivity of this second-story burglar, who has a soul worth saving; the other pawn is the implacable Nemesis, Aristide Valentine, the number-one bloodhound of the French Sûreté who chases Flambeau with a single purpose and plodding logic.

Christie sidesteps the paradoxical manner, the metaphysical concerns of Chesterton's Father Brown series when she creates her own "intuitional" detective, Miss Jane Marple, who unlike Father Brown is almost a fundamentalist as regards evil. Miss Marple accepts evil as a dominant force to be reckoned with; some are deeply tainted by it. For those who are too deeply committed to evil, there is no redemption possible. These criminals must be handled with severity and neither mercy nor compassion should be shown to them. Like Father Brown, Jane Marple views violence and criminality as acts of debased and corrupted character, resulting from some evil taint inherent in human nature, well-hidden and quiescent for the majority of men, but apt to flash out in anti-social forms in the most unexpected and highly placed persons. To Marple, all the world is a sink of depravity and contains numerous germs of evil; no social sphere is exempt.

The presence of evil is universal, but Marple tends to simplify the phenomenon inasmuch as outbreaks of crime follow several basic patterns, or so Miss Marple would have us believe. By seeking parallels between current and past crimes, by drawing forth the basic human elements, she finds truth. Thus the parallel consists in juxtaposing simple misbehavior patterns in village life with the puzzling acts of crime in larger spheres: Miss Marple does this by continually recalling what happened to so and so. All persons according to Marple's view of evil, have the capacity for evil expression, but most are able to resist. Those who opt for crime commit their evil deeds by over-extending their negative personality traits, by displaying quirks of thought, and by displaying compromising emotions. Jane Marple, like Father Brown, takes the physical residue of crime and relates backwards to identify the character or personality type—assuming certain personalities (or souls) commit certain acts of lawlessness. Since evil imbalances one's nature, Marple and Father Brown are sensitive to conditions revelatory of evil possession; they sense incongruous circumstances in personalities, contradictions in word and deed, unusual juxtapositions which jar, contradict or draw attention. Miss Marple, for example, is excellent at spotting a liar, be he adult villain or secretive girl scout. When large gaps occur in the developing puzzle pattern of crime, it is the quiescent intuition that springs forth to bridge the disparate parts.

Of equal interest is Christie's indebtedness to Gaston Leroux (1868-1927), the creator of Rouletabille, the young journalist turned detective who not only picked up a Watson stooge but becomes emotionally involved with the intended victim of a would-be murderer—this device will appear in *Trent's Last Case* and even Christie's Chaptain Hastings will tangle emotionally with a major suspect and practically ruin the detective work of Poirot in *Murder on the Links*.

Christie discusses in her *Autobiography* how she read and enjoyed Leroux's famous novel *The Mystery of the Yellow Room* (1907).[6] While it abandons altogether Gaboriau's preoccupations with police methods and functions, it introduces new interesting features. There is still the locked-room device, derived from Poe or influenced by Zangwill's *The Big Bow Mystery*. There is also the opposition between the professional detective Larson and a young journalist; both of them investigate the mysterious murderous assault on the heroine. The first puzzle is the hermetically-sealed room, locked from inside, watched from outside: how did the murderer get in and get out? With less melodrama, less complexity and fewer digressions than Boisgobey, Leroux drops clue after clue so that both the reader and Rouletabille see evidence building up strongly against Arthur Rance, then to another suspect, Barzac. Rouletabille, like Miss Jane Marple or Monsieur Poirot, focuses attention on close members of the family, ultimately moving on to discover a most likely and then a least likely suspect.

Among contemporary detective writers, Christie favored Elizabeth Daly, Michael Gilbert, Margaret Millar, Patricia

Highsmith, Elizabeth Bowen, Graham Green and Muriel
Spark. As Nigel Dennis points out: "She enjoys whodunits
which are quite different from her own."[7] She displayed less
enthusiasm for the hard-boiled school of detective fiction,
being repelled by its gratuitous violence, brutality and sadism.
As a result, she did not read Mickey Spillane and others. She
had a higher appreciation of the writers who through
originality, inventiveness and innovations infused new life,
new ideas and new force into the modern detective story.
Among these were Dashiell Hammett, Raymond Chandler,
Ellery Queen, the Lockridges and Georges Simenon. For
example, in an interview with Lord Snowden, she praised
Graham Greene's novels: "They are the sort of books that you
can't put down because he writes remarkably well."[8] On the
other hand she found Ian Fleming's work boring in
comparison to science fiction "which is quite enjoyable and
always seems to make sense."[9]

Though Christie was alive to the historical changes in
detective fiction from the 1930s to the 1960s, the major
influences upon her art were basically formulated and
operative during the first two decades of this century. From
1900 to 1920, Christie was exposed to major landmarks in
detective fiction such as A.K. Green, Collins, Conan Doyle,
Leroux, Chesterton. As we have seen, these writers were the
major forces which tempered and inspired her own craft. In the
first nine years of her writing career, she experimented with,
formulated and established her own concept of the detective
story and novel. She fashioned the elements of her own style
and content, and she established the major features and
characteristics of her fictive art including the concept of her
sleuths, the puzzle-problem, the attitudes toward police, the use
of dialogue and her especial sense of milieu and environment.

Christie made a natural transition from reading to
creative writing. Encouragement came from her mother who
had years earlier stimulated her to read. When Agatha was
recovering from a case of flu her mother suggested that she try
to write a short story. Although she protested that she could
not, her mother was positive in her insistence to the point of
providing a notebook and pencil. In two days Agatha finished
a work she called "The House of Beauty," not a bad effort, she

thought—though very romantic.[10] Another romantic novel written around 1915 she called "Snow Upon the Desert." With this effort she sought the professional advice of the widely published author who was also her neighbor, Eden Phillpotts. Phillpotts welcomed his young neighbor and offered the following advice:

> "Some of these things that you have written," he said, "are capital. You have a great feeling for dialogue. You should stick to gay natural dialogue. Try and cut all moralizations out of your novels; you are too fond of them, and nothing is more boring to read. Try and leave your characters *alone*, so that *they* can speak for *themselves*, instead of always rushing in to tell them what they ought to say, or to explain to the reader what they mean by what they are saying. That is for the reader to judge for himself. You have two plots here, rather than one, but that is a beginner's fault; you soon won't want to waste plots in such a spendfree way. I am sending you a letter to my own literary agent, Hughes Massie. He will criticize this for you and tell you what chances it has of being accepted, so you mustn't be disappointed. I should like to recommend you a course of reading which I think you will find helpful. Read De Quincey's *Confessions of an Opium Eater*—this will increase your vocabulary enormously—he uses some very interesting words. Read *The Story of My Life* by Jeffreys, for descriptions and a feeling for nature."[11]

Whether or not Christie pursued the "heady" reading list suggested by Phillpotts we can only guess, but she did profit from her contact with his literary agent, Hughes Massie. Massie read the manuscript; and though he decided he could not place it, he encouraged her to put this manuscript behind her and start another right away. Ironically, the subsequent affiliation with Hughes Massie Limited brought more wealth to that company than that of their established client, Eden Phillpotts.

The idea for what was to be her first published novel occurred to Christie some time around 1918. In the *Autobiography* she speaks of the characters who were forming in her mind, particularly a bearded neighbor whom she envisioned with an older wife. (This person may well have been Edward Noake, a portrait painter who lived with two elderly ladies in the Barton Road area. He moved to Italy and married an older woman.)[12] The plot for *The Mysterious Affair at Styles* took shape as Christie contended with the routine in the Torquay Hospital Dispensary. Her husband was serving on the front, and she was living with her mother at Ashfield and walking back and forth to the hospital. Although she had trained as a volunteer nurse, she was later needed in the dispensary; she took the Apothecaries Hall Examination which licensed her to dispense for a chemist. Thus the ingredients for a mystery story fortuitously emerged from her experience—the bearded neighbor became the villain; the older wife the victim; a chemist's shop the source for the fatal drug.

Again the immediate encouragement needed to write the story came from Christie's mother. She advised Agatha to go off by herself to a hotel in the remote Dartmoor area where she could write undisturbed. Her method then and in the future was to "talk" the novel into being. Christie says she must have walked miles working out the dialogue and fitting the details of the plot together. In a fortnight, she returned home with her finished novel.

Time elapsed, however, between the completion of *The Mysterious Affair at Styles* and its publication in 1920. As a novice in the field, Christie received several rejections before securing a publisher. When John Lane did place her under contract, Christie discovered too late that Lane had imposed "unfair" restrictions on her and her income for the next five books. Still, Christie achieved significant acclaim from her first published work to place her among the successful writers of *detective fiction*.

As one looks back upon Christie's achievement, several factors seem to have motivated her choice of detective fiction as her medium. First, given the person herself and her continuous involvement in fantasy, one might say that Christie was well disposed to take up detective fiction. Secondly, the tremendous popularity of detective fiction during Christie's formative years obviously presented models which were to influence her. Thirdly, the happy combination of imagination, practicality and respect for those late Victorian values became the mainstay of her fiction. Christie's world—the servants, money, class, traditions, concepts of good and evil—became the vital forces in her detective fiction.

For the sake of clarity, let us establish what we mean when we say that *The Mysterious Affair at Styles* is a work of detective fiction. Auden describes the genre in this way: "The basic formula is this: a murder occurs; many are suspected; all but one suspect, who is the murderer, are eliminated; the murderer is arrested or dies."[13] Haycraft puts it more succinctly: "the crime in a detective story is only the means to an end which is—detection."[14] Christie operated within the category of *mystery* fiction, writing some pure mystery stories—stories which involve mystery but not necessarily a detective nor a solution to the mystery; she also wrote thrillers—stories involving international adventure and crime; but the majority of her work is detective fiction.

The Mysterious Affair at Styles reflects the classical detective tradition upon which Christie was nurtured. It contains all the basic ingredients including a murder puzzle; a triad of victim-murderer-detective; a likely group of suspects; and a host of clues. As Cawelti points out, Christie "gives us the pure, concentrated essence of the classical art with just enough flavoring to keep it from becoming tasteless and sterile."[15] Though *Styles* was not to be her greatest work, her conception of the detective story was to remain constant from that point onward; for with this first novel, Christie discovered a medium which was both natural to her and successful.

Let us consider how this first novel combines Christie's various talents into a successful art form. First, Christie was drawing from personal experience, actually projecting elements of her own lifestyle into an imaginative structure. In fact, *Styles* contains characters who might have stepped out of Christie's own life. Among them is Cynthia Murdoch, the young, auburn-haired dispensary aide who is a mirror image of the youthful author herself working in the Torquay dispensary during World War I. Along with the chemist and the bearded neighbor, whom we identified earlier, she also introduces Emily Inglethorp, the aged matriarch of Styles Court—a woman very like her own grandmother, Margaret Boehmer Miller, the kindly step-mother of Frederick Alvah Miller. And the dark and mysterious Mary Cavendish bears an uncanny resemblance to Clarissa Miller, Agatha's mother. The Cavendish men are very like the males in Agatha's own family—debonair and charming, but weaker than the women. Like her own father and brother, Lawrence and John Cavendish are country squires who do not have to work for a living. Lawrence has studied medicine and John is a barrister, but neither engages in his profession. Emily Inglethorp holds the reins on the family money and property, allocating funds for her step-sons as needed. Their estate, Styles Court, is the symbol of the family's place in the community—a sacred trust to be cherished and passed on from Mrs. Inglethorp to her step-sons. We see the motifs operating in the story as those which shaped Agatha Miller Christie's own development: Family, Property, Money and the Marriage Game. Thus in the case of Emily Inglethorp, the intrigue of money and marriage precipitates her murder—for marriage to an "outsider" who is much younger and whose intentions are suspect rocks the very foundations of Styles Court. Although such motifs are found in other detective stories of the period, not all writers of the genre came by them as honestly as Christie and few expressed them as well.

The heart of the novel, the murder puzzle, is challenging but not overpowering. "One must assume that an infinitesimally small number of Agatha Christie's half billion readers ever understood or expected to solve her stories in advance of Jane Marple or Hercule Poirot," says Grossvogel. "What the detective story proposes instead is the expectation of a solution."[16] How Christie engages the reader in the expectation of a solution is the key to understanding her success. Essentially, she presents a *likely* puzzle: Emily Inglethorp is found dying in her locked bedroom, apparently the victim of strychnine poisoning. Whodunit is complicated not only by the locked room but also by the method of administering the poison. Was it placed in her coffee, her cocoa, or in her own medication? The identity of the murderer is not to be discovered until method and opportunity are established. Consequently, Christie provides floor plans and a detailed coroner's report.

The intelligence who sorts through the evidence, evaluates clues and interrogates suspects is the detective. Christie's detective, Hercule Poirot, is not an Englishman, but a Belgian whose foreign qualities make him all the more interesting and amusing. Since we will study Poirot more closely in Chapter IV, let it suffice to say here that he is significantly different from his peers yet engaging enough in manner to win the public's trust. Because he is a refugee from a neutral nation, he is not perceived as a threat; then, his friendship with Captain Arthur Hastings places him in good company. Hastings, recently discharged from military service and recuperating from a war injury, is the epitome of the British gentleman. As narrator of the story, he reveals the sequence of events in a straightforward and conversational manner. Either he takes the reader aside to discuss what he sees or he converses with one of the characters; for the reader the effect is more like eavesdropping than reading. For example, his introduction to Emily and Albert Inglethorp sets a tone which enables the reader to perceive Mrs. Inglethorp's magisterial bearing and the feigned courtly deportment of her husband:

The french window swung open a little wider, and a handsome white-haired old lady, with a somewhat masterful cast of features, stepped out of it on to the lawn. A man followed her, a suggestion of deference in his manner.

Mrs. Inglethorp greeted me with effusion.

"Why, if it isn't too delightful to see you again, Mr. Hastings, after all these years. Alfred, darling, Mr. Hastings—my husband."

I looked with some curiosity at "Alfred darling." I did not wonder at John objecting to his beard.[17]

Actually, Hastings and Poirot are the conversational pivots upon which the story depends for interpretations—or misdirection, as the case may be. As Christie acknowledged, her method of writing was to talk the story into being; and it is precisely this native talent for reproducing the appropriate expressions and nuances of conversations which makes her fiction flow naturally and easily.

The reader is presented with a first impression of the suspects through their interaction with Hastings. He meets Miss Howard as she is working in the garden in her "stout tweed skirt" and "good thick boots," a forty-ish women who speaks with a clipped, "telegraphic style" (p. 8). The vignette of Miss Howard is produced with quick, precise strokes; yet she is easily identified in her thick tweeds, speaking her clipped comments. She is a type not to be confused with the elderly Mrs.

Inglethorpe, nor the young Cynthia Murdoch, nor the mysterious Mary Cavendish whose "intense power of stillness" provokes the impressionable Hastings (p. 9). The characters become individualized through language cues which function as labelling devices. Thus Albert Inglethorp is distinguished by a long beard, a pince-nez and a "rather deep and unctuous voice" (p. 10). Dr. Bauerstein is also bearded, but he speaks with a German accent. Among the suspects, Christie builds a case for the possible guilt of each by using what Grossvogel calls tautological evidence: "The people in that landscape are as tautological as the landscape itself: an adjective or two are sufficient to call their identity to mind.... But once the murder has been committed, the tautological evidence can no longer be trusted."[18] Christie sets the reader and Hastings up for a set of reversals, challenging first impressions and ultimately discovering hidden character traits.

Tension develops as the preliminary investigation focuses on two likely suspects: Albert Inglethorp and Dr. Bauerstein. The two bearded "outsiders" are regarded with distrust by Hastings. Thus when he calls at Bauerstein's rooming house, he is shocked to discover that the doctor has been arrested. An old woman answers his query:

> "Good afternoon," I said pleasantly. "Is Dr. Bauerstein in?"
> She stared at me.
> "Haven't you heard?"
> "Heard what?"
> "About him."
> "What about him?"
> "He's took."
> "Took? Dead?"
> "No, by the perlice."
> "By the police," I gasped. "Do you mean they've arrested him?" (p. 133).

The incredulous Hastings matched with the village servant produces one of the typically light comic touches which enlivens the novel. Hastings' chagrin becomes even greater when he announces his findings to Poirot, only to be put down by the master detective. So average is Captain Hastings that he has assumed the obvious—that Bauerstein has been arrested for Mrs. Inglethorp's murder. (The reader may also have shared this assumption.) Not until Poirot explains that Bauerstein has been arrested as a spy does Hastings learn of his error. Despite the bitter lesson, Hastings is still reluctant to accept Albert Inglethorp's innocence even though Poirot warns him not to let his feelings about the man override his judgment. It is not until John Cavendish, Hastings' friend, is arrested that Hastings is forced to suffer some guilt over his rash judgment of Inglethorp.

But the murder puzzle is not solved yet, for Christie has still more reversals and surprises in store—including two instances of disguised identity. She exhibits her professional knowledge of drugs in her scientific explanation of how strychnine, when mixed with a bromide, will produce a lethal concentrate in an otherwise harmless prescription drug. After a lengthy trial sequence, the reader is finally presented with the truth—but only after Poirot reconstructs the crime.

It is interesting what Christie chose not to include in future novels and what she retained as part of her successful formula. First, she chose not to offer as detailed a description of the victim's death throes in subsequent works—though poison was to remain one of her staples. Although she often included inquests in her novels, and wrote a single famous work based on a murder trial, "Witness for the Prosecution," she did not incorporate trials into the plots of her later novels. Her treatment was aesthetically successful, but she provoked criticism from those in the legal profession who found fault with her handling of specific aspects of the law. She maintained, however, the classical tradition of the *dénouement* as the final scene for her novels. The country estate as the setting for the murder puzzle was to persist, though Christie extended her range from the country to the city and from England to the Middle-East.

As we examine components of Christie's style in the succeeding chapters, we shall look more closely at how the so-called formula worked for Christie and how she varied certain elements and invented new puzzles. Most of all, we hope to show how that delicate balance between complexity and simplicity which we have observed in *The Mysterious Affair at Styles* continues to appeal to the vast numbers of people who read Christie's fiction.

Chapter III
The Puzzle-Game

The heart of the classical detective story is the puzzle—
that complex structure which offers the reader intrigue and
intellectual stimulation. Agatha Christie, who was well versed
in the puzzle tradition, distinguishes herself from other writers
of the genre in her conception of the murder puzzle: "I don't like
messy deaths. Anyway, I'm more interested in peaceful people
who die in their own beds and no one knows why. I don't like
violence."[1] Though her puzzles may be shrouded in mystery,
the bloodstains are few; for Christie distances the reader from
the garish effects of murder by focusing instead on "whodunit"
and engaging the reader in the pursuit of the murderer. The
reader then moves with the sleuth as an armchair detective in a
detection process which is both an entertainment and a heady
challenge—a puzzle-game.

Among the most enthralling of puzzle-games are those
found in the detective story, for those puzzles operate on
multiple levels with varying complexities devised by the
ingenious author. The detection game offers, in fact, several
different player combinations: the game played between the
murderer and the sleuth, the game played between the reader
and the murderer, the game played between the reader and the
sleuth, and even the game played between the author and the
reader. Traditionally, the puzzle-game has followed certain
formulas; when Ronald Knox set up "Rules" for detective
fiction in 1918, he was codifying those conventions which had
already been accepted by most practitioners of the genre.
Consequently, the reader approaches detective fiction with a
particular set of expectations. The reader expects the mystery
and the challenge of the careful plot; he expects to find a puzzle,
but he does not expect to be tricked since the "fair" puzzle
places the means of solving the enigma within a given range of
difficulty. The fair play doctrine is an attempt to ensure

validity of evidence, adequate presentation of facts (but not enough to spoil the mystery), and readiness to grant the reader an opportunity to "play the game."

Some authors of detective fiction, including Agatha Christie, increase the dimensions of their works by weaving "games within games."[2] One such amusement is the "recognition game" in which the author refers to real-life murderers to highlight similarities between reality and fiction. A favorite murder case often referred to by Christie is the "Brides in the Bath," as the image of Dr. Crippen is seen in counterpoint to one of her murderers. In *Mrs. Mc Ginty's Dead*, for example, Christie employs clever allusions to newspaper accounts of famous murders and their crimes as an integral part of the clue-hunting and subsequent solution to the Mc Ginty murder. But Christie's most celebrated "game within the game" is her parodying of detective sleuths and their creators in *Partners in Crime*, a collection of short stories featuring Tommy and Tuppence—a detective couple.[3] This husband and wife team assume the mind-set, the techniques, the language and total style of illustrious practitioners of detection. Their role playing becomes a guessing game for the reader who is asked to identify such luminaries as Sherlock Holmes, Dr. Thorndyke, Father Brown, Inspector French, Max Carrados and even Hercule Poirot (fair game). The tone of these sketches is light and humorous as Christie playfully pokes fun at the over-worked devices and rusty machinery of the genre.

Christie was not above self-parody, particularly in the case of her female sleuth, Ariadne Oliver. When she places Mrs. Oliver in charge of a murder game in *Dead Man's Folly*, Christie makes a series of double plays to involve the reader in a game within the puzzle-game. Ariadne Oliver is invited to set up and supervise a Murder Hunt—a game similar to a treasure hunt in which participants are challenged to solve a theoretical murder. As the players enter the game area, they are given cards containing the first clue which, if interpreted correctly, will lead then to the next clues. Players carry score cards to be filled in as the game progresses with the name of the murderer, the weapon, the motive and the cover-up. However, Mrs. Oliver's game soon turns into a *real* murder in a clever reversal engineered by a clever killer. The reader is then thrust into a puzzle-game that is heightened by the interplay between the two games.

Game plans and "gaming" devices abound in Christie's detective stories. Actual games, as in Ariadne Oliver's treasure hunt, often become the frames upon which the puzzle-game is played. In the *Halloween Party*, a young girl bobbing for apples is drowned in the tub by a mysterious assailant; in *Cards on the Table*, the host is stabbed in a covert attack during a bridge game. And in *A Murder is Announced,* bemused neighbors drop in at Little Paddocks to participate in what they assume will be a new parlor game—a staged murder-game. To their astonishment, real gunshots and death ensue. A gaming device that Christie uses to tease the reader and to provide additional clues is a nursery rhyme conundrum. *Ten Little Indians, One Two, Buckle My Shoe, A Pocket Full of Rye, Hickory Dickory Death,* and *Crooked House* are among the novels in which a nursery rhyme functions as an advantage for the reader who may be able to discover whodunit by interpreting the rhyme correctly. These variations upon the essential puzzle-game reveal Christie's gift for maintaining a delicate balance between levity and horror in what might be considered a serio-comic perspective.

At the heart of the detective story is the puzzle-game. Although its structure is among the more complex, it possesses components common to all games: a goal (whodunit), a field or playing board (setting), players (murderer, suspects, sleuth), devices used to reach goal (clues), barriers and handicaps (cover-up schemes including red herrings), and rules for fair play (conventions of the genre). The individual author creates puzzles bearing his or her own imprint, for the uniqueness of the puzzle derives from the way in which the author perceives and then manipulates each of the components. Thus the game situation, which requires a playing area where the moves and countermoves are enacted, must be a thriving social environment. Christie's field may be a country estate, a transcontinental express train or a Nile River steamer—but it must be a commodious place with relatives, colleagues, fellow guests or travellers in active pursuit of their social routines. Though the victim may expire in the privacy of a bedroom, library or stateroom, just as often a murder occurs in a crowded drawing room. The targeting of the victim by the mysterious murderer in their midst serves to alert the rest of the group to danger and possible threats to their own lives. Since *bloody* murder is not the rule in a Christie puzzle, details of the crime are given as succinctly and clinically as possible; greater emphasis is then placed on the circumstances of the crime.

The game requires players engaged in a competitive struggle to achieve a goal. In the detective story, it is the murderer who makes the initial challenge which will subsequently plunge the victim, the other members of the community (who will become suspects) and the sleuth into a life-death struggle. Who is likely to be murdered? According to Christie, anyone—male, female, adult, child—anyone who in some way crosses the wrong person. The potential victim, Christie believes, is a person who *could* be killed—someone who is vulnerable. Given the closed society which Christie portrays, the victim is frequently a member of the inner circle who poses a threat to another person in the group. Although occasionally the innocent suffer, most often the victim is someone who has brought the event upon himself.

Likely victims are the compulsive babbler, much as Major Palgrave in *A Caribbean Mystery*, whose talk alarms the murderer; or the foolish Heather Babcock in *The Mirror Crack'd,* whose loose tongue reveals the tragic consequences of a stupid act. Even when children are murdered, as in *The Halloween Party*, the author deftly dismisses their deaths as the result of their own defective characters. Although exceptions to the rule occur, most victims possess personal flaws which render them unsympathetic characters—thus increasing the emotional distance between the reader and the victim. Christie also provides distance between reader and victim through *time*: she presents several mysteries in which a past murder or murders must be solved. In such novels as *Murder in Retrospect* or *Elephants Can Remember*, the emotional involvement with the victim is reduced to its minimal level, for with the passage of time grief is no longer an issue, but rather truth and justice.

No matter how well placed the victim is or no matter how sterling his character may be, Christie does not engage the sympathy of the reader; her focus is on the solution to the murder. By developing means of emotional distancing for the reader, she makes the puzzle solving all the more challenging. The focus then shifts from the victim to the murderer.

In order to discover the murderer, the sleuth must go through a process of elimination to reduce the number of suspects to *one*. Since anyone and everyone on the scene can be a suspect, the range and variety of suspects in a Christie puzzle is broad. Her typical method of building suspicion is through the gradual uncovering of information which incriminates the characters one by one, slowly expanding the circle of suspects. The circle widens until practically everyone is included; as likely suspects emerge from the group, possible motives and opportunities are established. As the reader begins to make judgments about certain suspects, Christie sets up reversals and complications. One of her favorite devices for surprising the reader is hidden identity; she develops the Janus-faced character in graphic terms, displaying over and over again how easy it is for a person to pretend to be someone else and how readily the public will be taken in. Impersonation, hidden, and mistaken identity dominate Christie's portraits. In *A Murder Is Announced*, for example, four cases of hidden identity out of a group of twelve suspects provide continuous surprises.

Perhaps Christie's most renowned case of hidden identity is to be found in "Witness for the Prosecution." In this short story the reader participates by following the defense attorney's activities and sharing his impressions. Attorney Mayherne is attempting to win acquittal for his client, a young man accused of murdering an elderly woman. But the pivotal figure in the case is Romaine Heilger, the accused's common-law wife: instead of testifying for the defense, as Mayherne had hoped, she testifies for the prosecution—offering evidence as to her hatred for her one-time lover. Luck comes to the rescue, or so Mayherne believes, when an aged woman with a grudge against Heilger offers to sell him letters written by Heilger to an unknown lover in which she discloses her intentions of incriminating the accused. When Mayherne introduces these letters in court, Heilger's credibility as a witness is destroyed—the jury rejects her testimony and acquits the young man. Belatedly, Mayherne (and the reader) discovers that he has been tricked. By playing a series of double roles, Romaine Heilger outwits all the other "players." While presenting herself as the accused's wife, she is in reality not his wife. And by *impersonating* an old woman, she fools even an experienced attorney. She accomplishes her coup by playing "a lone hand," by misdirecting the perceptions of all the other players—even to the final twist when she reveals that she acted to save the accused because he was, in fact, *guilty*.

Suspects can, wittingly or unwittingly, provide a cover for the murderer. They complicate the puzzle-game by their very presence, for each one must be investigated in the methodical process of elimination. When one suspect finally emerges as the dominant figure, this character will become the most likely suspect. Although Christie follows the conventions on how and when to reveal the most likely suspect, she varies her puzzles so that the reader can never assume that a particular suspect is the murderer. Consider Christie's *Cards on the Table* in which she sets up a puzzle with *four* likely suspects. In the Foreword to this novel she warns the reader that although some detective stories are "rather like a big race—a number of starters—likely horses and jockeys,...*this is not that kind of book*."[4] In this case there are four starters—all capable of murder—matched by four able sleuths. This particular novel also provides a good introduction to the "gaming" aspects of Christie's puzzles. Obviously not all writers of detective fiction present their cases with the challenge and sportive tone usually found in Christie's work. *Cards on the Table* actually includes a series of games—a card game, a cat and mouse foray, and a detection game.

The game begins when the victim invites four people who have gotten away with murder to dine with four notable sleuths: Hercule Poirot, Inspector Battle, Colonel Race and Ariadne Oliver. The victim, Mr. Shaitana, arranges for the party for his own sadistic pleasure as he baits individuals, insinuating knowledge of their hidden crimes and threatening exposure. However, Shaitana loses control of the game. Assuming the position of overseer, he relaxes in a fireside chair while his guests play bridge. While his guard is down, one of the players makes a secret, yet deadly move. Shaitana is discovered dead—stabbed with a dagger from his own collection. No one but the eight players has entered the room; consequently, everyone realizes that one of them is the murderer. Although each has been involved in the bridge contest, one individual has obviously made a successful *double* play.

At this point the detection game begins. The sleuths take up the challenge by selecting a particular "Starter" to investigate. Battle muses, "It's the sort of game that would have amused our late friend."[5] They investigate their chosen suspects with inventive moves and sleight of hand plays. For example, Ariadne Oliver insinuates herself into the confidence of Anne Meredith's roommate and discovers information which Miss Meredith has concealed.

However, it is Poirot who assimilates all the information gathered by the other sleuths and makes the appropriate deductions. His initial game plan is to examine the bridge score in order to determine who had the opportunity to leave the table and whose playing style matches that of the murderer. His assumption is that since the murder was unpremeditated and committed in a high-risk situation, the murderer must be the kind of person who is willing to take chances even when the stakes are high. If the reader accepts the validity of this premise and recalls Christie's warning that all four suspects are capable of murder, then the reader may possibly deduce the identity of the murderer. Early in the game, Poirot figures out who is guilty but he does not lay his cards on the table; instead he gathers evidence to prove his case.

The detectives are handicapped because there are no tangible clues aside from the bridge score. Behavior patterns, or what one might call "intangible clues,"[6] form the basis for the second stage of the investigation. By applying pressure to the suspects, the sleuths hope to elicit responses which will lead them to the murderer. Poirot, for example, tests out his theory that Anne Meredith is a thief by giving her the opportunity to steal. He reasons that she may have murdered a former employer to cover up a theft, but that this was a covert act. Would she have dared to commit murder in a room filled with people?

The puzzle is complicated further by a series of moves

designed to misdirect even the most astute players. A false confession, a possible suicide, letters of confession and an attempted murder—all lead to a combination of twists and turns until the murderer incriminates himself by revealing his style. Poirot is quick to note that in *kind* the murders of Shaitana and Mrs. Lorrimer, the latest victim, are similar: both are swift and daring. However, so perfect are the crimes that Poirot has to use the trick of deceit to entrap the murderer. In effect, he suspends the rules of fair play and fights back with the very tricks the murderer has used so successfully. According to the bridge score, Dr. Roberts bid a grand slam based on his partner's hand in the third rubber—a risky bid. This meant that he was dummy during that hand and would have been free to move around the room while the other players were concentrating on the game. Roberts could not recall any details of the hand, indicating that his attention was diverted. And the other murders committed by Roberts were similar in method—enacted openly, in public and in daring circumstances.

Dr. Roberts is actually a typical Christie murderer. Most of her murderers come from the same social class—doctors, lawyers, financiers, highly placed men and women. Husbands, wives, prodigal sons, brothers and sisters have all played the murder game. Nevertheless Christie is famed for her skill in hiding the murderer's identity until the last scene. The murderer never wears the self-advertising garments of villainy, for this would be tantamount to confession. Christie's murderer makes an initial appearance early in the story, but under the mask, the disguise or the subterfuge. Consequently the murderer has a double dimension: that of a respected member of the community, a cover that tends to fool the public; and that of the inner man, flawed by pride or greed, capable of murder. Since the real person, the inner man, can not be revealed until the cover is blown, it is the "cover" that receives the delicate strokes of characterization. Clues to the true nature of an individual's character are fewer and more subtle.

In the puzzle-game, the murderer makes the initial moves to thwart the efforts of the puzzle-solvers. A Christie murderer is astute in shielding himself with that well-devised fabrication known as a cover-up. Within the multitudinous schemes to be found in her stories the following are the ones that Christie's murderers use most frequently:

1. *Hidden Identity or Impersonation*: This procedure allows the murderer to move freely within a familiar environment without arousing any suspicion. For example, in *Third Girl* part of the murder team lives a double life assisted by a wig and appropriate makeup. In other situations, the murderer impersonates another person for the purpose of casting suspicion on that person; often this is part of a process of incrimination set up to make an innocent party the scapegoat, such as in *Lord Edgware Dies*.

2. *The Frame-Up*: This elaborate scheme of directing guilt to another person is perhaps the best cover for the murderer. We see it used effectively in *The Mysterious Affair at Styles* as well as in *The ABC Murders*, where the scheme is so cunning that it even convinces the duped party of his guilt. (In most cases, however, the frame-up victim fights back, providing added conflict to the plot.)

3. *The Red Herring*: The false clue, deliberately left by the murderer, confuses the police and usually the sleuth. In *The Clocks*, for example, the killer arranges a roomful of clocks at the scene of the murder, all set at different times; the significance of the clocks sends the police in all directions— away from the murderer.

4. *The Cover-up Victim*: The person who threatens to reveal the killer's identity is likely to be murdered. Numerous blackmailers meet their fates this way as do innocent individuals who are unaware of what they know. Gladys, the scatter-brained maid in *A Pocket Full of Rye,* has no idea that the tryst she runs off to keep in the garden will end in murder. She, and other cover-up victims like her, are doomed by the special knowledge that they may have gained from eavesdroppings, snooping or just being an involuntary witness.

One of Christie's most renowned puzzle-games, *The ABC Murders*, contains her most clever cover-up. In this novel, the murderer invents a scheme to divert attention from himself by hiding a single murder within a series of murders, and then by setting up a scapegoat to pay for the crimes. The game plan is to make the killer seem to be a demented individual who chooses his victims by alphabetical order. An ABC railway guide is left at the scene of each murder, and the victim's surnames, ranging from A through D, correspond with a town of the same initial letter. The significant victim, Sir Carmichael Clarke from the town of Churston, thus appears to be chosen in the same fashion as the other three victims. Actually, Sir Clarke is the brother of the murderer who hopes to inherit the estate; the ancient Cain and Abel motif is developed with a new twist.

The murderer personally invites Poirot to join in the game by sending him a series of letters indicating his intention of bringing violence to an unnamed party in a particular town on a specified day. While casting him in the role of opponent, the murderer then proceeds to taunt Poirot—belittling his detectival powers. As Poirot is sparring with the unknown killer, the reader is enticed into the game. Christie employs alternating points of view to inform (or mislead) the reader as to the activities of the most likely suspect: Hastings' first person narration reflects the case as Poirot and the police perceive it, while a third person narrator focuses on Alexander Bonaparte Cust, an individual whose identity is not yet known to either the police or Hercule Poirot. Consequently the reader alone possesses information that may either assist or handicap him, depending on the way he processes that information.

The character of the most likely suspect, Alexander Bonaparte Cust, develops gradually as the facts of the case come to light. Is Cust the murderer? His initials are not the only incriminating elements, for the reader knows this man has had the opportunity to kill since he was at the site of each murder. And Cust is a disturbed man who experiences headaches and periods of disorientation. At one point, the reader is a silent witness to Cust's washing blood off his hands. In fact, Cust believes he is guilty of the murders and eventually turns himself in to the police.

Though the reader may be convinced of Cust's guilt, Hercule Poirot is not. He questions the validity of Cust's alibi for one of the murders and discovers that Cust could not possibly have been responsible. It is at this point that Poirot wrests control of the game from the murderer, for if Cust did not commit this murder then why assume that he committed the other three? By looking at the puzzle from another angle, Poirot perceives that Cust must have been duped and that someone with a finely tuned mind must have devised the frame-up.

Ultimately, the psychology of the murderer becomes the guide to the correct solution to the crimes. Poirot tells Hastings: "The case is the man, Hastings. Until we know all about the man, the mystery is as deep as ever."[7] The key to the man is the letters: ironically, the letters reveal the killer to be someone quite different from the hapless Cust—the writer is vindictive, calculating and highly intelligent. The image of the letter writer leads Poirot to reconsider the other suspects in order to discover who would have had the most to gain from a single murder, and who would have been capable of constructing this elaborate cover-up. Poirot plays the game to the finish, correctly deducing who the murderer is and adroitly eliciting a confession.

In order to match wits with the murderer, the sleuth must sidestep the pitfalls of the cover-up and interpret the clues correctly. A fire burning in a hearth on a warm evening, an open window, a long-distance telephone call—the Christie puzzle includes commonplace clues like these, clues that the less astute observer might easily overlook. Of the two kinds of clues—genuine and false—the false clue or red herring is the major handicap because it not only obstructs the truth but also delays solving the puzzle. If the detective follows all leads until he has proven their authenticity, by a process of elimination the field narrows down to a select group of genuine clues.

The genuine clue is not complete until it is seen in relation to a combination of other genuine clues. For example, in *Sleeping Murder* a suitcase hastily packed with the *wrong* clothes becomes much more meaningful against a background of other clues which imply that the victim may not have left home of her own accord. The keystone of the puzzle, however, is that final clue—in a Christie puzzle, the one reserved until the eleventh hour. When it finally surfaces or is finally interpreted correctly (it may have been there from the beginning), the keystone of the puzzle fits the psychology of the crime and focuses on the killer and his method.

Although many Christie clues are physical objects or facts that can be used as evidence, other clues are found in people—in body language or personality quirks that reflect the individual's true character. These intangible clues often lead to the murderer. In some novels, for example, intangible clues in the form of body language lead to the correct solution to the murders. *A Caribbean Mystery* develops as Jane Marple assesses the expression on the face of Major Palgrave just as he is about to tell her about a wife-killer. And the look on the face of an actress as she greets a guest at a reception tells Miss Marple enough to help her solve the mystery of *The Mirror Crack'd*.

Devotees of Christie tend to expect certains kinds of clues, just as they look forward to favored settings and recognizable characters. In fact, part of the allure of the game is the element of expectation. As Cawelti points out in his study of the genre, the reader anticipates "highly predictable structures that guarantee the fulfillment of conventional expectations."[8] Authors have used variations of formulas since the inception of the detective story. For the reader, the formula has several positive functions: it sets up a series of conventions which the reader looks forward to encountering in subsequent stories; it permits the reader to relax, inviting a sense of *deja vu* and coaxing him into involvement with the story; and it encourages the analytical thinker to match wits with the other players in the puzzle-game. As we have seen thus far, Christie's puzzles are rendered in a basically traditional manner, yet with a uniqueness that reflects the author's personal and aesthetic values. To become attuned to Christie's style is not to be bored or to be able to predict the outcome of her puzzles, for her work cannot be reduced to a formula. Although the detective story is of necessity formulaic, Christie invents imaginative variations to the basic formula.

In using the Watson-narrator device, Christie was relying on a pattern developed by Poe and transmitted through Arthur Conan Doyle. This point of view appears in a large portion of her detective fiction, yet perhaps her most famous novel, *The Murder of Roger Ackroyd*, is a clever variation on this well-known device. In this novel, Christie effectively handicaps the reader who assumes that the first person narrator is providing an accurate and full account of the mystery. As Champigny observes in his study, Dr. Sheppard is not only the narrator, he is a diarist using a "tricky style."[9] And he is also a credible character—a physician who is respected in the community and an assistant to Poirot (substituting for the absent Captain Hastings).

The characterization of Dr. Sheppard is accomplished with subtle strokes. Christie purposely understates him to the point where the reader is lulled into false security and accepts him at face value as an ordinary, if not stereotypical, country doctor. Although the experienced reader *should* realize that no one is beyond suspicion, the reading public was taken by surprise at the outcome of this puzzle.

Did Christie play fair with the reader? In examining the fabric of the narrative, one discovers that the narrator's account is true in the sense that no false information is presented. Ingenuous as Sheppard may be, he does not lie. Instead, he omits certain details which then produces a false picture or, as Champigny says, "a fictional image of the basic narrative."[10] Commenting in her *Autobiography* on this technique, Christie points out that concealment and ambiguity with respect to "lapses of time" are the key factors in manipulating point of view.[11] The fictional image is conveyed by Dr. Sheppard's narrative from the point when he takes the reader to the scene of the crime and then through the process of discovery that follows. Only when Poirot readjusts the picture at the *dénouement* does the reader discover that Sheppard has killed Ackroyd and staged an almost perfect cover-up.

Solving this puzzle is made progressively difficult because Sheppard seems to recede into the background when a most likely suspect emerges. However, the master detective relies less on tangible clues and more on the psychology of the killer. The turning point occurs when Poirot senses that there is too much evidence, that a frame-up is likely. When viewed as a puzzle-game, we perceive that a deadly match is going on between Sheppard and Poirot. The reader assumes that the two players are on the same team, working together to solve the mystery of Ackroyd's murder. However, at the *dénouement* it becomes clear that Sheppard has played a reverse role, feigning support for Poirot while at the same time manipulating evidence to lead him astray. But Sheppard is no match for Poirot. We see this initially when Sheppard mistakenly identifies the renowned detective as a hairdresser, having jumped to that conclusion based on Poirot's fastidious grooming. Poirot, however, is a better judge of character, for he does not accept the doctor at face value. After investigating his background, Poirot makes the correct deductions.

Once Christie pulled off her coup in this novel, she did not use the same device again. The term "ackroydism" emerged subsequently as a generic label, but once the trick had been turned by Christie, other writers were not game to try an imitation—and neither was Christie. Nevertheless, Christie continued to experiment with point of view, achieving notable success in alternating points of view in two of her most famous novels, *The ABC Murders* and *Ten Little Indians.*

Another component of the traditional formula which Christie chose to modify is the basic triad of victim, murderer, sleuth. In two exceptionally fine puzzles, *Murder on the Orient Express* and *Ten Little Indians,* Christie complicates the riddling process by increasing the number of personae. In *Murder on the Orient Express*, complicity among twelve likely suspects produces red herrings and a proliferation of clues— none of which seems to point to the identity of the traditional murderer. The concept of a ritualistic murder, an execution carried out by twelve individuals, is so removed from the expectations of the reader that the mystification structure seems significantly different from the basic formula.[12] Actually though, only one element—the number of murderers—has been modified.

The puzzle-game which defies all conventions, however, is *Ten Little Indians.* In this novel, all the players change positions so that ten individuals play three distinct roles: victim, suspect and sleuth. One of the ten also plays a fourth role, that of murderer. Although there is not a conventional sleuth in the story, which is often billed as "a detective story without a detective," the characters participate in the detection process and so does the reader.

Ten people, including a housekeeper and caretaker, have been induced to go to a guest house on a remote island off the coast of Devon, where they discover themselves to be the only inhabitants. Although they seem to have nothing in common, it is soon revealed that each is secretly responsible for the death of another human being. An accusation of guilt blares forth from a recording naming the guilty parties and their victims, even to the date on which the deaths occurred. Though the accuser is anonymous, his tone is menacing. The ten claim that they are innocent of all charges, but when the first murder occurs that evening it becomes apparent that each of them is in danger. Unable to leave the island or to communicate with the mainland, they unite to unmask the killer. While each participates in the detection process, each is still a suspect (until he or she becomes a victim), since no outsider has been discovered on the island.

If one considers the story a puzzle-game, it becomes apparent that although there are ten players, one of those players is in complete control of all the moves. This person manipulates the others so that each will participate in a cat and mouse chase. Though one assumes that the profile of the murderer might be deduced by one or more of the potential victims, the game is complicated by the reality that each of the players has taken a life before. Thus the issue becomes not *who* is capable of murder but rather who is capable of this kind of murder scheme. (Not all the victims are murdered directly, but each death is brought about by the machinations of one person.)

The point of view provides the reader-participant with certain advantages. Though in public these individuals deny the charges brought against them, the omniscient narrator permits the reader to hear the truth when each character silently recalls the details of the crime. The shifting narrative focus from one group to the individual allows for moments when each of the guests is alone and privately acknowledges personal responsibility for his deeds. Nevertheless, the omniscient narrator does not reveal the murderer.

A riddle entitled "Ten Little Indians" is the only tangible clue. The riddle is found framed on the wall of each bedroom, and ten china figurines stand on the drawing room table. This riddle depicts the scheme which the murderer has devised: the ten guests suffer the fate ascribed to the appropriately numbered Indian. As each person is killed, a figurine mysteriously disappears from the table. At one point, Vera Clathorne—victim number ten—almost solves the riddle. The line, "A red herring swallowed one, then there were three," causes her to probe the demise of victim number seven. This leads her to the judge who is noted for his lack of mercy—and who is indeed a likely suspect. Clathorne comes very close to the truth, but fails. Still, the reader may possibly succeed at this point if the error in Clathorne's thinking is deduced.

As in most Christie puzzles, the pyschology of the murderer is the key to discovering the identity. The murderer is obviously obsessed with justice, assuming a judgmental position; the scheme is patently an execution plan. Judge Wargrave is the obvious suspect, yet he is reportedly shot and killed, victim number six; consequently one assumes that he cannot be the murderer. The problem then shifts from whodunit to *howdunit*. An account of how the judge carried out his plan is ultimately found in a bottle. Many purists feel that the use of this *deus ex machina* device is the single flaw in an otherwise brilliant puzzle. Obviously, Christie tried an unusual combination for this puzzle—an almost impossible design with ten people dead, including the perpetrator of the scheme. The novel can hardly be deemed formulaic.

As we have seen, Christie puzzle-games share common components, but they cannot be reduced to a simple formula. The puzzles we have examined reveal creative structures which depart from a single pattern. Although the seasoned reader can anticipate typical Christie devices and components, the variations upon typical designs render her better puzzles unique. (Granted Christie was not brilliant all the time, but she managed an amazing number of successes.) A Christie puzzle which may seem ordinary on the surface frequently develops into a full-blown mystery, revealing hidden dimensions, unusual variations, and surprising turns. Consequently, we challenge the assertion that anyone can "tune" in to Christie and figure out whodunit early on. While familiarity with her methods and ideas may dispose the reader to feel comfortable or to anticipate the use of certain devices, this disposition alone cannot solve the puzzle. In fact, familiarity often handicaps the reader whose assumptions may easily lead him astray.

Why then is Christie so successful at the puzzle-game? As

we look at the components, we find that she operates in a
seemingly traditional manner but that she is capable of
unusual twists and turns. The Christie puzzle is methodical
and often creative. Through various methods of distancing,
Christie maintains a playful tone—sorrow, blood, sadism do
not intrude upon the scene. From her predecessors in the genre,
Christie learned the conventions of the genre, the formulas, the
varieties of the puzzles; but out of her own genius, she invented
new game plans. She judged correctly those elements which
worked well for her, combining them into successful patterns
that have earned for her fame and fortune.

Chapter IV

Hercule Poirot: Dandy Detective

D.N.B. (1971-1980)

POIROT, HERCULE (184?-1976), detective, was born in Belgium in the 1840s. Though an only child, he is believed to have had an imaginary twin brother, Achille. M. Poirot became one of Belgium's foremost detectives, having assumed leadership of the Belgian Police Force until his retirement prior to World War I. During the war, he sought refuge in England and was given hospitality at Styles Court by the wealthy Mrs. Inglewood. When she was later found murdered, M. Poirot volunteered his professional services and found himself launched in another career.

His fame as a private detective grew with the solution to the mysterious affair at Styles. And instead of returning to the retirement in war-torn Belgium, M. Poirot established himself in London. At first he shared rooms at 14 Farraway Street with his British friend, Captain Arthur Hastings, who assisted him in his investigations. Eventually, however, he lived alone.

In 1929 Poirot decided to retire permanently. He rented a cottage in the country where he hoped to raise vegetable marrows. But the murder of the village's most prominent citizen, Roger Ackroyd, forced him back into action. Rejuvenated by his success in this case, Poirot returned to a London

flat, No. 203 Whitehaven Mansions. From this point on, he was consulted frequently and called upon to solve the most challenging cases in both England and abroad. He also traveled extensively during the 1930s and early 40s in the Middle East.

M. Hercule Poirot became known as the most well-groomed and cosmopolitan of all detectives. Though barely five feet tall, he struck an impressive pose with his egg-shaped head, his luxurious black moustache, his perfectly coifed black hair, his piercing green eyes, his impeccable attire. He was also a gourmet who frequented the Savoy and the Ritz as well as the better French restaurants in Soho. At home, however, he was content with a well prepared omelette, a cup of chocolate, or a sirop de cassis. A lover of the arts, especially of theatre, M. Poirot was often seen at significant London functions.

M. Poirot was even more famous for his "grey cells," his extraordinary mental powers which enabled him to outwit the greatest of criminal minds. The most challenging criminals with whom he contended include the mastermind of the international syndicate known as the Big Four (1927), the cunning murderer who slew his victim during a bridge game (1936), the perverted genius who devised a murder plan using an ABC Railway Guide (1935), and a group of executioners who performed their rites on the Orient Express (1934). Not one of these, however, was a match for the great Hercule Poirot.

Though his name was once linked romantically with the Russian Countess Vera Rossakoff, M. Poirot never married. He was, though, a man of intense loyalty and true friendship. His secretary, Miss Lemon, remained with him for the duration of his career, as did Georges, his trusted valet. Captain Arthur Hastings, who was his oldest and dearest friend, is convinced that he owes his very life to Poirot.

In his last years, M. Poirot suffered from heart failure. When the end came in 1976, he was working on a case at Styles Court—where he first began his English career in 1926. M. Poirot is buried in Styles St. Mary; there are no known survivors.

Hercule Poirot came to life on the southwest coast of England at the beginning of World War I. Agatha Christie literally walked him into being as the hero of her first detective novel, *The Mysterious Affair at Styles*. He was born old, a retiree of the Belgian police force. He emerged a short man, five feet four inches in height, with an egg-shaped head, glossy dark hair and a well-waxed mustache. His name, Hercule, belies his diminutive physical size; yet we are told that the great Hercule Poirot is a mental giant whose "grey cells" are second to none. With an ego to match his reputation, Poirot cultivates his personal eccentricities—his neatness, his preference for exotic food and beverages, his foreign mannerisms and expressions.

Although Christie contends that Poirot is based on impressions derived from the Belgian refugees she had seen during the war, in appearance M. Poirot resembles the *Punch*-like caricature of the typical Frenchman with his waxed mustache and dandified appearance. As one critic points out, Poirot seems to embody all the stereotypes of the foreigner "to the point of absurdity"—a touch which very likely is all the more endearing to the British reader.[1]

Specific literary ancestors of Hercule Poirot are difficult to trace. Christie says that Poirot is *her* original creation. Still, prototypes for Poirot appear in different characters from French detective fiction such as Leroux's Rouletabille, Robert Barr's Eugene Valmont, and A.E.W. Mason's Inspector Hanaud, and Mrs. Belloc Lowndes' Hercules Popeau. Each of these fictional detectives made his debut by the early 1900s, before Christie began writing. An avid reader of detective fiction, Christie consumed much of the popular literature of her day; and consciously or subconsciously, she must have been influenced to some extent by her reading.

Whatever the borrowing—whatever the inspiration— Poirot shares specific personal and professional characteristics with his literary ancestors. Poirot may have inherited his egg-shaped head from Gaston Leroux's Joseph Rouletabille, the sleuth whose "round" head held the brains to riddle the puzzles of *The Mystery of the Yellow Room* (1907) and *The Perfume of the Lady in Black* (1907).

Poirot shares other notable personality traits with Rouletabille—pride in extraordinary reasoning power, reliance upon intuitive flashes of inspiration and common sense combined with keen powers of observation. Rouletabille also has a Watson-type relationship with Monsieur Sinclair that suggests the Poirot-Hastings friendship. And both detectives struggle with locked room puzzles as well as with problems of disguise and impersonation. The confrontation scene also delights both Rouletabille and Poirot who summon their wide range of talents to stage grand finales.

In the comically conceived French sleuths of Robert Barr and A.E.W. Mason, Christie may have found additional models for Poirot. Though English to the core themselves, Barr and Mason viewed Frenchmen as excitable, temperamental, conceited and slightly ridiculous—attitudes which were projected into their fictional heroes.

The parallels between Barr's Valmont and Christie's Poirot are unmistakable. Both are aged, unmarried, retired police officials who are self-exiled from their own countries. London becomes their operations' center as they work closely with Scotland Yard. They are both prosperous in their vocation and enjoy the wealth which comes from assisting the upper ranks of society. They live in elegant style and dress with fastidious perfection. Although given to self-praise and conceit, each works hard and seeks challenging puzzles.

But differences also abound between Valmont and Poirot. Valmont's career is a limited one, while Poirot's is almost timeless. Valmont is thoroughly comic, while Poirot is basically a more serious character. Valmont is a failure, whereas Poirot is a success. Poirot is also a practicing

Christian humanist who shares the values of the Victorian gentry. Of the two, Poirot is the more gentle, personable and responsible.

Although there is little physical resemblance between Mason's Hanaud and Christie's Poirot, they share characteristic comic qualities. Mason openly revolted against the superman detective heroes of his day, choosing instead to create a more passionate, sentimental character who is given to bursts of intuitional inspiration—much like Hercule Poirot.

Certain mannerisms of Hanaud also foreshadow Poirot's. Both men are vain about their successes and inconsolable over their failures. They enjoy creature comforts, especially a cup of chocolate in the morning. And both are completely bourgeois in values. Though capable of banter and theatrics, they are remorseless defenders of the innocent and tenacious in their pursuit of justice.

However, a more curious literary parallel abounds in Hercules Popeau—the detective hero whom Mrs. Belloc Lowndes developed before the appearance of Christie's Hercule Poirot. How circumstantial this resemblance was has never been resolved; but surely both women must have read each other's work. Mrs. Lowndes, French by birth, depicts her detective as a solid agent of the law, a riddler of puzzles, a friend to the distraught—and she spells his first name correctly with a final s, as is customary in the French derivative. Notably there is nothing comic or eccentric about Popeau! But why does Christie misspell the name—was it her recurring problem with spelling or was "Hercule" another one of her comic twists?

Parallels also exist in Popeau's and Poirot's methods and in certain motifs and character traits. For example, in both Lowndes' *One of These Ways* (1929) and Christie's *The Mystery of the Blue Train* (1928) the scenes shift from England to Paris and then to the French Riviera. Jewel robbery, gambling casinos, jealous lovers, persecuted maidens, millionaires and a master criminal of diabolical cruelty set the stage for detectives of the French Sûreté. In both works, an old but experienced sleuth laments his age and yearns for the past; he befriends a young lady who becomes his catspaw and apprentice. In both novels the sleuth breaks the law when it is to his advantage to do so; and he also uses a strong young man as a sounding board and prides himself on bringing young lovers together.

In method and in recurring motifs, Poirot shares many of the traits of the most famous detective hero of all time—Sherlock Holmes, his English forebear. Admittedly, Christie was well versed in the Holmes tradition and even refers specifically to Holmes and Watson in her own works. Like Holmes, Poirot seeks clues and incriminating evidence to arrive at logical solutions. And the master-amateur relationship between Holmes and Watson is the prototype for the Poirot-Hastings collaboration. But as Haycraft indicates, Poirot distinguishes himself from the prototype in his "picturesque refusal to go Holmes-like on all fours in the pursuit of clues...."[2] Instead, by relying on his "little grey cells," Poirot moves beyond the limits of physical evidence to rare moments of perception. Christie also wisely curtails Hastings' role by the end of the second Poirot novel. In subsequent adventures the use of a variety of amateurs to assist Poirot adds a refreshing touch to what might have become a dull convention.

But of all the heroes of detective fiction—past and present—Hercule Poirot is among the most cosmopolitan. He is a man of the world—at home in London or Paris, his native Belgium or in the Middle East. His fame enables him to move in the best circles to become privy to the affairs of royalty and highly placed government officials. Yet he is accessible to worthy individuals from lesser society as well.

In the tradition of the sleuth, Poirot is a loner—a totally free person who can go almost anywhere at any time. He has no family; the reputed brother invented in *The Big Four* is nonexistent. Aside from Hastings, he has no close friends. His valet assists him in his preoccupation with attire and comfort. But the relationship stops there, for Poirot would never treat a servant as an equal. His secretary and his valet are part of the machinery of efficient living—no more, no less.

Poirot's loyalty transcends land, country and nationality. He serves justice on a universal scale without parochial barriers. Although at Styles, Poirot inhabits a cottage with other Belgian refugees, he is never part of an ethnic clique. He moves about independently but maintains his closest ties with members of police organizations, such as Scotland Yard, who continue to consult him. As a person, Poirot is a romantic figure—eccentric, impossibly free, incredibly gifted and yet comic.

Like Jane Marple, Poirot barely ages. He is in his sixties when we first meet him during World War I, and he thrives for fifty-five more years until his demise in 1975. And he changes very little during these years—becoming older but wiser and moving lithely with the times. Between 1920 and 1930 Christie composed five Poirot novels and numerous short stories; in the 1930s she wrote eleven more novels and more short stories. Thus the years between 1920 and 1940 account for almost half of the Poirot canon. Although some might argue whether or not this was Christie's best Poirot period, certainly all will agree that it was her most prolific.

In the 40s and 50s she averaged five Poirot novels a decade; and between 1960 and 1975 an additional five adventures appeared. During this time collections of stories were published, several focusing on Poirot. Ironically, though in numbers the adventures of the little Belgian detective far exceeded that of all her other detectives (doubling those of Jane Marple), Christie grew tired of him. Public demand necessitated her choice of Poirot as hero more than her own preference. Nonetheless, Hercule Poirot became one of the classic detectives, distinguishing himself as an individualized character among the many others in his field.

An examination of the Poirot fiction, reflecting the versatility and cunning of the detective in the various periods of his career, offers some insight into Poirot's success as a detective hero. As we shall see, Christie establishes the character of Hercule Poirot in the *early* novels and short stories of the 1920s. She captures him so exactly in fact that in future works he barely changes. Understandably Christie herself tired of him. But when the public continued to find appeal in the little Belgian detective, Christie managed to find "work" for him in a variety of challenging puzzles.

We first meet Hercule Poirot in *The Mysterious Affair at Styles* (1920). He is a refugee from the German invasion of Belgium who is sharing a cottage on the grounds of Styles

Court with other Belgian nationals. Mrs. Inglethorpe, the owner of the estate, has given the group hospitality. An extraordinary looking little man, Poirot is dignified in bearing—his luxuriant mustache is stiff and military looking; his attire is impeccable. A guest at the house, Captain Arthur Hastings, immediately recognizes him as the famous Hercule Poirot, formerly one of the most celebrated members of the Belgian police force.

Poirot's methods and his unique detectival skills are dramatically revealed when the matriarch of Styles Court is found poisoned in her bed, and the family invites Poirot to investigate her death. To save the family undue scandal, he works methodically and quietly, beginning with facts and details brought to his attention by Captain Hastings who is only too willing to assist him. Next, he undertakes an intricate on-the-spot examination of the murder scene. For this case he even plays the bloodhound, getting on his knees and smelling a stain on the carpet, taking samples of cocoa, checking spilled candle wax, noting the dead ashes on the hearth and the fragments of a destroyed will. Then he questions everybody, beginning with the servants. While police inspectors and constables tend to intimidate and upset the servants, Poirot's continental charm succeeds in disarming even the most recalcitrant. Throughout the proceedings, he exhibits complete control—nothing disturbs his aplomb.

To assist him in his investigation, Poirot employs a traditional Watson in the person of Captain Arthur Hastings, now recuperating at Styles from a debilitating war injury. Hastings is open, energetic and uncomplicated; he willingly becomes Poirot's sounding board and his leg-man. Although he worked for Lloyd's of London before entering the service, Hastings has always harbored a wish to become a detective like Sherlock Holmes or Hercule Poirot. Occasionally, Hastings is rebuffed by the master, especially when he lets his imagination run away with him, but usually he and Poirot remain on friendly terms.

Poirot also gets along well with the official police investigators. He and Inspector Japp, who has been assigned to the case, are old friends, having worked together before. But Poirot is much freer than the representatives of Scotland Yard;

he is mobile and has direct entree to the inner social circle. Despite his foreign background, he is accepted as one of the elite: his manners, his accent, his person mark him as cosmopolitan.

When John Cavendish, the son of the victim and also a friend of Hastings, is arrested for his mother's murder, Poirot takes up the cause to prove him innocent. After discovering a missing piece of evidence, Poirot arranges for all parties involved to meet in one room to listen to his explanation of the crime. Lacking sufficient proof to convict the real murderers, Poirot resorts to subterfuge to trap the guilty. Through cunning, he then succeeds in forcing the murderer and his accomplice to confess. He also helps to reunite John Cavendish and his wife in a final romantic ploy.

The components of the typical Poirot adventure are established in this first novel—Poirot's character and methods, his relationship with Hastings and with Scotland Yard, his kind of clientele, his type of case. Having found a successful formula, Christie develops Poirot as a more credible character in future adventures—but she makes *few* changes.

In the series of short stories published under the title *Poirot Investigates* (1924), Christie experimented with the aesthetic combination she created in her first novel. She develops the intricacies of Poirot's character and methods as well as the growing relationship between Poirot and Hastings. And she also parodies the Sherlock Holmes tradition in these fourteen short stories.

Christie pays homage to the Sherlock Holmes literature in these stories by borrowing various clichés from the master: the Watson, the shared rooms and the landlady image; the emphasis on eccentricity in the sleuth; the prosaic quality of the Watson character, the special relationship with the police; the range of investigations from society robberies to international intrigues; the inordinate pride of the master-sleuth; the lack of family or romantic involvement for the great detective; the reticence on pedigree and family origins; and the great reliance on puzzle situations.

However, Christie depicts Poirot with greater detachment and more humor than Doyle does Holmes. Poirot is humanized in these stories by focusing on his foibles, his weaknesses, his comic traits. Yet Christie conveys at the same time the image of a dedicated, hard-working human being. It was especially important for Christie to make her hero acceptable because he is an alien who has to win the British reader's trust. Consequently, although he has the veneer of a foreigner, Poirot possesses the manners, social graces, values and sentiments dear to the Edwardian Englishman. He is well read in the classics of English literature, and he can speak "correctly"— when he cares to drop his pose. But his *savoir faire* in high society is his greatest asset, winning for him the patronage of aristocrats and royalty—and creating the necessary snob appeal for the ordinary reader.

While Poirot's eccentricities may disarm the criminal, he needed to prove that he was "normal" to the law-abiding public. Friendship with a proven British loyalist, Captain Arthur Hastings, completely endorses Poirot's credibility. Having served in Her Majesty's army, Hastings is employed as a secretary to a member of Parliament at the time when he and Poirot share rooms at 14 Farraway Street. And the living arrangements appear to be congenial, as the reader observes in the *Poirot Investigates* collection.

That Poirot and Hastings may have had a homosexual relationship is suggested in Keating's study.[3] We do not support this theory—for to make such an assumption is to miss the cultural shading Christie uses to contrast the emotional Poirot from the staid, conservative Hastings. Poirot is also such a self-styled loner that he readily marries off Hastings at his earliest convenience. And Hastings remains happily wed for over thirty years until the death of his wife. Poirot and Hastings remain good friends—nothing more, nothing less. Poirot's sex life is never discussed. If anything, he is neutral. He has no sexual involvements, though he mixes well socially with both men and women.

Hastings' role as a professional assistant to the great sleuth is developed more fully in *Poirot Investigates*. Under Poirot's tutelage, Hastings has been trained to follow instructions and to respect the judgment of the "master." But he does get one opportunity to solve a case on his own in "The Mystery of Hunter's Lodge." Poirot is bedridden with influenza and remains in his room sipping a tisane while Hastings is dispatched to investigate the murder of Roger Havering's uncle. However, Hastings is under orders from Poirot to report fully each day and to follow instructions without question. At the scene of the crime, poor Hastings is almost duped by a clever impersonation act; he is impatient, prone to be tricked by red herrings, and far too gullible. But he is faithful in reporting back to Poirot. From his sickbed, Poirot fingers the culprits by relying on Hastings' information and on his own famous "grey cells."

Poirot's skill as an armchair detective continues to mark him as different from the "bloodhound" type. While his assistant may scrounge around for miniscule traces of incriminating evidence, Poirot's activity becomes increasingly cerebral. In fact in "The Disappearance of Mr. Davenheim" he accepts a five pound bet from Inspector Japp of Scotland Yard to discover Davenheim's whereabouts without even leaving his chair. Poirot succeeds in proving motive, opportunity and method—much to the chagrin of Japp who must hand over five pounds.

Even genuises make mistakes. Poirot, as the reader soon learns, is fallible—and human. In "The Chocolate Box," his only failure, Poirot reveals to Hastings how he once made a fool of himself and almost sent an innocent man to the guillotine. As a member of the Belgian police force he was sent to investigate the suspicious death of a French deputy. After gathering incriminating evidence, he was about to make an arrest when the most unlikely individual confessed to the murder. Poirot recalls his shock and also his personal shame in making such a great error, blaming himself for not recognizing the truth—for the evidence was there in the chocolate box. The story tells Hastings as well as the reader that the famed Hercule Poirot can make a mistake and still be respected all the more for admitting it.

The break in the relationship between Poirot and Hastings occurs in *Murder on the Links* (1923). In this novel, Christie moves from the Holmes-Watson parody into a more original approach to her detective. Poirot becomes his own man in this adventure—eccentric, yes, but certainly capable as he deals with a love-stricken Hastings and a sardonic French detective. Poirot has been called to the French coast by a wealthy client who is found murdered shortly before Poirot arrives on the scene. Here we see Poirot mingling with ease and radiating his special charm to gain entree to the family circle. Hastings, on the other hand, is almost debilitated by his love for the mysterious young woman who becomes a prime suspect in the murder case.

So complete is Poirot's confidence in his detectival skills that the taunts of an arrogant young member of the French Sûreté do not deter him. The youthful Giraud strikes at Poirot's most vulnerable area—his age. He chides him about his out-dated methods: "You cut quite a figure in the old days, didn't you? But methods are different now."[4] Though Giraud bristles with efficiency and crawls about in search of clues, it is the old-timer, Poirot, who succeeds in solving the case.

Poirot is also ready now to establish himself *without* Hastings. The inept Arthur Hastings does not seem to realize that the young lady whom he loves shares the same feelings for him. In this case, the "herculean" task involves bringing the two lovers together—and, clearing the young woman of a murder charge. Happily, M. Poirot succeeds. Hastings goes off to Argentina to manage a ranch and live happily ever after with his bride. And Poirot is alone.

Oddly, Poirot does not open a professional office in London. Instead he decides to retire. In 1926 we find him in a rented cottage, a newcomer to the village of King's Abbot, where he is raising vegetable marrows (squash). But the impending doldrums of retirement are fortuitously shortlived, as Poirot is called upon to investigate the murder of Roger Ackroyd. This is the novel which stirred cries of "foul and unfair" from detective fiction devotees protesting Christie's violation of one of the unwritten rules of the genre. But breaking with tradition in this work was Christie's declaration to the world that she had confidence in herself and in her sleuth. Why would she risk rejection otherwise? Assisted in this case by Dr. Sheppard, the village physician, Poirot solves the almost perfect crime. He succeeds alone—without Hastings and despite the efforts of Dr. Sheppard!

Retirement now out of the question, Poirot returns to his career. In *The Big Four* (1927), Hastings visits England and discovers that his old mentor has become a celebrated consulting detective. They engage in another adventure together in which Poirot matches wits with a cunning criminal who calls himself "the destroyer." This man, once a professional actor, is an expert at disguise. But Poirot outperforms the whole cast of criminals—he upstages even the destroyer.

Poirot's life is threatened. When a powerful bomb explodes injuring Hastings, the end comes for Poirot. We learn that he has been killed. Hastings mourns the loss of his friend and pledges to avenge his death. Achille Poirot, the little-known brother of Hercule (shades of Mycroft Holmes), enters the fray and a marvelous double play thwarts the master plan. Alas! all is not lost—we learn that Poirot has no brother, that he himself has been operating in disguise to trap the Big Four. His act has been so perfect, in fact, that not even Hastings suspected.

The *femme fatale*, the only one in Poirot's life, comes to the rescue here—the Countess Vera Rossakoff. In this relationship Poirot comes as close as he ever will to a romantic entanglement. The Countess is a charming Russian aristocrat, a member of the old regime, who operates outside the law. She makes her first appearance in "The Double Clue" (1925) where she is responsible for stealing a fabulous collection of jewels. She would have kept the gems had it not been for Poirot's "pressure" to return them. But she returns the favor when she helps Poirot and Hastings to escape just before a massive explosion destroys the Big Four.

Crime continues to pay for Poirot. His fees from wealthy clients enable him to assume a more luxurious lifestyle. He moves from the rooms on Farraway Street to a chic flat, 203 Whitehaven Mansions. This crescent-shaped building is new and contains the latest in conveniences and appointments. Oddly, Poirot furnishes his flat in ultra modern decor, with lots of chrome and geometric shapes. His taste seems to belie his continental background—or perhaps the stark, sleek lines are meant to set off his baroque appearance.

Though Poirot has always looked like a dandy, he can now afford to indulge himself in silk scarves, fur-lined overcoats, and patent leather shoes. While a landlady looked after him on Farraway Street, he now has a valet—as befits a gentleman. Georges comes from the best stock, having served Lord Edward Frampton before taking a place with Poirot. We learn that Georges not only cares for his master's wardrobe and prepares unusual culinary delights, but he also assists him occasionally in his sleuthing. He is often a sounding board for his master's ideas; he penetrates the servants quarters, returning with vital bits of information; and he aids Poirot in several experiments.

With his increased income Poirot has the opportunity to frequent the best restaurants as often as he pleases. A lover of the Cordon Bleu cuisine, he avoids English tearooms and ordinary village cafes. He disdains the English breakfast, preferring only hot chocolate and an occasional croissant. He dislikes beer, abhors whiskey and serves his guests brandy or a sirop.

Business is so good, in fact, that Poirot hires a secretary. Miss Lemon, who may be the same woman who once worked for Mr. Parker Pyne, is cool and tart as her name suggests. We know little about her background, except that she has a sister. But she is the epitome of efficiency—and, one observes that she does not cramp Poirot's style in any way.

As his reputation grows, Poirot becomes a specialist in solving certain types of crimes—not the ordinary ones, but the most complex crimes which often implicate persons of position. He is also noted for vanquishing the enemy; in his battles with individual criminals the master thief or murderer never enters the lists again. The criminal seldom escapes justice; he is either imprisoned or executed, or he may be permitted to take his own life gracefully through an overdose of drugs.

Although Poirot does not undergo any radical changes in character over the years, his challenges tend to become more trying. In the stories and novels of the 1920s, M. Poirot meets and vanquishes a complete gallery of rogues. During the twenties, a favorite lament of Poirot is that the great criminal minds are disappearing, thus making his work less interesting and less challenging. But as he moves from 1928 through the thirties, this tune changes for he now comes up against the most creative criminals of all time—those who are noted for their assurance, their arrogance and their cunning.

M. Poirot finds himself battling a challenging duellist who deliberately involves him in the murder game, attempting to play with the detective as cat with mouse, controlling most of his actions and reactions through cunning deceptions, misrepresentations, hidden motives, impersonations, red herrings and sheer brilliant counter-plots to confuse, misdirect and foil the Master Sleuth. Among these great murder "chess-games" played by Poirot and the murderer are *Peril at End House, Lord Edgware Dies, Murder on the Orient Express* and *The A.B.C. Murders.*

The duel between Poirot as protagonist and a clever murderer as antagonist becomes tinged with personal animus, pride, disdain and desperation on the side of the criminal. Though the identification of the murderer is often delayed to the end of the novel, we meet him or her early enough to obtain by indirection an organic sense of character revelation and psychology. In *Peril at End House,* for example, the double role of the victim is a dazzling *tour de force,* a brilliant puzzle which only the very astute detective can solve. Poirot triumphs in this case, but this glory is not as evident in *Lord Edgware Dies* (1933). Hastings tells us that Poirot was so unhappy about the direction of this case that he actually despaired at one point of ever arriving at the truth. When he belatedly arrives at the correct solution, Poirot does not experience any satisfaction, for he feels this case is one of his failures. Even the murderess puts him down: "I never thought you'd be so horribly clever. You don't look clever."[5]

Among the most amazing minds to oppose Poirot is the collective genius revealed in *Murder on the Orient Express* (1934). This case is particularly interesting in its outcome, for Poirot winks at the letter of the law and allows the murderers to escape the legal consequences of their acts. We find that Poirot believes in a "higher" moral law—an Hebraic settling of accounts. This private interpretation of justice runs through Christie's works, culminating vividly in Poirot's last case, *Curtain.* But the most insulting murderer whom Poirot encounters is the clever manipulator in *The A.B.C. Murders* (1935). This villain writes belittling letters to M. Poirot ridiculing his powers and daring him to solve a series of murders which are announced in boastful terms beforehand.

Another group of audacious antagonists challenge the master by daring to commit murder in the midst of a group of people, including Poirot himself. Such villains are found in

Death in the Air (1935), *Murder in Three Acts* (1935) and *Cards on the Table* (1936). A woman is murdered on an airplane filled with people in *Death in the Air*, yet no one—not even Hercule Poirot—has noticed the attack. Since there is no chance of an outsider being involved, one of the passengers in the cabin must be the murderer. To Poirot's astonishment (and Inspector Japp's delight), the great detective himself becomes a prime suspect in the case because a likely weapon is found behind his seat cushion, and because he "looks guilty." But the murderer is no match for Poirot who soon clears his own good name and unmasks the guilty party.

Even on holiday, Poirot is plagued by crime. With both the desire and the means to travel, he enjoys taking trips—even though he complains continually of sea and air sickness. And when he travels, Poirot does so in the grand style. His prime reason for going abroad is usually to take a holiday, but often he is called upon to solve a murder. At least four of his holidays in the Middle East turn into perilous journeys as Poirot encounters dangerous criminal foes. (As we will note in Chapter VIII, Christie's travels with her archeologist husband obviously are reflected in these settings.) Such novels as *Appointment with Death* (1938), *Murder in Mesopotamia* (1936) and *Death on the Nile* (1937) are what might be called travel-murder books.

The work which Christie thought to be her best "foreign travel" mystery is *Death on the Nile*. Here we find Poirot attempting to escape from a cold, wet London by taking a holiday in Egypt. But while taking a steamer trip down the Nile, a young heiress is murdered and Poirot, also aboard the steamer, takes charge of the investigation to find the killer. Although he had hoped to enjoy his leisure, Poirot immediately shifts into high gear and narrows the circle of suspects to the two unlikely culprits.

From the 1940s on, Poirot's adventures decrease in number and in geographical range. His base tends to be his apartment in Whitehaven Mansions where, by appointment, clients come to consult him. A trip to the dentist in *The Patriotic Murders* (1940) unwittingly leads him into intrigue as the doctor is murdered in his own chair right after Poirot's visit. (How Christie must have enjoyed that touch!) Yet in most instances he is called upon by a third party to investigate a crime.

One of the obvious reasons for Poirot's more sedentary state is his advancing age. If he were in his sixties in 1915, how old must he be in 1940? The young woman who seeks his help in *Murder in Retrospect* (1943) is reluctant at first to employ Poirot when she sees how old he is. Despite his dyed hair, he is clearly showing his years. But he succeeds in proving to the girl that his "grey cells" are still young, and that any detective worth his salt should be able to solve a mystery without taxing himself physically. Notably, Poirot is not a complete armchair detective yet, for he still goes out to meet those individuals who can remember information to help him solve a crime that occurred sixteen years earlier. By assessing the characters of those involved along with details of the crime, Poirot works out the solution. This case and *Elephants Can Remember* (1972), one of his last cases, are both concerned with righting a wrong which occurred in the past, and both draw upon Poirot's talent for ferreting out evil.

The contrast between the now-aging Poirot and his younger subjects is highlighted in those novels of the late 1950s, *Hickory Dickory Death* (1955) and *Cat Among Pigeons* (1959), which deal with murders committed in student residences. The glaring typographical errors of his impeccable secretary, Miss Lemon, bring Poirot to the problem confronting Miss Lemon's sister, who is manager of a youth hostel in *Hickory Dickory Death*. The experienced old man of the world is able to prove to even the most enlightened of the students that he is still the master. One notices here especially that Poirot has suprahuman powers in sensing evil—a lawyer he consults in this case is convinced that he must be psychic as Poirot proceeds to tell him the contents of a sealed document. But Poirot stresses in these cases that human nature has not altered over the years.

The aging Poirot becomes involved more frequently with Mrs. Ariadne Oliver. She becomes his assistant in those situations requiring an insider of social consequence, bringing clues and hypothetical solutions to the master who then reevaluates her hasty conclusions. For the most part, the Oliver-Poirot duo works well as a study in contrasts: the large and disorganized Mrs. Oliver versus the petite and meticulous

M. Poirot. The combination produces a comic effect, and well-mannered humor unmatched in other Poirot combinations gives Poirot a vitality and wit unexpected for his age.

Throughout his career Poirot with other individuals who supply him with various kinds of information—police inspectors, other private detectives, and the typical amateur who wittingly or unwittingly assists. One such interesting youthful assistant is Colin Lamb, supposedly an alias for the son of Superintendent Battle, who consults Poirot in *The Clocks* (1963). By now Poirot has obviously aged. When the young man brings a problem to Poirot, he finds him in his apartment sitting in his armchair sipping a tisane. Proclaiming that his grey cells are as good as ever, Poirot proceeds to prove that he can solve the mystery right from his armchair. He sends an emissary to Somerset House for special information, however; and ultimately he cannot resist being personally on hand to give his solution. One notices that part of Poirot's function is instructive as he plays the role of teacher, passing his legacy on to the new generation of detectives.

Poirot comes full circle in *Curtain* (1975). When he and Hastings return to Styles for a final adventure, signs of aging and decay pervade. Styles Court is now a guest house split up into smaller quarters, furnished in a cheap modern style and managed by an elderly couple. Weeds have taken over the once lovely gardens and the ravages of suburbia intrude upon the estate. Hastings, now a widower with grey hair but still straight and distinguished looking, is appalled to find his old friend Poirot in a wheelchair and suffering from heart failure. Although his hair and mustache are dyed jet black, Poirot can no longer hide his age. But he assures Hastings that the grey cells are still functioning very well, and that the two of them have a final crime to solve together.

In this case, Hastings is Poirot's eyes and ears as it is his function to report all that goes on to his disabled friend. Poirot explains that the murderer is a person like Iago who provokes certain people to commit crimes, deriving sadistic pleasure out of violent acts which he himself cannot carry out. The problem is made real for the reader as Hastings himself becomes caught up in the murderer's web: the stalwart old soldier is prodded into thinking that his daughter is being seduced; to protect her, he plans to kill the undesirable man. After Poirot thwarts Hastings' plan, he tells him: "Everyone is a potential murderer—in everyone there arises from time to time the *Wish* to kill—though not the will to kill."[6]

Before the curtain falls, Poirot gives the award winning performance of his life. We learn that he is really able to walk, that he wears a wig and a false mustache, that he has been putting on an act to trap a murderer. But not only does he engage the criminal in a psychological battle; in this case he assumes, for the first—and last—time in his life, the role of judge and executioner. Poirot proclaims, "I am the law.... By taking [X's] life, I have saved other lives."[7] We discover later that Poirot drugs and then shoots the guilty person, making it look like suicide. He then arranges his own death, knowing that by rejecting medication he will not survive an on-coming heart seizure.

In this final case, Poirot is totally *alone*—Hastings is present but is too emotionally involved to function as an effective Watson; no policemen are called to the scene; and Georges, Poirot's valet, has been replaced by a stranger. Never has the great master detective had this kind of problem to solve before. (Physically, Poirot is declining—his armchair has been replaced by a wheelchair.) How then does he set about capturing the criminal? In effect, he decides to stop a crime and contain the killer by using the methods of the criminal—subterfuge, trickery and manipulation of the law.

Christie composed *Curtain* during World War II, most likely as an effort to put her affairs in order should she not survive the bombing of London. Yet this novel reveals a decided shift in her thinking as she permits Poirot to take the law into his own hands. Perhaps the panorama of death and injustice which she witnessed during these wartime years is reflected in the retributive justice Poirot metes out in his last case. During the war, Christie lived alone and spent her days working in the dispensary of University Hospital—walking back and forth from her flat amid the bombs. She lost her son-in-law in battle. And she was separated from her husband who was serving his country in the Middle East. Perhaps Christie's wartime experiences may account for *Curtain*.

Why did Christie plan the demise of her most successful

detective? As we have seen, Christie had a proprietary attitude toward her privacy, her wealth, her family, her possessions. She was the kind of person to consider Poirot her exclusive artistic property. It is understandable then that Christie made certain Poirot would be laid to rest so that no one could usurp him after her own death.

Still, the treatment of Poirot in *Curtain* is unique in the history of detective fiction. No other creator of a detective hero has killed off a leading character with such bizarre precision. Not even Jane Marple suffers such a fate. Why does Christie put an end to Poirot in this manner—making him a murderer or public executioner as well as a suicide? After all, Poirot had been a strict moralist, a man who had never had blood on his hands.

In *Curtain* Poirot faces a diabolical foe, the embodiment of evil, who uses other people as a catspaw in his murderous schemes. When all ordinary means of bringing him to justice fail, Poirot takes the law into his own hands. He acts alone but with the conviction of his conscience. Yet Poirot's intellectual pride at outwitting this criminal hints of ignoble motivation. The ultimate rationale then is a pragmatic one—murder or execution is sometimes necessary for the protection of society (just as it is in time of war). Thus Poirot's actions may be viewed as a kind of self-sacrifice in behalf of his fellowmen. (Not all readers, however, may be willing to accept this ethic.)

The puzzle upon which *Curtain* is structured is among Christie's most unusual and challenging. Variations on *Ten Little Indians* can be found in the unusual character of the murderer, in his methods and in the prolonged solution to the problem. The annihilation of the murderer involves a cover-up—a murder staged to look like suicide (but with a clue: the bullet enters at the center of the forehead resembling the "mark of Cain"). The death of the detective appears to be "natural" although suicidal intent is revealed later. As in *Ten Little Indians*, the finesse comes in an epilogue which tells all—finally completing the puzzle.

Despite the challenge of the puzzle and the rationale with which one may approach the case, the reader may feel uncomfortable if not because of the shifting of the moral balance then certainly because Poirot is out of character here.

Poirot fans may well have difficulty watching their hero laboring in a debilitated body bearing the ravages of age and illness. The end is indeed unseemly and perhaps unfair for the great detective, his triumph bittersweet. Christie releases Poirot from his earthly tasks only after he plans his own death and arranges his own funeral. One would have hoped that Christie might have shown more good humor and tenderness here instead of such clinical precision.

Though Christie became bored with Poirot and wanted to dispose of him years before the publication of *Curtain,* the public became increasingly fond of him. Why? Poirot is a memorable character. His egg-shaped head, his foreign mannerisms, his eccentricities, his comic pretensions—all combined to distinguish him from his peers. Poirot became "a person" fleshed out in his temper tantrums, his flights of fancy, his compassion, his flair for the dramatic. And readers came to respect him.

As a detective, Poirot was traditional in method. Neither a "blood-hound" nor a complete "armchair detective," he employed a felicitous combination of common sense, deductive reasoning, and flashes of intuition to solve his cases. His "grey cells," which became his trademark, mark him as a clever, cerebral type of sleuth. To Poirot, therefore, came the most ingenious puzzle—those cases of the 1930s and 1940s composed during his creator's prime.

Will Hercule Poirot, master sleuth, achieve immortality as a detective hero? We believe that he will indeed. As a fictional character, he is unforgettable; as a detective he is often brilliant; and as a riddler of puzzles, he is a master. Ironically, though Christie did not see fit to permit Poirot to live, she endowed him with the gift of immortality—her most creative puzzles.

Chapter V

Miss Jane Marple: Little Old Lady Sleuth

D.N.B. (1970-1981)

MARPLE, JANE (185?-), amateur sleuth, was born in Chichester during the 1850s, the older daughter of the Reverend Marple, Vicar of the Chichester congregation. Miss Marple was educated at home and then studied in Paris as a teenager at a young ladies' school. She was subsequently engaged to be married, but the engagement was broken. Her younger sister married and became the mother of the successful writer Raymond West.

Miss Marple never married. She lives alone in the village of St. Mary Mead, where she has resided for over fifty years. A lifelong member of the Church of England, she has continued to remain active in church affairs. Her exceptional dedication to the community has taken various forms over the years. Miss Marple has been responsible for training young girls from the local orphanage in the art of housekeeping. She is also an unofficial counselor to the troubled, especially to the young and lovelorn. As the eldest member of the village, she has assumed the role of local historian; contributing to her success in this area are her unusual powers of observation and her vivid memory. Her hobbies include bird-watching, gardening, knitting and gossiping.

Her career as an amateur sleuth began in the late 1920s when she became hostess for a social group who dined at her home and then enjoyed a parlor game of riddling detection puzzles. Among her notable guests at these functions was Sir Henry Clithering, former head of Scotland Yard, with whom Miss Marple was to share an enduring friendship. It was in 1930s, however, that Jane Marple first came to public attention: she succeeded in trapping the culprits responsible for the murder at the vicarage. In 1942 she defended the honor of her friends, the Bantrys, when the body of a young girl was discovered in their library.

Fame brought Miss Marple outside the community of St. Mary Mead in the 1950s to assist acquaintances who were plagued by evil in such villages as Lymstock, which was threatened by poison pen letters and murder; and Chipping Cleghorn, which was beset by a murderer who announced his plans in advance.

Occasionally, her successes were touched with private sorrow. In 1962 a happy reunion with an old friend from her Paris schooldays ended tragically as Miss Marple found herself at the scene of a murder. The following year she was called upon to pursue the murderer of one of her protéges, young Gladys, whom she had trained for service.

Wherever she has gone, Jane Marple has proved unrelenting in her

105

struggle against evil whether in the great homes of England, such as Rutherford Hall and Gorston Manor, or in her travels. In 1964, after a serious case of pneumonia, Miss Marple traveled to the Caribbean to recuperate; but even here she became involved in the pursuit of a killer. The following year she spent a week at her favorite place in London, Bertram's Hotel. After she had barely tasted her tea and seed cake, Miss Marple sensed that all was not well at this elegant hostelry—and the pursuit was on. A house and gardens tour which she took in 1971, however, almost proved fatal as Miss Marple fought for her life in a hand-to-hand struggle with a killer.

Recently, the astounding story of one of her earlier triumphs was made public for the first time, though it occurred back in the 1940s. Miss Marple, in this case, assisted a young woman who wished to discover the truth about a murder "sleeping" for over twenty years.

Though age has now necessitated retirement from most of her activities, Miss Jane Marple is alive and well—living quietly in the village of St. Mary Mead.

The little old lady with snowy white hair and blue eyes knitting fleecy pastel items pursues an unlikely avocation. Miss Jane Marple is an amateur sleuth. Though deceptively fragile and uncommonly shrewd, she assumes her place comfortably in middle class society as a "lady" with a special talent for solving mysterious crimes.

But this lady is someone with a mystique of her own. The niece of a Canon of Chichester and the aunt of a famous writer, Jane Marple appears to have spent most of her life in the village of St. Mary Mead. Though once engaged to an unsuitable young man of whom her mother did not approve, she acquiesced to her mother's judgment and seems happily to have accepted her single state.

Independent status, excellent eyesight, and a nose for gossip dispose her well for her role as amateur sleuth. But her special talent, a keen understanding of human nature, is her most distinguishing feature. By analyzing character correctly and, by analogy, typing people accurately, Miss Marple is capable of focusing on the guilty and protecting the innocent. Guided by feminine intuition and reinforced by a strong moral sense, she devises her own methods for trapping suspects.

Despite her unassuming appearance, this little old lady has attained world-wide fame. Other writers have employed female sleuths before Christie breathed life into Jane Marple— notably Anna Katharine Green's Amelia Butterworth (1898) and Grant Allen's Hilda Wade (1900). Although Amelia Butterworth is middle-aged, and almost twenty years younger than Marple, she too is genteel and astute, "a woman of inborn principle and strict Prebyterian training."[1] As a member of New York society, she has access to certain inner circles where her sense of evil is employed to ferret out guilty secrets. But unlike Jane Marple, Miss Butterworth is merely employed and then outdone by an astute member of the police force who uses her as a catspaw to solve complex crimes.

In contrast, Hilda Wade is a young woman in her early twenties whose exploits are motivated by her desire to clear her father's name. She shares Marple's insight, however, for she too "recognizes temperament—the fused form of character, and what it is likely to do."[2] Another female who also bears some slight resemblance to Marple is Stacy Aumonier's Miss Millicent Bracegirdle (1923). Like Marple, she is a spinster from a rural British town, but this sister of a vicar is much less daring and self-sufficient than Jane Marple.

Among those authors who shared the literary scene at the beginning of the century with Christie, such as Mary Roberts Rinehart and Mrs. Belloc Lowndes, none created a female detective with the longevity and fame of Miss Marple. In the late 1930s Patricia Wentworth developed Miss Maud Silver, a retired nurse with a stern sense of morality and a gift of clairvoyance. Yet Marple, who emerged at least ten years prior to Silver, remains the prototype and the more celebrated character.

One can also cite similarities in personal qualities and methods between Marple and her male counterparts. Chesterton's Father Brown, for example, relies upon an unassuming presentation of self and brilliant flashes of intuition for his success—much like Marple. Ramsey perceives Marple as "a neat combination of the Old Man in the Corner and Madame Defarge."[3] One might also draw a parallel between Marple and Sergeant Bucket: both share the innocent, benign appearance, the ready sympathy for the wronged innocent, the implacable pursuit of the guilty. However, amid any number of like combinations, Marple distinguishes herself from her fellow literary detectives.

First, Jane Marple abounds in shocking incongruities.

Seemingly fragile and often enfeebled, she jaunts about with great energy. Though supposedly restricted by a "limited" income, she often splurges in elegant social arenas. This benign, white-haired lady is a female bloodhound; she not only believes in the presence of evil, but also suspects everybody of possible evil.

Because she is gentle, elderly and very proper, Marple does not seem to pose a threat to anyone. In fact people tend to overlook her—at first. But they are soon brought up short, for this Victorian spinster is a powerhouse. Her deceptive appearance and lulling naiveté disarm criminals (and readers), who are caught off guard until they feel the cool steel beneath that fleecy wool.

Above all, Marple is human—this is her most salient feature. Christie managed to capture in Marple the final life spark of a dying generation. As she confided to interviewer Bernstein, Christie drew Marple's character from real life: "My grandmother lived to be 92, so she was a great study to the end. I had a great aunt of the same age and a lot of things they approved and disapproved of were representative, and they both contributed to Miss Marple."[4] The two sisters, Mrs. Margaret Miller and Mrs. Mary Boehmer, as we have noted earlier, had a profound effect on young Agatha. Images of these elderly ladies knitting soft garments, shopping at the Army and Navy Stores, training young servant girls are among the facets of the composite Jane Marple.

The literary genesis of Marple can be traced to obscure beginnings in *The Mystery of the Blue Train* (1928), then to fuller development of character in the *Tuesday Club Murders* (1928-32) and in *Murder at the Vicarage* (1932). The village of St. Mary Mead appears for the first time in *The Mystery of the Blue Train* as does a crafty old lady named Miss Viner who was to become the prototype of Miss Marple.

If in the village of St. Mary Mead Christie recreated English village life, in Marple she fleshed out its virtues, values and customs. Marple's fictional model, Miss Viner, is an aging spinster who, through her Victorian-style letters, conveys news of the village to a young female friend abroad. In these letters are vignettes of vibrant village females, local gossip and details of daily routines. Christie devised Miss Viner's letters as a medium for weaving the fabric of the village of St. Mary Mead. When Christie later placed Jane Marple in the same village, she made her more than a letter-writing commentator. Marple is given a vital role to play in the village; she is involved in the central action of the community as she investigates the disappearance of the family silver, questions the new curate's odd behavior, or chides the young women "in service" who speak out of turn.

In the loquacious Miss Viner, Christie developed the talent for which Jane Marple was to become most famous—skill in anecdotal conversation. Marple spins off tales of family problems, village scandals and words to the wise that lead naturally into the arena of detection. Marple's "small talk" is the source for character revelation, social commentary, clue-gathering and confrontation drama.

How did Marple become involved in the detection game? "The Tuesday Night Club," the title story of the *Tuesday Club Murders* collection, reveals that a select group of people gathered socially at her home; as after-dinner entertainment, each presented a detection puzzle to be solved by the rest of the group. (The individual stories of this collection precede publication of *Murder at the Vicarage,* indicating that Christie tested out the viability of her new sleuth in short story form first.)

With Miss Marple presiding, this inner circle of the "right" people includes among others the former head of Scotland Yard, a famous actress, and Raymond West (Marple's nephew). With unassuming grace, Marple proceeds to astound everyone with her uncanny success at riddling the various puzzles. Her method is to listen carefully, question, draw upon an analogy, and arrive at the correct solution.

In one of her stories, "The Bungalow Mystery," Miss Marple prevents a crime from being committed. She realizes that the young actress who is describing a robbery is actually telling her plans for a future crime she intends to "stage" in order to trap her husband and his mistress. As the older and much wiser woman, Marple cautions the actress about involving herself in such a scheme.

For the most part, the brief episodes developed in these short stories do not show Marple at her best because the medium is too confining. Marple requires space and time to move about in a community to cast her spell. We find, for example, better Marple in the final story of the collection, "Death by Drowning," an adventure that does not take place in theory as after-dinner entertainment, but *live* in the village of St. Mary Mead. No longer the armchair detective, Marple rises to the occasion by assisting Sir Henry Clithering, the former head of Scotland Yard. Together, they apply their skills to discover the murderer of a pregnant village girl. Though this case confirms Marple's talent for detection, at the same time the short story reveals the serious limits of the form and indicates the need for a larger canvas.

Murder at the Vicarage, the first novel in the Marple series, establishes Marple as a credible character. With the novel as her medium, Christie found the scope needed to shape Marple's world—the parameters of the village, the various social circles, the characters who were to become the "living features" of the community. Thus the village of St. Mary Mead functions as part of and because of Miss Marple: we know her through her role in the community.

When murder rocks the serenity of the vicarage, Marple emerges quite naturally as a likely amateur sleuth. Her Victorian upbringing, her conviction of the presence of evil, her feminine intuition, her method of perceiving analogies—all prepare her for the role. And her penchant for gossip puts her steps ahead of the local police. Not foiled by false clues or the masking of identity, she cuts through to the core of the mystery.

Notably, the portrayal of Marple in this novel differs from that in succeeding works. Here she is blatantly a busybody with time on her hands, eager to watch more than just birds with her binoculars. (Happily, the binoculars disappear after this portrait.) And gardening is more like a "cover" than a true avocation as it provides unlimited opportunities for observation and gossip. Marple is glib at times, evincing a know-it-all attitude. In subsequent works these obtrusive traits are modified, and Marple is depicted as less of a snoop and a more credible amateur detective. In time, Christie refined her perception of Marple and shaped her into a more human character.

The salient feature of this first fully-drawn portrait is the firm establishment of Marple as a trusted member of the community: she has roots in the village and church affiliation, and family—a nephew, but the maiden aunt role is expanded by her gratuitous knitting of little garments for the youngest members of the community so that she emerges as the archetypal great aunt. A consistent principle of character is also identifiable: Marple's ability to sense evil and type people, just as she groups flowers and birds. Certain detectival methods are also established such as her keen observation, probing conversation, clever linking of clues, and the staging of a confrontation drama to trap the guilty.

With *The Body in the Library* (1942), Marple's reputation is assured. Now a recognized local authority on crime, she sallies forth to the rescue of her friends, Colonel and Mrs. Bantry. The body of a young woman has been found in the library of their home—creating a well of suspicion and talk among the townsfolk. To preserve the good name of the Bantrys and to avenge the unfortunate girl's murder, Marple sets about solving the crime.

Marple moves with calm assurance as she traces leads and evaluates clues. No longer a rank amateur, she has acquired investigative skill: she scrutinizes marriage records and examines wills at London's Somerset House. By using the right psychology in her interrogation of a dissembling girl guide, she connects disparate clues. With the cooperation of police officers, she then sets the trap for the guilty parties. Clearly the armchair detective role is not to be hers, for Marple proves herself capable physically and mentally.

Despite her increasing fame, Marple's services are not for hire. She does not earn a living through detection; usually she enters a case at the request of a friend or to satisfy her own curiosity. But once committed, Marple is dogged in pursuit of the truth. Unlike Poirot, Marple does not traffic with master criminals; but one can depend on her to ferret out evildoers in the small communities she knows well and also those within the range of her occasional travels. The type of malefactor she tends to encounter is usually a respected member of the community who commits a crime in order to cover up a guilty secret or to satisfy greed for the family fortune or to dispose of an unwanted spouse.

In *The Moving Finger* (1943), Marple comes to the rescue of the village of Lymstock, which has been plagued first by a series of poison pen letters and then by murder. We observe the ease with which Marple moves about this community, for though it is not *her* village, she is sensitive to the villagers' expectations and customs. Clad in her well-cut tweed suit, Marple is readily accepted. Unlike Poirot who must prove that a foreigner can be trusted, Marple is thoroughly English and beyond reproach. And she uses this entrée to full advantage.

Marple alone gets to the heart of the problem in Lymstock. Though the local police are convinced that the poison pen murderer is a woman, Marple is not easily put off. She understands people, especially women, and she herself is experienced in the art of gossip, for the letters are a perverted form of gossip. After careful examination of the evidence, she concludes that the poison pen writer is not a woman—for the psychology is all wrong. Then, winning the confidence of townspeople, she soon learns of essential family gossip and recent village scandals. The break in the case develops when Marple recognizes that young Agnes, one of the housemaids, is not telling the truth; and soon admonishes her into a full revelation and then uses her to trap the murderer.

Although *The Moving Finger* takes place during World War II, Christie includes nothing about the war—even though one of the characters is an RAF officer recuperating from injuries received, presumably, in combat. The reverberations from the bombs and the destruction and the food shortages do not disturb the gentle decorum of the village. Even *Sleeping Murder*, the novel which followed in sequence but which was saved for posthumous publication, is also untouched by the war. However, those novels which Christie published from 1950 onward describe the sweeping changes which England experienced *after* World War II.

From the 50s onward, Christie's novels treat the decline of the old lifestyle from a mixture of nostalgia for the past and distrust for the future. She focuses on the changing family structure, on the effect of new money, on the loss of tradition, and on the decay of the estates of the gentry. In these novels, Marple functions as the Victorian nurturing mother—the last of a dying breed. As a soother and healer, she always knows what is right and what is wrong; her domestic skills range from managing people to running a large home—and to solving crimes.

With *A Murder is Announced* (1950), we find alterations in village life-style with the infusion of strangers on the once thoroughly familiar terrain. Chipping Cleghorn is a village besieged by a series of murders, but it has other problems which Marple uncovers when she is called upon to help. Now, times have changed. Complaints about servants, refugees, lax police, food shortages abound. We learn that the subtler links that had held together English social life had fallen apart. These stresses have weakened society's moral fiber. Rackets provide cover for embezzlers, blackmailers and legacy hunters who prey on innocent villagers.

When murder occurs as guests are sipping sherry at Miss Blacklock's home, the village is torn apart by suspicion and fear. Two more murders intensify the situation. A refugee cook is driven into terror spasms at the sight of the police; strangers hide under aliases; legitimate heirs conceal their true identity.

Marple places herself in personal danger in her effort to trap the murderer. When she emerges from a hiding place in the nick of time to prevent a fourth murder, she grapples hand-to-hand with the assailant and, but for the timely intervention of the police, might have been the next victim. Interestingly, despite having aged twenty years since the *Murder at the Vicarage*, little old Miss Marple is showing no signs of decline.

But when Marple is propelled into a country home debased into a corrections institution and into that twilight zone between aberrant psychology and criminality, she loses her vitality. *Murder With Mirrors* (1952) is set at an institution for delinquent boys, where Marple's girlhood friend resides with her husband who runs the facility. While the subject of juvenile delinquency is timely and the murders which occur are challenging, Marple is out of her element. Without the usual delights of the village—the shops, the varieties of people,the gossip, the social gatherings—the milieu is lifeless; the novel is lackluster.

When the setting fits Marple, as it does in *A Pocketful of Rye* (1953), all parts of the novel work together successfully,

Yewtree Lodge, a large estate of the newer variety—lacking in taste and old money—forms the background for this mystery. With the economic shifts following the war, a new breed of moneyed individuals have bought into old land. Among them is financial wizard Rex Fortesque, the owner of Yewtree Lodge.

Marple enters the scene uninvited after the deaths of Fortesque, his young wife and Gladys, a housemaid, formerly employed by Miss Marple. Outraged that the unfortunate Gladys has been murdered in such an unseemly fashion, Marple sets out to find the villain. When she appears at the doorstep of Yewtree Lodge, she says the right things to the right people and is invited to stay. She is welcomed particularly by the family matriarch, an aged aunt who shares similar values. Clearly, Marple is in her element here as she interviews members of the household, mothers the young people and soothes the staff.

While times may have changed, Marple's old-fashioned methods and ideas still succeed. She talks and then listens; then ultimately the truth spills out. The motive for the crime in this case is as old as mankind—greed. And Marple's discovery of the motive is reinforced by her own inbred notion about the nature of evil, that the crooked cannot be made straight. The "bad seed" in the family eventually reveals himself as Marple puts the pieces of the murder puzzle together.

The ravages of time and fortune set the tone for Marple's next exploit. In *What Mrs. McGillicuddy Saw* (1957), Christie takes us to another estate, a dilapidated one this time. Rutherford Hall is in disrepair; its grounds are overgrown with weeds and unkempt shrubbery. The town has impinged on its borders, leaving it ignominiously shunted in on all sides.

Time has taken its toll not only on the estate but suddenly on Jane Marple herself. No longer able to get around as she used to, Marple employs a young emissary, Lucy Eyelesbarrow, to infiltrate Rutherford Hall. (Marple is convinced that the body of a murdered woman is buried somewhere on the grounds.) Although she stays nearby at the home of a former housekeeper, Marple is removed physically in this novel; she directs Lucy Eyelesbarrow's activities, but does not participate in the tense moments of discovery.

This adventure marks a crisis in Marple's career. She is

nearly ninety years old—enfeebled, deaf, rheumatic. To her sorrow, gardening is forbidden as too strenuous for her failing heart. She tries to knit, but the continual dropping of stitches and the unravelling of the wool brings tears to her eyes. Could Christie have been planning to retire Marple at this point?

But Christie decided instead to rejuvenate Marple. In *The Mirror Crack'd* (1963), Marple should be at least ninety-five years old, but she seems years younger. In fact, Marple appears to have reached a comfortable plateau. However, the village of St. Mary Mead has changed drastically. The old homes have been sold off, a housing development blots the countryside and even Mrs. Bantry has been displaced. Now a widow, she lives in a small cottage on the grounds of her former estate, while the family mansion is currently owned by an actress who has renovated it in the Hollywood style.

A reception given at the house attended by the villagers becomes the scene of a murder. Marple, who is among the guests, shrewdly picks up details of the scene—odd gestures and suspicious behavior, traces of drugs and indications of corruption within this once "honorable" house. The increasing rootlessness among the new generation, Marple feels, has taken its toll. She connects the breakdown in law and morality with the alterations in British social life. Even in St. Mary Mead, Teddy Boys armed with knives haunt the new housing development, and the Mayor himself is said to be "one shade" this side of the law. Women have gone off to work in factories; the children are left unsupervised; and strangers roam through the village.

Ironically, the motives for murder do not change, nor does the threat of murder come from the outside. When Marple perceives vengeance as the motivation for murder in this case, she soon discovers that the murderer is not a stranger. The primal act of destruction is rooted in human history—in relationships, in the weakness of certain individuals—for people rarely deliberately kill those they do not know.

During the final years of her career, Marple does a surprising amount of traveling in spite of or because of her health. *A Caribbean Mystery* (1964) finds Marple at a British-run hotel on the island of St. Honore. The hotel is a gathering place for an assortment of couples and singles who enter into congenial company, at least until murder invades the premises. Although she is supposedly recuperating from a bout with pneumonia, Marple swings into action and prevents a final murder from being committed.

On holiday this time at a lovely old London hotel, Marple encounters a world of intrigue *At Bertram's Hotel* (1965). Capitalizing on public nostalgia, this hotel caters to a clientele willing to pay for a true rendition of the Edwardian period with its comfortable overstuffed chairs, well-made mahogany desks, genuine English tea and impeccable service.

Initially Marple enjoys the amenities of the hotel and the company of its genteel guests. And she busies herself with shopping forays to the Army and Navy Stores—just as she did in the good old days. But she soon realizes that all seems to be too good to be true.

Against this antiquated background, a modern drama is actually being played involving an international crime syndicate, precocious teenagers and varieties of concealed identity. Christie manages to fuse the vitality of the present with the traditional shock of Marple assets—gossip, eavesdropping, observation and just plain snooping.

Marple has become increasingly concerned about the young, in a grandmotherly fashion. As we indicated earlier, at a point in time Christie and Marple reached the same age, shared the same bodily aches and pains, and had the same concerns of the older generation for the young. The realism and intensity with which the views of Marple are articulated here seems to reveal the author more than ever in the lament about modern lifestyles and the dangers of not maintaining a proper home for the protection and education of the young.

Six years later we find Marple even more involved with young people as she attempts to solve a mystery rooted in the past. *Nemesis* (1971) describes the role Marple plays against the evil which has almost ruined a young man's life and which has actually claimed the lives of four innocent people, two of them young women.

Marple is older here; she requires periods of rest, but she is reasonably active. In fact she accepts an opportunity to complete a mysterious mission which involves traveling on a homes and gardens tour. A need to discover the truth and to clear a family name motivates Marple far more than the monetary reward offered, for she is really acting as evil's nemesis in this case.

With heroic fortitude, Marple places herself at the very center of evil—in the house of three elderly sisters. Suggestions of witchcraft and deterioration pervade everything as Marple attempts to solve the mystery of two earlier murders. The house and the grounds of this estate are in disrepair; the sisters are aging and exhibit strange, erratic behavior. But Marple's intrinsic sense of the presence of evil leads her to uncover the truth. Though a seemingly fragile old lady shrouded in her pink wool shawl, Marple confronts the murderer—and comes very close to being annihilated herself in the process.

Nemesis is parallel in theme to the Poirot mystery, *Elephants Can Remember*, written during the same period. In both novels, Christie reshapes the past—reaching back in time to right wrongs which were never corrected. Memory is a major factor in both cases, for though age eventually limited Marple and Poirot physically, both retained their mental acuity.

In anticipation of Marple's last case, *Sleeping Murder* (1976), the public assumed that Jane Marple would die—just as Poirot had in *Curtain*. The surprise then came not only in the solution to the mystery but also in the discovery that Marple is permitted to *live*.

Nostalgia pervades this work as Christie takes the reader back to Devon again, to *her* home—to the familiar house with a view of the sea, to the nursery covered with floral wallpaper. When the young heroine of the story, Gwenda Reed, arrives from New Zealand, she buys a house in the seaside village of Dillmouth. Gwenda, however, becomes haunted by a sense of *déjà vu* after she moves into the house. Fearing hallucinations, she consults Marple who reassures her of her sanity. Marple is practical; she does not believe in ghosts, nor does she believe that Gwenda is mentally ill.

In this mystery, Marple seems to *know* who the culprit is right from the beginning. She advises the young couple not to delve into the past, that danger and some painful truths may emerge. Gwenda is convinced that her step-mother was actually murdered in the very house she has bought; yet Marple feels that it is better to let "sleeping murder" lie. Still,

Gwenda and her husband, Giles, decide to pursue the truth.

At one point, Giles Reed says of Miss Marple, "Poking here or prying there, or asking a few questions. I hope she doesn't ask too many one of these days."[5] The comment might have been a foreshadowing of what was to happen to Marple while assisting the Reeds, for Marple is most helpful in gathering information from former servants and local people who recall the former inhabitants of the house and who knew Gwenda's family. One can only conjecture, but it does seem likely that Christie intended for Marple to be placed in danger—perhaps to give her life in a heroic last act—foisting herself between the killer and his intended victim. (After all, Poirot does just this to save Hastings and his daughter.) But such is not the way the novel develops. Instead, Marple assaults and disarms the murderer.

Nostalgia prevails instead. The last scene finds Jane Marple and the Reeds in safe harbor—in Torquay, far from the scene of the crime—calmly discussing the case on the lovely terrace of the Imperial Hotel. Harmony has been restored, the evil exorcised in the serenity of Torquay.

But why is Marple spared? Given the prototypes for Jane Marple—Christie's grandmother and aunt—and given also the likelihood that Christie herself identified in later years with Marple, it was probably impossible to destroy her. While Christie's creative integrity might have spurred her on to make an appropriate aesthetic end to her most lovable detective, it was very likely impossible for her to do so—requiring in fact a kind of psychic suicide.

The public waited eagerly for this last Marple mystery. In fact, the paperback rights for *Sleeping Murder* were purchased by Bantam at a record 1.75 million dollars *before* publication of the hardback novel. The record amount of money attests to the popularity of both the author and her famous female sleuth. And the subsequent popularity of the work is best told by its place on international bestseller lists.

But what does the future hold for Marple? Will this little old lady fade into the dusty archives of detective fiction? We believe that Jane Marple will endure. She possesses that unique combination of warmth and vitality needed to endear future generations of readers. Marple is a credible character;

she represents common sense and solid values—attributes which have universal appeal. And then she has been immortalized in the village of St. Mary Mead, that mythic environment of the English country village. Marple is naturally associated with the village and its timeless charm. To those who remember the pre-war English village, the Marple novel affords a trip back. To those who have never been there Miss Marple's world offers unique atmosphere and unequalled ambience.

Chapter VI

Sundry Folk:
Christie's Lesser Known Sleuths

Agatha Christie created a range of detectives—male, female, young, old, British, foreign, professional and amateur. Several detectives, though not as celebrated as Hercule Poirot or Jane Marple—reveal other dimensions of the talented Christie. Among these are Harley Quin and Mr. Satterthwaite, a strange nonprofessional duo; Parker Pyne, private detective; Tuppence and Tommy Beresford, undercover agents; and Ariadne Oliver, novelist and amateur sleuth. Except for Parker Pyne, no one else in this group advertises his or her talents on the market or earns a living through detection. However, all of them have a select clientele and perform successfully in different areas of detection.

Symons points out that the sleuth in detective fiction "was most often an amateur, because in this way the reader was able easily to put himself in the detective's position, and he alone was upon occasion allowed to be above the law, and to do things which for a character less privileged would be punishable."[1] Christie's sleuths follow this tradition in their use of extra-legal methods such as ruses, subterfuges, burglary, lying, coercion and entrapment. Because they are not affiliated with the police establishment, they handle cases which are too personal or too explosive to be brought before a public agency— matters of the "heart" or situations of potential scandal. And they are different in character and treatment from other detectives—including Christie's own Hercule Poirot and Jane Marple. Distinguished by their romantic and often fantastic adventures, these lesser known sleuths reflect that hidden dimension of Agatha Christie—the intensely emotional, self-revealing romantic component which she disguised under the pseudonym of Mary Westmacott in her six romantic novels.

Unique among all Christie's detectives is the Harley Quin—Mr. Satterthwaite duo. In this creative combination, Christie fused the mystery puzzle with the pure romance of the fairy tale tradition. The short stories in *The Mysterious Mr. Quin* (1930) collection recount the exploits of a magician-like detective and his assistant as they avert marital disasters, right the wrongs of the law and solve some strange crimes. In most cases they change the erring course of a client's life so that he or she will "live happily ever after."

Harley Quin is a derivation of the famed Harlequin, the clown with metaphysical and supernatural dimensions whose roots extend back to the sixteenth century Italian Commedia dell' Arte. The pantomimes featuring Harlequin were very popular in England during Christie's early years, finding ready audiences in London as well as in towns like Torquay which had its own theatre. As a child, Agatha went to the elaborate Christmas-time pantomimes with her grandmother and attended performances near her home in Torquay. She also frequented the theatre in Paris during her study there; at that time the Commedia dell' Arte tradition, an integral factor in the comedies of Moliere, continued to influence French comedy—particularly at the theatre Moliere's troupe founded, the Comedie Francaise.

Although Christie's fascination for Harlequin began in the theatre, she expressed her interest in other mediums—in a collection of poems about Harlequin and Columbine and in fiction through her own character, Harley Quin. Though traditionally a comic character, Christie's Mr. Quin was, as Christie acknowledged, "a friend of lovers, and connected with death."[2] The extremes of love and death reflect her personal concerns during those years between 1926 and 1930 when she had been traumatized by her mother's death, the breakup of her first marriage, her own disappearance episode; and then revived by her remarriage.[(These influences are treated more explicitly in two romances of the same period—*Giant's Bread* (1930) and *Unfinished Portrait* (1934).] As she matured as both a person and a writer, Christie did not develop another Harley Quin series. But for the reader of the Christie canon, Harley Quin and Mr. Satterthwaite continue to spark interest perhaps because they are so different from her other detectives.

Mr. Harley Quin is the most solitary, most elusive, most non-human of any Christie character. In fact, he is the most symbolic of all her characters, possessing youth and agility as well as magical powers of inspiration and invisibility. He has power over the minds and destinies of those in whose lives he chooses to intervene; his very presence evokes a supernatural aura. Christie develops Quin through descriptive imagery, ingenious deeds and through his relationship with his emissary, Mr. Satterthwaite.

Satterthwaite complements Harley Quin, for he is old whereas Quin is young; he is welcome in the best social circles, whereas Quin is a stranger; he is earth-bound, whereas Quin is transcendent. In addition, Mr. Satterthwaite is depicted as the wizened elf who carries out the master's orders: "a little bent, dried-up man with a peering face, oddly elflike."[3] When Mr. Satterthwaite first meets Harley Quin, he becomes so charmed by his powers that a totally new facet of life opens up for him. A person who had remained on the sidelines for most of his life without becoming involved with people, Satterthwaite is inspired to action by Quin.

"The Coming of Mr. Quin," the first story of the series, introducing Harley Quin and Mr. Satterthwaite, establishes the nature of their relationship. The occasion is a New Year's Eve party at a house in which the former owner had committed suicide. Mr. Satterthwaite is among the guests who are startled at the appearance of Harley Quin who seemed "by some curious effect of the stained glass above the door, to be dressed in every color of the rainbow."[4] Christie suggests through this imagery that Mr. Quin indeed is the embodiment of the famed Harlequin. When discussion among the guests turns to the mysterious suicide, Mr. Satterthwaite becomes aware that a major drama is being played in the stately hall, and that it is Mr. Quin who is staging it. By enlisting Satterthwaite's aid, Quin dramatizes his perception of the alleged suicide, uncovers a murder and restores faith to the threatened marriage.

Although he is jubilant at Quin's feat, Mr. Satterthwaite is still not fully aware of who Harley Quin is. Mr. Quin merely tells him to study the harlequinade for it repays attention. As Quin leaves, the rainbow effect again colors his body before he fades into the night. On one level, the reader is learning about the harlequinade; and on another level, Satterthwaite is experiencing an infusion of the romantic spirit. As he becomes increasingly aware of Quin's influence on him, Satterthwaite realizes that his "dull" life has become suddenly lively and meaningful. He looks forward to more encounters with his supernatural mentor, but he cannot contact Quin who is elusive and ephemeral. He can only expect spontaneous and surprise visitations which presage an unfolding human drama for both sleuths to observe and to moderate.

Harley Quin emerges as a magical figure with increasing symbolic dimensions. With each story, Christie heightens aspects of his power and reinforces his identity. Quin drops in unexpectedly in "A Shadow on the Glass," arriving after a double murder has occurred. This time he sits under a red-shaded lamp which makes his face look like a mask while his check-patterned coat has a motley appearance. Satterthwaite is already on hand as one of the guests at this picturesque country manor called Greenways House (Greenway House is the name of the home acquired by Christie in 1938). But with the arrival of Harley Quin, Satterthwaite, who has taken a secondary position up to now, is inspired to solve the murder puzzle. Quin's influence is not overt, as Satterthwaite examines the evidence, sifts through the clues, and deduces who the real murderer must be. The truth spares the most likely suspect from the scandal of being charged with murder, and it also brings a marriage proposal—the happy ending to what might have been a tragedy. We see in this story that Satterthwaite is no longer so passive, that Quin's influence is beginning to transform him into a more assertive person.

Association with Quin means excitement for Satterthwaite. When he unexpectedly finds Quin at a country inn called the Bells and Motley (the symbolic regalia of harlequin), he anticipates witnessing a spectacular event. But Quin delineates their roles clearly: he tells Satterthwaite that although he (Quin) is the inspiration for great deeds, it is Satterthwaite himself who performs the conjuring tricks. The stage is set once again as the innkeeper reveals that his daughter's lover has been accused of murdering the missing Captain Harwell. Although Scotland Yard has had no success thus far in solving the mystery, Satterthwaite follows a series of hunches and arrives at the truth—under Quin's tutelage. "The Bells and the Motley" story concludes predictably with the inn-keeper's daughter being reunited with her lover who is now free to marry.

Quin possesses the magic to restore innocence and to transform the world to an almost Edenic state. Satterthwaite functions as a disciple-in-training who is learning to perceive the romantic outlook needed to transform reality. In "The Sign in the Sky," Satterthwaite is despondent over the indictment of a friend on a murder charge. He wanders about pondering the problem, finally arriving at his favorite restaurant—the Arlecchino (Italian for "harlequin"). To his surprise, Quin is there, seated at the table that Satterthwaite usually occupies. The reader assumes this is not a coincidence, and that the great magician perceived Satterthwaite's need for him. But also we may infer that Satterthwaite himself may now be capable of calling forth the spirited Quin. Quin himself encourages more autonomy on the part of his disciple: rather than provide the solution, as he had done in the first case, Quin tells Satterthwaite to trust in his own judgment and pursue the truth. Once again, through Quin's inspiration, Satterthwaite saves an innocent man and reunites a pair of lovers.

Love relationships and the reuniting of estranged but true lovers dominate this collection. Two of the stories are particularly interesting in their treatment of the extremes of love: "The Soul of the Croupier" depicts enduring selfless devotion, whereas "The Face of Helen" describes the destructive quality of possessive, self-centered love. The first story is highly romantic, predicated upon a man's giving up his business and trailing around the world after a beautiful woman who has rejected him—ultimately to be united with her in Monte Carlo. Quin oversees this unlikely turn of events. "The Face of Helen" is more intriguing as the puzzle is based on a clever scheme by a rejected suitor to convert a wedding gift into a lethal weapon to kill the unsuspecting bride-to-be. In this case, Quin inspires Satterthwaite to perceive the real intentions of the rejected lover. Satterthwaite is bothered by the inconsistency of the lover's behavior and suspects danger, indicating that his sensitivity toward evil is growing. When he calls upon Quin, it is out of a personal conviction that something is wrong.

Less maudlin than some of the other adventures in the series, "The Voice in the Dark," deals with seances, ghostly noises, and a persistent spirit which bring Satterthwaite to the home of Lady Stranleigh who fears for the safety of her daughter. When Lady Stranleigh herself is found dead by drowning in her bath, murder is suspected. The puzzled Satterthwaite seeks Quin at the Bells and Motley. With minimal direction, Quin steers his charge to the correct course. Once inspired, Satterthwaite uncovers a bizarre case of switched identity and a cunning plot to bilk a woman out of her inheritance. (This case provides a respite from love affairs.)

Death is the other focus of the stories, death in the form of murder or suicide. Suicide in these cases is always the result of the loss of love. A typical case is recounted in "The World's End" where Satterthwaite discovers a young woman poised on a cliff contemplating a fatal leap. He learns that her fiance has been imprisoned for stealing a valuable jewel and that she cannot face the future without him. Perched at the edge of the same cliff, appearing out of nowhere is Quin who sets in motion a series of discoveries leading to the recovery of the jewel and the release of the falsely-accused young man—and the reunion of the lovers. A similar motif is repeated in "The Man from the Sea," only this time it is a young man who is lovelorn. Quin makes his appearance and together with Satterthwaite he reshapes a would-be tragedy into a romantic comedy. These stories have a pattern similar to the plight of the heroine in *Unfinished Portrait*, Christie's autobiographical romance; for in each situation, the main character contemplates suicide by leaping off a high point because of an unhappy love affair. A variation on the suicide motif is found in "The Dead Harlequin." In this story the key to the puzzle is the fact that the alleged suicide victim was happily married—thus casting doubt upon the probability of suicide and leading to the discovery of murder.

The final story in the collection, "Harlequin's Lane," reinforces the total effect of the group. The setting is Ashmead (a derivation of Christie's childhood home, Ashfield); behind the house is Harlequin's Lane, sometimes called Lover's Lane. This land extends from the village into a tract of wasteland marked by a rubbish heap. The estate belongs to Mr. and Mrs. Denham who have invited a group of guests to a house party where special entertainment has been planned; among the guests are Quin and Satterthwaite. Satterthwaite is delighted to find Quin on hand and takes the opportunity to praise him for his good deeds, especially in assisting unhappy lovers. But Quin reminds him that it is Satterthwaite himself who has accomplished the deeds.

To Satterthwaite's surprise, he discovers that their hostess is a former renowned Russian ballerina who gave up her art to live in obscurity with her British husband. During the pantomime, provided as entertainment for the guests, she discovers that her husband loves another woman. Later, when Quin dances the role of Harlequin to her Columbine, the dance revives her love of art and romance. Deciding to leave her faithless husband, she travels down Harlequin Lane accompanied by Quin. When Satterthwaite pursues them, he finds the woman dead—on the rubbish heap, a sacrifice to love (we presume). Satterthwaite is confused and the reader may well be confused too, for the symbols do not function clearly at the end of this story.

Can the consummate artist, having exchanged her life of art for love, live after her husband betrays her? Perhaps Christie is presenting a double sacrifice before us. The woman who gave up her art for love of a man can also sacrifice her life when bereft of both art and love. (Self-sacrifice is a romantic motif which dominates Christie's early works.)

Quin then gives a final admonition to Satterthwaite, advising him that win or lose, love takes its toll but it is still more important to have loved than not. Realizing that he has learned more about life by following Quin's romantic spirit, Satterthwaite feels that he has become more in touch with life and the human spirit.

When Quin fades away, he has made his last major appearance in the Christie canon.[5] But Satterthwaite survives to serve as a consultant to Poirot in *Murder in Three Acts* (1935) and in *Dead Man's Mirror* (1937). His encyclopedic knowledge of the upper echelon of society and his keen observation of acquaintances are useful qualities. In these novels, Christie has a larger canvas to develop complex puzzles.

Parker Pyne

Two years after the publication of the Quin-Satterthwaite stories, Christie published *Parker Pyne Investigates* (1934)—another collection of stories with a romantic motif. Though much more real than Harley Quin, Mr. Pyne—private investigator—plays similar theatrical games to solve his client's problems. On the front page of the morning pager Pyne has placed this personal ad: "Are you happy? If not, consult Mr. Parker Pyne, 17 Richmond Street."[6] Those in need of his services are usually surprised at his methods, for in most cases, Parker Pyne does not function in the traditional detective roles. He does not usually solve murders; he does not chase criminals; and he rarely interacts with the police. Instead, he is an impressario who brings would-be actors on a stage to play roles contrived to produce a moment or a lifetime of happiness for a grateful client.

To those seeking help, Pyne looks reassuring with his "bald head of noble proportions, strong glasses, and little twinkling eyes."[7] Having spent thirty-five years in a government office compiling statistics, he has developed a theory of investigation based on the science of statistics. He perceives himself as a kind of doctor of the soul who treats unhappiness as a disease that can be diagnosed, treated and cured. Though he handles most cases, there are times when Pyne will advise a client that no treatment is available for a particular problem. And like Quin, Pyne attempts to restore order to a troubled society and frequently intervenes in personal problems which threaten heartbreak or scandal.

We meet him in his London office with a secretary, Miss Lemon (whom he apparently later bequeaths to Hercule Poirot), and an entourage of employees who have a flair for the dramatic. When consulted, Pyne analyzes the prospective client's problem, decides on a plan of treatment and then engages one of his employees to implement his plan. The plot sequences involve reuniting estranged couples, making life interesting for the bored leisure class, solving jewel thefts, unmasking impersonators and averting or solving a murder.

Bringing together happily married couples is Pyne's primary function, however. His first client, Mrs. Parkington, brings him "The Case of the Middle-Aged Wife." Mrs. Parkington is unhappy because her husband has fallen in love with a younger woman; in desperation, she seeks Pyne's aid. Pyne's approach is unusual—theatrical, in fact. His treatment involves engaging a young man to play the gigolo role; Pyne then directs a scenario in which Mrs. Parkington "swings" with the smart set in the company of her handsome escort. As the pace of the fling increases, the errant husband finds his wife much more attractive. The Parkingtons are finally reunited, for Pyne's expensive drama succeeds though his fee is high. Like Poirot, Pyne is fond of fabrication, even lies, if they bring results.

But the jealousy ploy does not always work. An ironic sequel to the former case is "The Case of the Discontented Husband." This time, it is the wife who strays—overcome by the charms of a younger man. After Pyne assigns one of his regulars to "vamp" the worried husband, the scheme backfires as the husband falls in love with the young actress who is supposed to be baiting his wife. Pyne eventually brings husband and wife together—though the husband is slightly reluctant. This story has comic dimensions and a light tone, revealing Christie's gift for humor. A touch of the same wit prevails in "The Problem at Pollensa Bay" where Pyne stages a drama between a young man and the kind of girl no mother would want for her son. Pyne has been consulted by a young couple who are being driven apart by the man's possessive mother. The trick, this time, is on the disapproving mother whose attitude changes drastically when she sees her son succumbing to a seductive, scheming female—abandoning his fiancée for the "other woman." Naturally, the respectable fiancée looks better by contrast and wins her future mother-in-law's confidence.

Unlike the conjuring tricks of Harley Quin, Mr. Pyne's methods are pragmatic and often simple, yet they require an understanding of the needs of his clients. When bored members of the leisure class turn to Pyne to change their lives, he assesses the kind of change each person really needs. For example, in "The Case of the Discontented Soldier" two clients, both unhappy with their drab lifestyles, appeal to Pyne for excitement. Perceiving that what they really need is a crisis to

bring them together, Pyne calls upon another professional—
Mrs. Ariadne Oliver, the novelist. She devises a sensational
plot with fake assailants and an old-fashioned treasure map to
highlight the distress of a young woman and the gallantry of a
retired soldier. Last seen, treasure map in hand, the couple
heads for a honeymoon in Africa. We have the light-hearted
adult fairy tale here with the damsel in distress and a prince
charming (aging though he may be) to rescue her. An even
thicker plot is conceived by Mrs. Oliver for another one of
Pyne's clients—Mr. Roberts, a middle-aged family man
dissatisfied with his humdrum existence. "The Case of the
Bored Clerk" involves the eager Roberts being sent across
Europe pursued by jewel thieves, rescuing a beautiful girl and
receiving a medal of honor for his heroism. Roberts gets his
moment—and short-lived though it is, he is satisfied.

One of the most extreme instances of Pyne's changing the
lifestyle of a bored client occurs in "The Case of the Rich
Woman." Mrs. Rymer, a widowed millionairess, wants to know
how to use her money to achieve maximum personal
happiness. Perceiving that she is unhappy because she is
unloved and idle, Pyne literally changes her identity: he drugs
her and places birthmarks on her body, and then sends her to a
desolate farm surrounded by people who insist she is Hannah,
a farm laborer. She herself becomes convinced of her new
identity. After some time elapses, Pyne returns and explains
how he tricked her. What does she do? Abandoning all claim to
her wealth and former ties, she decides to stay on the farm—
and marry Joe, a farmer. The story is another version of the
tale of the princess who could not enjoy her gold, but who finds
happiness as a simply dairy maid—thanks to the efforts of the
good fairy. This story is less successful than some of the other
Pyne adventures because its tone is so serious and the romantic
elements so contrived.

Shifting identity and the masking of identity, a familiar
motif in fairy tales, recurs throughout the Christie canon. One
story in the Pyne collection is an outstanding example of the
felicitous blending of the fairy tale and the modern mystery
puzzle. In "The House of Shiraz" Pyne discovers a strange
tragedy involving two women,the mad Lady Esther and her
companion Muriel King. When Lady Esther fell to her death,

her companion assumed the lady's identity, claiming her title, her money but—alas—her madness as well. To preserve the screen, Muriel is forced to pretend madness. Realizing three years later that she may be in danger of really losing her mind, Muriel comes to Pyne for help. The story has a happy ending, for Pyne convinces her to give up the game and marry the man who has been pining away for her—thinking her dead all these years. The plot is romantic—especially the ending where marriage is offered as the solution to the problem.

The illusion versus reality game takes another form in the series of stories where Pyne aids those victimized by jewel thefts. Each of the stories has a unique twist, the kind of reversal which has made Christie famous. In "The Case of the Distressed Lady," Daphne St. John asks Pyne to assist her in restoring a diamond ring which she has stolen from a friend. She suggests that a paste copy and the genuine stone may be switched unnoticed, so that the theft will not be discovered. But Pyne is suspicious, and manages to trap the lady at her own game by using a "double cross." This is one of the few cases in which Pyne has to deal with a criminal mind.

Trickery and jewel theft challenge Pyne on several occasions, a typical case is "Have You Everything You Want" where a woman consults Parker Pyne about the strange behavior of her husband. Pyne investigates and correctly deduces a cunning scheme to steal the lady's jewels. The gallant Pyne restores not only the jewel but also the errant husband. And in "The Pearl of Great Price" the theft of pearl earrings threatens a romance when an innocent young man is falsely accused. Here again Pyne uncovers not only simple theft but a much larger game of illusion in which the twists and surprises make for a good mystery.

In two cases, Pyne becomes involved in murder. "The Gate of Baghdad" reveals Pyne's skill in applying the more traditional detective methods to discover the murderer of Captain Smethhurst as he lay sleeping in a bus. He uses a similar approach to detect the poisoner of Lady Grayle in "Death on the Nile." In these two cases the reader can readily see some similarities between Pyne's exploits and those of Hercule Poirot as both travel to the Middle East anticipating a vacation but find themselves embroiled in murder and

intrigue. In fact, the Poirot novel, *Death on the Nile,* possesses
the same title as the Pyne short story. What can be seen as well
is the differences between the two detectives. Poirot is the more
fleshed out of the two; for though eccentric, his peculiarities
render him more human. Pyne, in contrast, is more elusive—
much more the magician or the good fairy of romantic
tradition. Details of his person and lifestyle are not developed,
for the focus of the short stories is on plot rather than
character.

Pyne's character does *not* develop in the series; he remains
the same quiet "Mr. Fixit" throughout, although his
adventures vary. However, unlike the Quin-Satterthwaite
series, the Pyne stories are leavened with humor—a touch
which enlivens the reading and lightens the burden of the plot.
Still, Christie creates some good moments with Quin,
Satterthwaite and Pyne; and each of these sleuths has a claim
to reader appeal.

Generally speaking, those characters Christie develops
more realistically with humorous touches tend to be among her
more successful; and those characters given the fuller scope of
the novel are among her best. For these reasons, her detective
couple Tuppence and Tommy—and her novelist, Mrs. Ariadne
Oliver—are particularly successful characters. They claim a
wider reading audience and offer the necessary resilience to be
fleshed out in continuing adventures.

Tuppence and Tommy

More like twins than lovers, Tuppence and Tommy, the
young detectives presented by Christie in 1922, play at
detection much like schoolmates. Although Tommy has the red
hair, Tuppence has the vibrant personality. Together they
operate in complementary fashion: Tuppence uses her
intuition and Tommy relies on deduction. They marry, have
children and supposedly age, yet they never lose their love of
adventure. Christie traces their fortunes through five works
spanning fifty years: *The Secret Adversary* (1922), *Partners in
Crime* (1929), *N or M* (1941), *By the Pricking of My Thumbs*
(1968) and *Postern of Fate* (1973).

Christie's only married detective combination, this couple

was among the first in the field. Such detective couples as Pam and Jerry North, and Nick and Nora Charles appeared later. The genesis of the young pair was derived primarily from Christie's own experience. Tuppence (Prudence) Cowley, like the young Agatha, had served during World War I in a hospital; and Tommy, like the young Colonel Christie, had served in the military.

Through this couple, Christie engaged in role playing, an activity she transmitted into fiction. The red hair, for which the young Agatha was noted, was ascribed to the male counterpart of the fictional couple (Inversion is one of Christie's favorite techniques). But this couple very likely reflects Christie's conception of the ideal couple. They are depicted from youth through retirement, mellowing in time (along with their creator). Even in retirement they continue to pursue the detection game—and a game it is, for certainly their adventures are among the most light-hearted and humorous in the entire Christie collection.

"Tommy, old thing!" "Tuppence, old bean!" When Prudence Cowley and Thomas Beresford greet each other in *The Secret Adversary* (their first adventure), their responses set the tone of their relationship—friendly, bantering and supportive. These two young people, old childhood friends, meet up with each other at the end of World War I. Tommy is just demobbed like everyone else, broke and at loose ends. He was a lieutenant in intelligence work, twice wounded and had met Tuppence again in the hospital, where she worked as a nurse. Prudence Cowley, called Tuppence, left her home during the war and came to London, and worked in an officer's hospital. The full description of her wartime duties recalls Christie's own efforts.

Tommy has red hair, a pleasantly ugly face, yet the look of a gentleman and a sportsman. Tuppence is not beautiful; but her little elfin face radiates character and charm—with grey eyes and black brows. As with many of Christie's young sleuths, Prudence comes from a well-educated, genteel family, for she is the fifth daughter of an archdeacon.

The grim ravages of war have greatly depressed Britain's labor-market; for ten long, weary months Tommy has been job hunting, but there are not any jobs. There is no home for

Tommy to return to since his parents are deceased and his rich
uncle is still angry at Tommy's side of the family for some past
family quarrel. Tuppence does not want to return to life at her
home, for it is all drudgery, dullness and stagnation. Both
youngsters crave the excitement, adventure and sense of
danger they enjoyed while the war was on.

Tuppence suggests that they form a company, "the Young
Adventurers Ltd.," whereby they might combine their talents
to solve other people's problems. As they become immersed in
foreign intrigue, espionage and potential revolution, their
individual talents emerge. Tuppence operates almost
completely through intuition, while Tommy is preeminently
logical; the head of British Intelligence considers him devoid of
imagination, hence thoroughly logical and dependable.

The happy-go-lucky adventurers make fun of the danger
they court. Tommy, new to the game of sleuthing, gets involved
in some complex tailing of suspects. He stalks a gang into their
lair and hears their violent plans for a reign of terror and
revolution in Britain (before he is coshed and imprisoned).
Tuppence, disguising her sleuthing under a maid's uniform,
recruits her own Baker Street Irregular—a "juvenile
adventurer," a lad called Albert who helps her with the chores
of detection and is literally fascinated by her hints and
innuendoes of dangerous detection exploits forthcoming: he
primes for his task by reading *Garnaby Williams, the Boy
Detective*. This elevator boy turned detective proves to be a
most able assistant. (He also grows physically older,
paralleling the aging of his older friends.)

Success in their assignment brings two very positive
results: Tommy is reunited with a wealthy uncle who grants
him an allowance, and he is also given a permanent position
with British Intelligence. Tuppence agrees to marry Tommy,
thus assuring her also of security. Typically, the amateur
detective has to be able to afford his or her "sport." It really is
not until the Beresfords attain their upper middleclass status
that they become free to continue their adventures.

Six years later finds the irascible Tuppence staring out of
the window of a London flat, lamenting the fact that life has
become dull. British Intelligence, however, saves the day (and
perhaps the marriage) with a proposal that the Beresfords

operate a detective agency, Blount's Brilliant Detectives, in order to trap a spy. *Partners in Crime*, a collection of short stories, details the various exploits undertaken by the two. Tommy, who assumes the position of private detective with Tuppence as his secretary, takes the limelight as he acts out his fantasies by taking on the characteristics of various fictional detectives. He becomes Sherlock Holmes, Dr. Thorndyke, the Brothers Okewood, the Old Man in the Corner, the Blind Problemist and even Hercule Poirot. These episodes are among Christie's most humorous as she proves her skill at satire, poking gentle fun at her colleagues and also at her own detective Poirot. For Christie enthusiasts, this collection also provides a compendium of what Christie herself had read and obviously studied.

Yet curiously these satirical vignettes are not in keeping with Tommy's character. The solid British man of decorum and good sense suddenly becomes the clown; the young man supposedly devoid of imagination suddenly is capable of changing personality to accommodate impersonation. Tuppence would be completely in character as the clown here, but perhaps it would be inappropriate for a female to play the roles of the leading detectives of the period—all of whom seem to have been male. Tuppence, nevertheless, remains Tommy's assistant throughout, overcoming her boredom through participation in his assignments.

Tuppence and Tommy experience a variety of adventures together—most of which are humorous and fast-paced. For example, what seems to be a simple case of breaking an alibi turns out to be a most perplexing mystery: how can one woman be in two widely spaced places at the same time? This is the problem found in "The Unbreakable Alibi" brought to Blount's Brilliant Detectives by a young man who has a bet with his lover: only if he can solve the mystery of the alibi can he marry her. Her boast is that "I can produce an alibi that nobody can shake."[8] Tommy and Tuppence discover that witnesses have vouched for her presence in London while at the same time eyewitnesses swear she was staying at the Castle Hotel in Torquay. Obviously this breaking of Miss Una Drake's alibi will be a case patterned on the Inspector French type of investigation. Everyone knows he does alibis, and Tuppence has learned the exact procedure: "We have to go over everything and check it. At first it will seem all right and then when we examine it more closely we shall find the flaw."[9] As Tommy and Tuppence check out reliable witnesses they discover that yes, indeed, this woman was in two separate places at the same time. And though the sleuths diligently try to break the one or other alibi, they are not successful until Tuppence makes a startling discovery. The alibi is then broken. Mr. Montgomery Jones can claim Una Drake as his bride, and the Beresfords can chalk up another sleuthing success.

By accident and indirection, Tuppence and Tommy provide another great service, this time to the lady of the story titled "The Clergyman's Daughter." They answer an appeal from Miss Monica Deane, an impoverished minister's daughter, who has inherited a house from her rich aunt, but the treasure lost by the deceased can not be found. The poor girl and her widowed mother barely have the means to keep up the Red House after they move in; they are reduced to taking in guests. But soon after they move in, strange noises and poltergeist manifestations frighten their paying guests away. Beset by financial difficulties and the strange physical phenomena the girl approaches Blount's Brilliant Detectives to investigate the mysteries. The Beresfords believe that the cause of all the mysteries lies with the buried treasure somewhere in the Red House. By clever questioning of bank officials, Tommy uncovers the fact that the rich aunt did indeed withdraw a substantial fortune in gold and notes, and he reasons that the hoard had been buried by the cautious old aunt before she died. Tommy invites confidences by inventing and telling lies about his old aunt "who on the outbreak of the war, drove to the Army and Navy stores in a four-wheeler, and returned with sixteen hams."[10] Here is another of the grandmother images which Christie often wove into her fiction, based on reminiscences of her own "auntie-grannie."

By skillful deduction, Tommy suspects that certain people are scheming to empty the Red House so they may continue to search for the treasure they know is buried there. A thorough check of the dead aunt's papers leads to the discovery of an anagram which Tommy cleverly deciphers.

The concluding story of this volume, "The Man Who Was 16," not only concludes the adventures of the Beresfords, but also spoofs the methods of M. Poirot. Chief Carter approaches the couple in their office with praise for their success at catching no fewer than five notorious personages. So successful, in fact, are Tuppence and Tommy that Moscow is sending a special agent to liquidate them. This agent is a fluent linguist and a master of disguise.

Realizing that this may be his most demanding case, Tommy decides to assume the methods of the famed Hercule Poirot. By using his "grey cells" to counter the super spy, Tommy focuses on the problems of recognizing this agent, who will be in disguise. Scotland Yard installs wire taps in the Beresfords' office to filter all contacts and places numerous police agents on emergency call, but the young detectives meet the danger head on and alone.

The master spy, disguised as Prince Vladiroffsky, invites Tuppence to lunch. With Tommy's consent and with a backup of agents from Scotland Yard, Tuppence lunches with the Prince at his hotel, goes up to his suite of rooms—at that point both of them vanish. Has Tuppence been drugged, disguised and then removed from the hotel by the master spy?

The police are stymied. Tommy, however, uses his "grey cells" and deduces correctly that Tuppence and her captor are still in the hotel. Tuppence is soon found drugged and weak but alive; her captor is divested of a wig and make-up and taken away by Scotland Yard. Snaring this master criminal becomes the crowning point of their young careers as Blount's Brilliant Detectives prepare for retirement, their task now complete. When Tuppence announces that "our baby" is on the way, we assume that the Beresfords will live happily ever after, raising a family.

But twelve years later, at the beginning of World War II, the Beresfords reappear in a fully developed spy-thriller entitled *N or M* (1941). Now middle-aged with two grown children (twins), Tuppence and Tommy are slower-moving and bored. The war is in its second year; the German armies are overrunning Europe; and England is reeling from unpreparedness, defeats and fear of invasion. The Beresfords have missed the excitement of spy-hunting in those golden years of their youth and yearn to become involved in the war effort. Though they crave activity, they are frustrated at being rejected from serving because of their age.

Opportunity knocks when Tommy is recruited to help track down some German agents in England. Though Tuppence is not "invited" by British Intelligence to participate, she cannot contain herself and resorts to eavesdropping for details. Both she and Tommy then plunge into the spy hunt, each operating independently of the other. They soon discover that detection involves no fun and games in this venture.

The grimness and the austerity of war-time conditions color their attitudes and feelings with a somber cast. After all there is a terrible war going on, with death, horror and fear of invasion haunting all persons. Christie has put her finger on the pulse of the English populace threatened by invasion and death, and she has recaptured the restlessness, the anxiety and the everyday concerns of a rationed, uprooted and disoriented people beset by shortages, military draft, military reverses and fear of spies and fifth columnists. Amid the thrills of the spy hunt come reverberations of bewilderment at democratic inefficiency, disgust with their country's unpreparedness and distrust and hatred at aliens and refugees. Everyone quivers with tales of spies dropping down from the sky and moving about in disguises; above all, the English direct their hatred against the fifth columnists among the British people themselves who are willing to work for the enemy and betray their country and its ideals.

This is the stage upon which Mr. and Mrs. Beresford set forth on their own patriotic and dangerous quest for the German agents who are acting under the code names of N or M. Together they focus on the center of spy activity, a seaside hotel on the south coast of England (in a resort area which resembles the Devon Coast where Christie grew up and where she owned a country home). This Victorian style inn houses a mixture of eccentrics and "old pussies." Christie sparkles here as she captures the various traits of the guests with their small talk and trivial activities, their concerns and their entertainments. She paints a gallery of portraits and at the same time provides a realistic depiction of the effects of war upon the average citizen.

Tuppence comes into her own in this mystery as she is the one who infiltrates the hotel's social circle, posing as a tiresome, middle-aged woman who knits helmets in khaki wool for British soldiers. In a child's nursery rhyme book, Tuppence uncovers a mysterious code which eventually leads to the identity of the spies. She risks her life at one point; then becomes incarcerated in a bleak, seaside fortress with little hope of rescue. However, the dogged and faithful Tommy finds her and saves the day. Together the Beresfords manage to avert a national disaster and capture the spies.

Tuppence becomes a more interesting character with age. She relies less on Tommy and exhibits an intrepid resourcefulness of which the conservative Tommy seems to approve. In *By the Pricking of My Thumb* (1968), Tuppence is older but she seems to have become more stalwart over the years. While Tommy is away on business, she attempts to discover the whereabouts of an elderly woman who has been discharged from a nursing home. She starts by tracking down an old house that appears in a painting once owned by the woman. To find the house she uses railroad charts and then methodically seeks the view of the house from the various trains—a view which she remembers but cannot place.

Persistence pays off as Tuppence locates the house and begins to investigate its history and its role in the community. She employs the techniques that only one Prudence Cowley Beresford, daughter of a vicar, might carry off with aplomb. She has tea with the elderly ladies of the village, visits the local gossips, endears herself to the vicar—but gets coshed on the head for her trouble. A worried Tommy eventually arrives on the scene to assist her, but it is Tuppence who solves this riddle.

Postern of Fate (1973), the final adventure of Tuppence and Tommy, depicts an older couple looking forward to retirement. In years and attitude, this couple resembles Christie and her husband. In fact, Tuppence slides back in time to recover remnants of Christie's childhood home, Ashfield. The Beresfords have bought an old estate in the coastal town of Holloquay (a variation on Torquay, Christie's childhood village); in the process of restoring the house, Tuppence discovers a deadly secret.

For Tuppence and Tommy fans, the nostalgia which pervades this last adventure may be more significant than the plot, for the reminiscences become a channel for Christie's comments on her former home, on children's books and toys. The house in this novel is Ashfield, Christie's first home. Passages describing the house in the novel are almost identical to those in Christie's *Autobiography* describing Ashfield. The glass enclosure which Tuppence finds on the side of the house, for example, is the same structure described in the *Autobiography*. Truelove, the child's riding cart that becomes a plaything for the adventurous Tuppence, is not only described but is also replete with a photograph in the *Autobiography*. The nursery at the top of the house is Agatha's; it is here where Tuppence discovers a message in a child's book. The many children's books which Tuppence delights in rereading are those which Christie herself read. Aside from giving Christie, the author, the pleasant fantasy of restoring that house long since torn down, these sequences help to humanize Tuppence and to sustain that adventuresome spirit so characteristic of the young Tuppence.

Despite encroaching years, Tuppence and Tommy can still play the detection game. Tommy continues to rely on his contacts in British Intelligence for information, while Tuppence strikes out on her own, captivating old spinsters and churchmen, visiting nursing homes and supporting local charities. The kind of information the Beresfords receive is complementary and enables them to solve the mystery together.

Having come full circle from youth to retirement with the Beresfords, we find that they have become increasingly credible characters over the years. Christie has fleshed them out into a couple whom the reader may relate to—almost ordinary in their appeal. Tommy, one of the "good old boys" who has the right connections, is less dynamic than his wife; for Tuppence rises above the role of "Mrs. Tommy" to become more of an individual. In fact, having none of the eccentricities of a Poirot, Tommy needs the ebullient Tuppence. The more facile portrait of Tuppence reveals Christie's insight into the dynamics of the female world, especially in the role of the upper middle class wife—her motivation, her daily routine, her involvement in the benign events of village life. Christie projects much of her self into Tuppence to develop a character whom many readers consider their favorite sleuth.

Mrs. Ariadne Oliver

From another facet of her life, Christie has drawn upon the experiences of the female writer in her characterization of that likable sleuth, Mrs. Ariadne Oliver. Here Christie is patently role-playing as she literally puts herself into her own detective stories. Nowhere in the annals of detective fiction do we find an author parodying herself as Christie does through Mrs. Oliver.

Novelist, widow, amateur sleuth—Mrs. Ariadne Oliver appears in eight Christie mysteries, spanning almost forty years. Like Ariadne, the ancient Greek princess, Mrs. Oliver holds the thread to the mystery but does not solve it herself—she assists a man whose task it is to face physical danger and solve the puzzle. More intelligent than the Watson-type assistant, Mrs. Oliver is valuable as a consultant and is respected for her accomplishements. Though a widow and a professional writer, she is not a truly liberated female for she plays the traditional female role in deferring to the male to complete the task. But the uniqueness of Mrs. Oliver is in her reflection of Christie herself. With gentle humor, Christie herself plays the detection game—moving about Hitchcock-like in the Ariadne Oliver stories.

To promote the joke on herself, Christie exaggerates the idiosyncracies of Mrs. Oliver. The apple motif which runs through these stories is her most flagrant exaggeration. Mrs. Oliver makes her entrance in 1934 carrying a large bag of apples; from then on, apples abound. The meticulous Poirot is struck by one of her discarded apple cores (how Christie must have enjoyed that touch); but the unabashed Poirot merely greets Mrs. Oliver courteously, for he does respect her (*Mrs. Mc Ginty's Dead*). In *The Halloween Party*, Mrs. Oliver who has been called upon to assist at a children's party almost loses her taste for apples—a child has been murdered, drowned in a tub of water used for apple-dunking. But the apples remain a symbol for the multifaceted Christie herself—prolific writer, tantalizer of the public taste, lover of mystery. As Poirot remarks in *The Halloween Party*, the elusive Mrs. Oliver does not like to be interviewed. She "manages" such interviews by retelling the same old stories about herself and her love of apples. Thus the apple joke may indeed be on the public—give them apples, if not the facts.

Ariadne Oliver is Christie's artistic projection of self; the fictional character is a surrogate, candid creation from physical appearance to habits and values. "She was an agreeable woman of middle age, handsome in a rather untidy fashion, with fine eyes, substantial shoulders, and a large quantity of rebellious grey hair..." (*Cards on the Table*).[11] In descriptions such as this, Christie seems to be describing herself fairly, emphasizing those aspects of her person—her eyes and hair—which she felt were her most distinguishing features. She also offers little glimpses of herself at home, writing in her room at the top of the house surrounded by walls papered in a forest-like design covered with exotic birds. She appears to need an outlet for her complaints about writing and the tremendous effort involved in producing the finished work. But she confesses that her bankbook keeps her going. The home continues to represent tranquility and security even for Mrs. Ariadne Oliver, successful writer. She looks forward to returning home, escaping from the public eye, believing that all authors are really reticent people, comfortable only with their fictional companions.

Mrs. Oliver's comments about her "Finn" are most revealing. Just as Ariadne Oliver has created a detective who is a "Finn," Christie created a detective who is Belgian, M. Hercule Poirot. The parallel here is obvious. Mrs. Oliver recounts the number of letters she has received from readers commenting upon her Finn's accent and his inappropriate expressions. But she is stuck with him and caught between the readers who are dedicated to her Finn and those who criticize him. Then she has herself found him tiring and would dearly love to dispose of him, if only her readers would permit it. (Ultimately Christie does just this to Poirot.) In the Oliver-Poirot stories, the two offer an amusing contrast—the large and casual Mrs. Oliver and the small but meticulous Hercule Poirot. Here Christie gets the chance to write, direct and act in her own show by using the persona of Mrs. Oliver.

When Oliver makes her first appearance in the pages of *Parker Pyne Investigates* (1932), she is a resident author working for Parker Pyne who employs her to prepare exciting and imaginative scenarios for his boredom-ridden clients. We find Oliver in a room at the top of Pyne's establishment typing away from several notebooks amid "a general confusion of loose manuscripts and a large bag of apples."[12] Pyne gently chides her for using old hand-me-down cliches from spy thrillers in the scenario she prepared for "The Case of the Discontented Soldier." He desires more originality than situations like the hackneyed one of the hero imprisoned in a cellar filling up with water. She informs him that originality does not go over well with her readers who demand old situations because they "are used to reading about such things. Water rising in a cellar, poison gas, et cetera. Knowing about it beforehand gives it an extra thrill when it happens to oneself. The public is conservative, Mr. Pyne; it likes the well-worn gadgets."[13] Oliver's reputation at this stage is already great, for she has produced forty-six successes of fiction and all of them are on the bestseller lists in England and America.

Soon Oliver abandons the Pyne stable of writers to concentrate on her own career. Even at that, she is most anxious to break down the barrier between fiction and reality and prefers to solve a real-life murder mystery. Her opportunity to function as a true detective comes in the novel *Cards on the Table* where she forms part of the detective foursome invited by the exotic Mr. Shaitana to his bizarre dinner party; here, four undiscovered murderers dine with three famous detectives and the famous authoress of detective novels herself. During Shaitana's dinner, Mrs. Oliver is referred to as the one who wrote *The Body in the Library*—a direct biographical reference to Christie, revealing quite openly the identification she develops with Oliver. When the shocking murder in their midst is revealed, Oliver recoils at the crude use of a stiletto to end their host's life: "I could invent a better murder *any* day than anything real. I'm *never* at a loss for a plot. And the people who read my books like untraceable poisons."[14]

Poirot turns out to be an avid and critical reader of Oliver's many novels. In fact, Poirot's categorizing of her plots resembles a résumé of Christie's own favorite plot surprises:

"One of your neatest tricks. The rubber planter arranges his own murder: the cabinet minister arranges the robbery of his own papers. At the last minute the third person steps in and turns deception into reality."[15] When challenged on a point of accuracy, the aroused Oliver bristles: "As a matter of fact, I don't care two pins about accuracy. Who is accurate? Nobody nowadays."[16] She presents her formula for a successful plot: plenty of bodies, a cover-up murder of a witness, and exotic untraceable poisons (for readers like them). If Oliver is truly a projection of Christie's alter ego, then these comments reveal as much about creator as creation. This, then, may be Oliver's special role in these novels—to serve as outlet for her creator's random thoughts on the craft of writing mystery stories.

Christie develops Oliver as a comic foil for Poirot in six more novels: *Mrs. McGinty's Dead* (1952); *Dead Man's Folly* (1956); *The Pale Horse* (1961); *Third Girl* (1966); *Halloween Party* (1969); and *Elephants Can Remember* (1972). Although the situations differ, Oliver's character is consistently portrayed. A sleuthing sounding-board, Oliver plays a triple role in these detective novels displaying her talents: she performs in her own right as an amateur sleuth drawn to murders and to attempted solutions of them; she appears often with Poirot and serves as friend, foil and helper to the great detective; she emerges as an amusing caricature of Christie herself in the assigned role of the disorganized, aging, opinionated, overweight, flamboyant authoress of detective stories whose untrammeled imagination produces a humorous contrast to the person of Poirot. Still, as a most eccentric authoress of detective novels, Oliver becomes so *outre* in conception that though she shares distinguishing traits with her creator, she emerges as an out-size parody of lady mystery writers. Even further, as Oliver describes her writing methods, her concept of fiction and the problems of her hero's development, the reader senses resemblances to Christie's own approach to her work, to Christie's own difficulty with the characterization of Poirot and to her strained impatience with the demands of her reading public.

From Harley Quin and Mr. Satterthwaite, to Parker Pyne, Tuppence and Tommy, and Ariadne Oliver, Christie comes full circle in her range of detectives. Although each of these characters in some way is drawn from the author's personal experience, they reflect different dimensions of the Christie personality. Harley Quin is the most romantic figure (and perhaps the least successful—for his presence is gimmicky when the symbolism fails). Pyne is made more resilient by the infusion of humor. Tuppence and Tommy combine romance and realism to provide a light, enduring youthful dimension to their adventures. Ariadne Oliver's exploits, though occasionally serious, reinforce Christie's essentially comic characterization—a woman novelist and sleuth who, like the author, does not take herself seriously and who enjoys playing games with her readers.

Chapter VII
Christie's Prestigious Policemen

Detective stories need policeman. Law enforcement officers are called upon to provide support and background for the solution to the puzzle and to assume the role of the arm of justice in bringing the case to the courts. In her conception of the British police, Agatha Christie is conservative and stereotypic: she reflects attitudes and expectations of the role of the police that have been projected in the pages of the various novelists who preceded her and in the real life practices of the police in Britain.

However, Christie transforms her police officers into human beings to whom the reader can relate: she humanizes them, providing family backgrounds and details of appearance and personality; she presents them in a series of novels to create familiarity for the reader; and she "couples" them with the appropriate sleuth to serve as a memorable assistant or foil. But most of all, Christie is selective—not all her police figures are developed in detail and those whom she treats with greatest deference are either of the upper class or in positions of power. Consequently, though a large number of individual policemen and detective inspectors appear solely in the story, others appear serially in several works—these include Sir Henry Clithering, Colonel Race, Detectives Slack and Melchett, Inspector Battle, and Inspector Japp.

The image of the British policeman has always been a positive one. The "bobby," as the constable is called, is known for his friendliness, courtesy, and social concern. Unlike his French counterpart, his function is not a judicial one as his work is separate from that of the courts. But the "gendarme" evokes a bitter prejudice from a public who consider the French policeman a political figure comparable to a spy or a bounty hunter because he works with the prosecutor for the conviction of suspects. This attitude is projected in the French "roman policier" which focuses on the tyranny of the police system.

The British attitude toward the police contrasts sharply with that of the French, for policing in Britain was designed *not* to be secretive, militaristic, or politically repressive. As Murch points out in her study of detective fiction, "the English policeman is regarded by the public as their safeguard;" consequently, the public "will assist the police whenever they can."[1] Because British policemen are unarmed and must also be residents of the community they serve, they are usually familiar figures who are well respected by the public.

In detective fiction the emerging image of the police investigator reflects the cultural differences of the French, the British, and the American traditions. The publication in 1828-29 of the *Memoires* of the infamous Vidocq, the former criminal who left the ranks to join and structure the newly formed Paris Sûreté, had the greatest single effect upon the image of the police in detective fiction. Gaboriau and Boisgobey, the foremost French detective story writers, modelled their police heroes after Vidocq. Poe, an American who had never been to Paris, employed the Vidocq image and the French milieu for his detective stories of the 1840s. Developing from this tradition, which bred distrust for the police, came the need for the righteous amateur sleuth and the rivalry between the successful amateur and the less admirable professional.

Although the British were less disparaging in their treatment of the police, still the amateur sleuth usually had to cope with police jealousy and resistance. Conan Doyle's treatment of the police is an obvious example of the less competent professional never reaching the heights of the revered sleuth, Sherlock Holmes. Still, among the vintage detective stories, two British policemen rise above the ranks to distinguish themselves—Dickens' Inspector Bucket (*Bleak House,* 1851) and Collins' Sergeant Cuff (*The Moonstone,* 1868). In her analysis of the amateur detective-police relationship, Mooney asserts that Collins' Sergeant Cuff "shares honors with Dickens' Inspector Bucket as the prototypical solid, responsible, capable professional police detective in the British tradition."[2] Noteworthy also in the American tradition is Anna Katharine Green's Mr. Gryce *(The Leavenworth Case,* 1848) who consistently outwits the amateur sleuth.

Agatha Christie's works reflect this positive British tradition. Although her detective stories are obviously detective-centered, not police-oriented, still Christie's detectives rely on the police; for no detective, however gifted or resourceful, can function without the machinery of the official police. The police are official; they are a necessity because of the social structure; they have the historic and economic organization, the vast forces, the latest technology, and the collective experience to deal with all varieties of crime.

Thus, one encounters in Christie's detective fiction various official police Inspectors or Superintendents of the Detective Force, who will sleuth and investigate as members of a larger, more complex organization—such as Scotland Yard or its Criminal Investigation Division known as the C.I.D.—thus insuring the cooperation and utilization of a well-oiled organization geared to supply any demand required of the detective be it photography, dossiers, fingerprints, laboratory tests, or psychological profiles.

While the bulk of the crimes solved in the Christie canon are handled by the private investigator, the amateur sleuth, or the "young adventurer" stumbling on the tracks of crime and onto the lair of a gang of master-criminals, even these sleuths must and will collaborate with the official police establishment. This must be done for social and moral reasons—otherwise there is the danger that the Super-Sleuth may turn into a Super-Man—assuming the role of sleuth, judge, and executioner as well—a rogue revenger responsive to individual moral norms and not to the standards of society.

For Agatha Christie there are three basic types of police figures including the village constable, restricted and parochial; and the Detective-Inspector or Superintendent of Detectives who operates out of Scotland Yard headquarters and is sent forth to aid the county authorities, who are naturally less-equipped in experience and facilities to handle crimes in the counties which may have national political significance. Then there is the secret agent, trekking all over the world, attacking various problems ranging from drug-smuggling to international jewel thefts, restoring lost honor. Often, one encounters an ex-policeman who after many years in the colonies has retired from service and has come home to England for a deserved rest after hard years of service only to find himself dragged into the solution of crime as a private investigator, working on his own, but still capable of calling upon the official arm of justice for aid. This was the role assumed by Luke Fitzwilliam in the novel *Easy to Kill* (1939).

The structure of a Christie detective work requires a dénouement featuring the complete capture and immobilization of the villain, the destruction of the fiend's plots, and the restitution of the innocent and the falsely accused. Though the major instrument in the re-ordering of the disrupted social order may be the master-sleuth or a number of amateur sleuths, the final work of apprehending the murderer and carting him or her to justice is done by the officers of the law. The police Inspector or Superintendent closes the case, achieves the honors, and restores the proper balance of justice and harmony in the social structure. Thus, the final frame of a Christie detective opus shows the minions of law leading the culprit off to prison or to a mental institution. The other variant permits the Master-Criminal to escape the clutches of the law by execution only by a suicidal exit with a convenient secret vial of poison.

Agatha Christie's fictional sleuths spring from the Doyle-Gaboriau-Hanaud variants which she discovered in her personal reading of popular detective fiction. Nevertheless, Christie is capable of various points-of-view and various shades of treatment, ranging from caricature to serious portrayal, from a la Arsene Lupin high jinks to ultra-solemnity a la Holmes. She can be serious, humorous, whimsical, and self-parodying in her portraiture of the professional policeman, according to her mood and purpose. However, her views of the functions of the police are conditioned by her realistic perceptions of the police as an integral part of the social environment of each community. Thus, she sees the omnipresent men in blue as appearing everywhere as bastions of law, order, and respect—from the village constable, the Bobbies, on up to the Superintendent of the C.I.D.

But among those police figures she portrays most favorably, Christie stresses the elitism of rank. The touch of snobbery one senses in these portrayals is consistent with Christie's keen class consciousness, which is reinforced by her method of distinguishing characters by social position. As with all her characters, Christie focuses on the policeman's manners and worldliness, for she is more interested in the *man* than in the techniques and mechanics of criminology.

Christie is less complimentary of the police figures serving, usually, in the lower ranks and usually with the county police, rather than in the Metropolitan Police Force, located at Scotland Yard. Her treatment of these differences reflects the culture of the county police as well as Christie's own snobbery. Since the village and county forces derive their members from the community where these men have their roots, they are sometimes too well known to the citizenry. The range of command extends from the Chief Constable, usually a prominent figure who has risen with distinction from the ranks, to chief inspectors and then on down to the local constables, who are familiar figures on the local scene with their helmets and truncheons. The county manages its own law enforcement unless a special case arises and Scotland Yard is called in to assist. Though Christie is adept at humanizing her police characters, she makes distinctions between negative and positive qualities—emphasizing the foibles of certain policemen in the lower ranks. We see this especially in the early Marple novels, *Murder at the Vicarage* (1930) and *The Body in the Library* (1942).

Attitudes toward the levels of command are fleshed out in the characterizations of Inspector Slack and Colonel Melchett, the Chief Constable in *Murder at the Vicarage*. Although Melchett is accepted and respected by the community, Slack is—as his name suggests—less capable and often rude in his dealings with the public. In this case, he even impedes the investigation of the murder. At first, Slack stirs up resentment with his treatment of the maids who are engulfed in hysteria, and he wastes time suspecting the butler. The Chief Constable, Colonel Melchett, is called in: he "is a dapper little man with a habit of snorting suddenly and unexpectedly."[3] Colonel Melchett, with tact and some common sense, aids in the investigation. He refuses to call in Scotland Yard for he has trust in Slack's ability: "He's a very smart man. He's a kind of ferret. He'll nose this way through to the truth."[4] The villagers soon discover that the police have no sense of humor and are apt to suspect everyone. Both the Colonel and the Inspector learn to lean on the Vicar for information. In fact, even Slack becomes more friendly to the Vicar and takes him along on his village interviews. The Vicar notes that the Colonel and the Inspector do not see eye to eye on clues, suspects, and evidence. The high point of this investigation for some villagers is the Inquest with its local color, gory details, gossip, and parade of witnesses.

Inspector Slack is especially contemptuous of the efforts of Miss Jane Marple. However, ultimately he is forced to admit that only through her efforts was the crime solved and the murderers arrested. Miss Marple has her revenge by not telling the police all the details of her detective methods or her conclusions. With the conviction of the guilty parties, Miss Marple allows the credit to fall to Inspector Slack. The public believes this policeman's zeal and intelligence brought the criminals to justice; he takes all the credit and nothing is said of Miss Marple's share in the business.

The full range of the police hierarchy is seen in *The Body in the Library*—the discovery by the Bantrys of a body in their library brings the police. First comes Constable Palk, slow moving, slow thinking, and deferential to the upper crust: since "His habit of giving in to the gentry was lifelong."[5] He is followed by Inspector Slack who on arrival displays his usual prejudices and overbearing attitude. Immediately, he wonders if the butler knows anything; he then proceeds to upset the shocked servants. Slack angers people with his rudeness: he dashes about in useless activity and cuts short witnesses who try to aid him. Even Colonel Melchett dislikes Inspector Slack for his arrogance and industry. Melchett is accused by Slack of putting his respect for the "old school tie" above justice. A second murder in a neighboring county brings in Superintendent Harper who dreads collaborating with another chief constable, but he likes Colonel Melchett and finds him cooperative and able. Superintendent Harper is gracious towards Miss Marple and relies upon her aid for information. Sir Henry Clithering, once commissioner of the Metropolitan Police, is also on the scene. He declines to be an amateur sleuth and is on the retired list, but he advises Superintendent Harper to use the special gifts of Miss Jane Marple.

When the police are told that Miss Marple is once more on the scene, Colonel Melchett jokes to Slack that she "Put it over us properly once, didn't she, Slack?"[6] Sir Henry Clithering himself has great respect for Marple's past achievements and lauds her ability to solve mysteries. He asks her for her famous parallels, and she readily obliges. Miss Marple startles the police when she proves that the first two murders are connected, and she produces a bomb-shell when she says she knows who the third victim will be. She performs her usual sleuthing magic and graciously explains her method of reasoning to the police and allows *them* to wrap up the case.

As a foil for Miss Marple, the less competent policeman is comic as well as self-effacing. Although Slack and Melchett are treated with satiric touches, the eminent Sir Henry Clithering is in a class by himself. His courtly style contrasts with the less sophisticated bearing of his "country" colleagues; for Christie makes obvious class distinctions in her portraits of these three men in terms of lower, middle, and upper class behavior.

Sir Henry Clithering is the most aristocratic and among the most distinguished of Christie's policemen. Though retired, this former Commissioner of Scotland Yard, commands respect from the public and from members of the police force. In recognition of his outstanding service to the nation, Sir Henry has been accorded the privileges and honor of knighthood. Although no details of his personal life are presented, he reveals his true character in his bearing, his comments, his actions, and in the reactions of others to him. Sir Henry is introduced in *The Tuesday Club Murders* (1928-1930) as that "well-groomed man of the world." He complements the amateur sleuth, Jane Marple, for both of them reflect gentility and each seems to recognize this refinement in the other. When he is called into action again in *The Body in the Library* (1942), he exhibits his superior policing talents as he guides the local police to focus on the real murderer. Here again, Miss Marple assists and it is Sir Henry who recognizes her unusual skills.

While the younger generation does not seem to appreciate the values of the past, Sir Henry shares with Miss Marple a steadfast belief in human weakness and an awareness of evil that only age and experience permit. Miss Marple's insight into human relationships is complemented by Sir Henry's decisive actions. For example, several of the stories in *The Tuesday Club Murders* collection are limited to discussions of probable solutions to past crimes. In these situations, Sir Henry defers to Miss Marple who always seems to sense where the guilt lies. However, in actual situations such as in "Death By Drowning," Miss Marple channels her information to Sir Henry who then acts upon it to produce the necessary evidence to convict the guilty party. In the subsequent novel, *The Body in the Library,* Sir Henry helps two old friends—Colonel Bantry and Jefferson Conway. Bantry, a retired army officer, has become the object of village gossip ever since the body of a woman was found in his library. Conway has suffered a personal loss since the murdered woman was like a daughter to him. Jane Marple is on the scene again this time providing Sir Henry with the most significant clues to solve the case. Even though he enters late on the scene, Sir Henry's role is significant here because his skill in dealing with people and his diplomacy in handling the local police prove him to be an individual of distinguished ability. And his rapport with Jane Marple reflects the positive relationship between the amateur and the professional detective.

Sir Henry Clithering emerges as the ideal police official—polished, intelligent, yet unobtrusive. Aesthetically, he complements Miss Marple but does not dominate or detract from her role of amateur sleuth. Typically, those policemen who operate well with Jane Marple are like Sir Henry—strong, quiet gentlemen who respect her lady-like demeanor and her skill at detection. These men are the "soldierly" types like Inspector Nash (*The Moving Finger,* 1942) and Inspector Neele (*A Pocketful of Rye,* 1953). Reith indicates in his study of the British police that up until the early twentieth century many police officials were appointed from the ranks of the military.[7] The types of officials Christie describes often resemble military men, many of whom could have been in office during Christie's early years and could have left a permanent impression on her. Since Clithering is a bachelor with no apparent heirs, Christie creates a legacy for him in a god-son, Detective Inspector Dermot Craddock. Lest the good die out, Craddock comes under Sir Henry's tutelage in *A Murder Is Announced* (1950), where the elderly Sir Henry passes on his experience to this god-son. He advises the young man to rely on the talents of Miss Marple, whom Craddock initially perceived as old and feeble. Ultimately though, Inspector Craddock and Miss Marple succeed as a team in solving a series of murders, to their credit and to Sir Henry's as well.

Another soldierly figure and bachelor is the most enigmatic of all the Christie investigators of crime—the suave, distinguished-looking, international crime-buster called Colonel Race. He makes his first appearance in 1924 in the novel entitled *The Man in the Brown Suit* as a debonair, world traveler to exotic places. It is obvious he is working for the British government as a crime figher, but we are not told the exact nature of his assignment or his connections, because his identity and operations are ultra-secret. Colonel Race is a mysterious super-agent, working out of the mysterious M.I.5 branch of criminal investigation.

His beat is the entire world; he had been active in India, South Africa, the Nile, and other places in pursuit of diamond smugglers, spies, saboteurs, and other malefactors operating on a vast international scale. His private and home life are unknown; his character as a human being is an enigma, for he shuns social functions and does not seem to rest long enough to establish either a family, a lover, or a circle of close friends. His work takes him into the reaches of high society where he is well known and where his skills as a sleuth are called upon by distraught family members, maidens-in-distress, or other police and detectives already on the scent of a master-criminal. Often Colonel Race is able to perform his official mission while rendering service to others in need. This handsome sleuth is tall, with a soldierly bearing, dark hair, and bronzed face—all these attributes make him most attractive to women. When we first meet him, he is about forty years old and beginning to gray at the temples. Full of the necessary social graces, he mixes well with people, though he can be formidable and intimidating upon occasion.

Through the point of view of the heroine in *The Man in the Brown Suit,* Anne Beddingford, the reader becomes better acquainted with Race. Suspicious of Race's cover as an archeologist, she gradually learns who he is. She discovers that Race is a Secret Service chap, and that he has led a most exciting and adventurous life. To her great surprise, Race reveals that he has inherited the vast fortune of Sir Lawrence Eardsley—this financial security gives him even greater independence and status. As in the past, Race has journeyed to Africa on a secet service mission. This time he succeeds again: stolen diamonds are recovered; a smuggling ring has been smashed; murderers have been caught; and the master criminal of subversion and violence has been destroyed.

During one of his jaunts to England, Race becomes involved with Hercule Poirot in the bizarre events of *Cards on the Table* (1936). On the basis of his secret service exploits, he is invited to become a member of a sleuthing foursome matched against the other quartet of guests—four undiscovered murders. Working with Poirot and Superintendent Battle on this case, he has little opportunity to dominate either the action or the resolution. Now a man of fifty, Race is still handsome and bronzed like a tropical big-game hunter. Yet his role is minor in this novel, as he defers to Poirot whom he perceives as the better man to pursue the murderer in the case.

Race works well with Poirot since both of them observe a professional courtesy towards one another. Race perceives Poirot as the most skilled ensnarer of the typical murderer, and Poirot respects Race's undercover activity in pursuit of secret agents. When they meet again in *Death on the Nile* (1937), Race helps Poirot to solve the murder of a young heiress who was their fellow passenger on a cruise ship sailing up the Nile. Race is particularly useful in this case since he is so gregarious and politic in dealing with the passengers on the ship. Actually, Race almost becomes Poirot's Watson—assisting him and fielding his questions and theories. Ultimately though, Race gets his man—an international criminal who controls a coalition of saboteurs.

Colonel Race makes his last appearance in *Remembered Death* (1945) as he helps to solve the murder of an old friend. Although he is now over sixty years of age, Race is tall and still the erect military figure. In this novel he reveals that he has worked for the M.I. 5, the top secret counter-espionage service, at one time controlling the operations of the Counter-Espionage Department. Known and respected by the pillars of British imperialism, he has been privy to state secrets. But he is still capable of solving a crime on the domestic front. Though over sixty, Race uses his powerful shoulders to break down a door and rescue the endangered heroine of this mystery, bringing his adventures to a successful and dramatic close.

Like Sir Henry Clithering, Colonel Race is a loner—a man of the world, not a family man. In a sense, these two aristocratic police types are Christie's most romantic figures. Although the reader is given details of their appearance and regaled with tales of their adventures, these men do not have that stoic quality which characterizes her other well known, serialized agents of law. Her most successful detective characters, Inspectors Battle and Japp, are realistically conceived and much more human.

The "squarely built middle-aged man with a face so singularly devoid of expression as to be quite remarkable" is Detective Inspector Battle of Scotland Yard.[8] Battle is a far cry from the romantic Colonel Race or the aristocratic Sir Henry Clithering. Nor is he like the caricature of the policeman as bumbling, vulgar, and inefficient. In the tradition of Dickens' Inspector Bucket, Battle moves quietly but decisively. He is first introduced in *The Secret of Chimneys* (1925) where he confronts three major operatives who are disguised and whom Battle must unmask in order to solve the mystery.

Battle proves he has the personality and bearing to carry out this difficult task. Maintaining cool control over his emotions, he is never shocked, never ruffled or angry; he never displays any overt emotion. He is not diverted by vanity and the need for adulation; instead he immerses himself in his work as a "company man." Though Battle is a large, heavy man, he can move with cat-like tread—often appearing without any warning. His bulk belies his athletic ability, for he can easily vault out of windows, dash about, and use his strength as a battering ram.

In *Chimneys,* Christie begins to warm up to the character of Battle, but she develops him more in those subsequent novels which portray him even more realistically. If he fails to develop as a credible human being in this first novel, it is understandable given the complex clutter of personae, fantastic plot lines, and myriad interrelationships—all of which tend to steal the limelight from the police and diffuse it over a broad area.

When Battle reappears in *The Seven Dials Mystery* (1929), he is tested again by a multifaceted mystery: espionage, a crime syndicate, and murder. He becomes a confidant and benefactor to the amateur sleuths and serves as well as Scotland Yard's man on the scene. Through the point of view of the young heroine, the reader sees Battle as he appears at a first glance—unimpressive, even average. But as the plot thickens she discovers the many dimensions to his character. At one point, she is startled to find Battle disguised as a footman until he assures her that the disguise is a deliberate one to give warning to criminals that the police are on the spot (Shades of Sherlock Holmes). The ultimate shock is the discovery that Superintendent Battle is a member of the masked Seven Dials Gang, a counter-espionage organization dedicated to the protection of the nation. Battle clearly triumphs in the finale when he sends the heroine into the arms of her prospective husband and captures the Master Criminal who threatens the well being of the free world.

Battle is seen in relief next to other well established Christie sleuths in *Cards on the Table* (1936). He works along with Hercule Poirot and Colonel Race to track down the murderer of Mr. Shaitana, their host at a dinner party. However, his methods clearly distinguish him from his peers as he proceeds to crack the case. Battle moves quickly into action, plans a strategy for questioning the guests, and deftly culls cooperation from his colleagues. Battle never regards M. Poirot's questions as foolish: he knows all too well the results they produce. In interviewing the four major suspects, Battle is gentleness itself: "I'm not a cruel man."[9] Never does he insult suspects, indulge in brutality, or use methods of third degree on any suspect or prisoner. If he carries a weapon, he almost never calls it into action. Battle never sheds blood; his main weapon is his understanding of the ways of the criminal mind, and his reliance upon standard methodical methods of investigation. And he knows how to use special gifts of his fellow-sleuths. For example, he knows M. Poirot is adept at the use of psychology, so he asks him to probe the suspects along those lines. Battle respects the strange methods of the little Belgian even though he sometimes fails to comprehend Poirot's purpose. Battle is plain English homespun, as he himself acknowledges: "I don't deal much in these fancy approaches. They don't suit my style."[10] He sees himself as "a straightforward, honest, zealous officer doing his duty in the most laborious manner—that's my style. No fancywork. Just honest perspiration. Stolid and a bit stupid—that's my ticket."[11]

As the four sleuths occupy themselves with shadowing and questioning the actions, backgrounds, and thoughts of the suspects, Battle's investigation takes him to Wallingford to question Anne Meredith. He uses a series of impersonations to check out the local gossip on Anne and her house-mate: in one place he pretends to be a London builder; in another spot he is a week-ender seeking a cottage to rent; and finally he passes himself off as the representative of a hard-court tennis firm soliciting business. Major Despard sees Battle hovering over the girls in a suspicious manner, and he warns them to be on guard for Battle is a "man of remarkable ability." In pursuit of particular knowledge about a past event in Doctor Roberts' dubious professional life, Battle realizes he must obtain details from a former maid concerning patients who died mysterious deaths. For this purpose, Battle uses Sergeant O'Connor, "The Maidservant's Prayer," a most strikingly handsome policeman with attractive physique, dashing good looks, and "a roguish and daredevil spark on his eye which made him so irresistible to the fair sex."[12] Sergeant O'Connor, in disguise woos, entertains and pumps the needed information out of his fair prey. In this manner Battle employs *all* the facilities of his department.

Superintendent Battle makes a belated and brief appearance at the end of the novel *Easy to Kill* (1939). His contribution is minimal since most of the action and detection is in the hands of the retired ex-policeman, Luke Fitzwilliam who is slowly solving the complex series of murders in Wychwood Under Ashe. Battle's usually expressionless face has less than usual to express. Agatha Christie's insistence on the woodenness of his visage deters both suspects in the novels and readers from giving the Superintendent appropriate recognition.

All this stiffness, unnatural dignity, and frozen face are shunted aside in the novel *Towards Zero* (1944), for here Agatha Christie has gone a long way in making a credible and likeable human being out of "wooden face." She achieves this by portraying Battle as a worried husband, and a sensitive father and companion to a nephew who is also in the police system. In this novel we see Battle as a family man with a wife and five children. Of particular interest is his youngest daughter, Sylvia, who is sixteen and a student at a school near Maidstone. The Battle family is shocked by a letter from Sylvia's headmistress who relates that this daughter has confessed to a series of petty thefts in the school. The irate Battle confronts the smug headmistress. He knows his daughter is weak, suggestible, but certainly not a thief. He realizes that his defenseless daughter cracked under the headmistresses' accusations, confessed to the thefts, and took the blame for something she did not do. Battle tells the headmistress's accusations, confessed to the thefts, and took confess, tells her to get the police in on the case immediately, and takes his daughter away.

This picture of Battle protecting his innocent child from the web of evil and guilt thrown upon her by an unfeeling headmistress and a calculating criminal who drove the victim to desperation and confession to crimes she did not commit becomes the central motif of *Towards Zero*, for Battle will later rise to the defense of another innocent driven to the point of desperation, madness, and suicide by the complots of an arch-destroyer. As the central figures in the major drama gather together for the house party at Lady Tressilian's at Gull's Point near St. Loo, the Battle family is upset by a change in their annual holiday plans. Rooms have already been booked for them at a place in Brighton, but Superintendent Battle must stay in London and work on an urgent case. He sends "mums" and the five girls on to their promised vacation trip. Later when his work load slackens, he will spend some time with Jim, his nephew. Inspector James Leach is a member of the local police, and Battle enjoys relaxing in his company while imbibing the holiday pleasures of Saltcreek as well.

But their visit is jolted by the news that Lady Tressilian has been brutally murdered. The Chief Constable asks Scotland Yard to put Battle on the job. Nephew and uncle work together on this case, and their first task is to assemble the entire family and guests around the dining room table for an inquiry. Though Superintendent Battle pays lip service to the tradition that suspects are innocent until they are proven guilty of a crime, Superintendent Battle regards "everyone connected with a murder as a potential murderer."[13] (These are the exact sentiments of M. Poirot.)

It is revealed that Battle is an avid sports fan who had attended the tennis matches at Wimbleton where he admired the expert playing of Neville Strange. Battle relates well with the members of the family and the house party: he keeps his place and distance and is respected and permitted to examine the premises. While the family is down in the dining room, he has all of their rooms searched for incriminating clues. The plethora of clues—bloody clothes and a blood-stained niblick— set the suspicious Battle to wonder if a frame-up against Neville is in progress. Cleverly, Battle proceeds to pretend to build a case against Neville, but secretly places all servants and household guests under observation.

When Battle's investigation slows to a stop, he thinks of Hercule Poirot; remembering the great powers of the Belgian detective, Battle wishes he had M. Poirot here on this case. As he thinks of M. Poirot's various strategems, he recalls two that help him on this case: always keep a murderer talking, for everyone is bound to speak the truth sooner or later; watch out for departures from symmetry of behavior or symmetry of room arrangements. Continued questioning of suspects reveals that malignant hatred could be a possible motive for murder, and a thorough re-search turns up a yellow glove and the true murder weapon—the heavy ornamental top of a massive andiron. The net of suspicion and evidence draws in on one suspect. Battle, following the dramatic flair of M. Poirot, invites all suspects to ride with him on a launch out into the bay. Then in a clever confrontation scene, Battle breaks down the defenses of the true murderer and extracts a confession. By endorsing a patent falsehood, Battle tricks the murderer into confessing. Like Poirot, he is not above using trickery to achieve his end—the exposure and arrest of a killer.

By the year 1945, Battle has retired from the New Scotland Yard and another generation of Inspectors and Superintendents hold down the Yard. Still, Battle's presence is felt in the men he has trained who acknowledge him as their mentor. In an effort to create a living coterie of "her people," Christie makes reference to Battle and his retirement, to the fact that he is writing his memoirs, and still tends his garden. She also creates a living legacy through his son, a device she used before with Colonel Race and his god-son. This time the reader must infer (another one of Christie's games) that Colin Lamb, the hero of *The Clocks* (1963), is the son of Superintendent Battle. Lamb confesses to Hercule Poirot that although he is a marine biologist by training, he is a secret service agent by persuasion. He then explains that he does not use his real family name because he does not want to curry favor through his famous parent—now retired, tending his garden, and writing his memoirs. Poirot asks how the former Superintendent is faring, and the reader must assume that this can be none other than Battle who is the unnamed father. Christie seems to be reinforcing the concept here that the good does not die out, but that it lives on in those who have been touched by it.

The majority of Christie's policemen are portrayed consistently; like Sir Henry Clithering and Colonel Race, they age but do not change in character. With Superintendent Battle, Christie began to develop less stereotypical characters. When we first meet Battle, he is rigid, somewhat "wooden" in personality, repressing all emotional responses. But, as we have seen, Christie gradually makes him much more human—introducing his family and developing closer ties to Poirot.

However, one detective whom Christie presents initially as lower middle class, unattractive, over-eager, and not especially amicable, changes *dramatically*—this is Detective Inspector Japp. Less imposing than Battle, he is a small man with less poise and polish. Yet Japp rises from among the least admirable of Christie's policemen to one of the most outstanding, a man who has emerged from the ranks to become a leader. These changes are revealed in the attitudes of Poirot and Hastings toward Japp and in the dialogue between them, for Japp becomes increasingly articulate with age and experience.

The ubiquitous Detective Inspector Japp is the peculiar-looking police official who makes most of his appearances on those cases featuring M. Poirot. Japp is first seen at the inquest held in *The Mysterious Affair at Styles* (1920). He appears to be ludicrous, little, dark, ferret-faced. Yet he must have excellent credentials as a detective to have been promoted to his present rank. M. Poirot greets Japp as an old friend—both men worked together on a case in 1904 in Brussels. Japp has the highest respect for M. Poirot and praises the Belgian sleuth to Superintendent Summerhays. Japp obeys a hint from M. Poirot not to be too fast with the planned arrest of the victim's husband. Though Japp pursues his investigation in the official manner, he still leans heavily on the work done by M. Poirot. The Master-Sleuth despairs of Japp's approach to crime solution: "I am disappointed in Japp. He has not method,"[14] nor does he have the tact, the style, and the poise needed for maximum cooperation and respect from suspicious servants and staff. Evidence of Japp's incompetence comes when the wrong man is arrested and tried on flimsy evidence for the murder of his stepmother. Only through the efforts and brainwork of M. Poirot is the true murderer unmasked and caught, and even then the great sleuth graciously surrenders the honor to Japp who will take full credit for solving the case.

Though Captain Hastings carries on a perpetual resentment and contempt for Inspector Japp, in *Murder on the Links* (1923), he admits that "The Scotland Yard inspector had more than once introduced us to an interesting case."[15] In return, M. Poirot helps to bring many a difficult case to a conclusion, even if it involves trickery as occurs in "The Tragedy at Marsdon Manor." Japp and M. Poirot also work as a team in "The Mystery of the Hunter's Lodge;" Hastings makes a mess of the case to Japp's amusement. Even though M. Poirot, in true armchair detective style, correctly singles out the murderer in the case, Japp is unable to get together the necessary evidence to insure a conviction.

All through the stories in *Poirot Investigates* (1925), Poirot often works with Japp, since he is the representative of Scotland Yard sent to handle cases of jewel robberies, murder, or stolen documents. In all cases, M. Poirot's grey cells provide the answers to the mysteries and crime puzzles; and Poirot graciously permits Japp to garner the kudos, though occasionally a large check falls into Poirot's hands from satisfied clients. In "The Disappearance of Mr. Davenheim," Japp begins to wonder if the brain power of Poirot is so phenomenal that the Belgian can literally solve a case without moving from his chair. The unbelieving Japp bets Poirot a wager of five pounds that he cannot figure out what has happened to the missing banker, Mr. Davenheim. Though Japp pities Poirot who seems debilitated by the late war, Poirot does riddle the mystery of the banker's disappearance. The chagrined Japp sheepishly loses his bet and sends the five pound note on to the winner by mail. M. Poirot, in remorse for getting the better of his colleague, will use the money to pay for a dinner for himself, Japp, and Hastings.

In this series of cases investigated by M. Poirot, Japp's main function seems to be that of arresting officer. Sometimes when Poirot wishes to gain entrance into a crime scene before the police arrive, he will use Japp's name as a key. Such was the case in "The Adventure of the Italian Nobleman" where the only true instance of a valet-butler being the cunning murderer is established in the person of Graves the butler who brutally murders his employer for gain: it will be the tardy Japp who will have the honor of arresting the "respectable" Graves, an incident which will prejudice Japp forever against butlers.

The history of the exploits of Detective Inspector Japp complements the history of M. Poirot. Japp is the operator of the police machinery which supports Poirot's crime-busting activities; Japp is the force that provides official sanction to Poirot's sometimes questionable tactics, unethical and often illegal; however, Japp is the recipient of all honor, glory, and fame spinning off from the successful solutions provided by M. Poirot. When contrasting his methods of sleuthing with those of the so-called "bloodhound" school, Mr. Poirot cites Japp as a prime representative of that tradition spanning from Gaboriau to Doyle. The growing challenge of *The Big Four* (1927) brings Japp into closer working alliance with M. Poirot. Japp, jaunty and dapper as usual, informs M. Poirot that a Secret Service operator, Mayerling, was captured, gagged, and poisoned by the gun of four Master-Criminals. Japp is the detective chosen to work with Captain Kent of the U.S. Secret Service in combating the activities of The Big Four.

In the attempt to trap the Master-Mind of the "radium thieves," Poirot arranges with Japp's assistance a stake-out, a surveillence, and a trap to catch Mr. Ryland and rescue Hastings from their clutches. Unfortunately, the clever Master-Criminal turns the tables on the Master-Sleuth by having a footman impersonate him while Ryland himself is home lying in bed. This is one of the few times Japp is able to chide Poirot for a maneuver which misfired. Japp complains to Poirot of the pretty mare's nest in which the Master-Sleuth has involved Scotland Yard: "First time, I've ever known you take a toss."[16] The determined Poirot, outsmarted so far by the wily Big Four, devotes all of his time and efforts to fighting their plots. To this end, M. Poirot works closely with Japp, giving the Inspector help and hints on how to handle the various cases stirred up by the busy Big Four: their first task is to quiet outspoken critics, then to steal valuable inventive plans, and then to manufacture engines of mass destruction from radium radiation and energy rays.

Naturally, all of Poirot's gratuitous aid is most profitable to Japp. Hastings contemptuously states that Japp received much renown in solving various cases which were resolved primarily from hints made by Poirot. Thus, it is Japp who drags M. Poirot into "The Yellow Jasmine Mystery." As M. Poirot carefully examines the murder room at Croftlands, Japp anticipates learning some of Poirot's methods of clue-gathering. Instead, Japp misreads clues and is forever chasing red herrings—much to the annoyances of Poirot, who finally sorts out the various threads of complication and explains them to Japp. During a dinner in a Soho restaurant, Hastings and Poirot are joined by Japp who relates the story of the death of a famed chess player during a Grand Masters challenge. Intrigued by Japp's reference to a possible murder attempt on

Savaroff, the surviving Grand Master, Poirot senses the hand
of the Big Four behind the case and thus enters and solves "A
Chess Problem." In the case of "The Baited trap," after Poirot
rescues Hastings and routs the gang in their Chinatown hide-
out with a bomb, a thorough search of the underground den is
made by Japp and his men. Though Hastings often sneers at
Japp's parasitic dependence on Poirot's sleuthing, yet it is
Japp who has been most valuable in rescuing both him and
Poirot from danger.

Evidence of the depth of the friendship existing between
Japp and M. Poirot is provided in *Peril at End House* (1932),
when Hastings and M. Poirot go to the Cheshire Cheese to see
Japp for an early dinner. It has been years since the two sleuths
last met, but Japp still has his fun mocking Poirot's mustache,
his attempt to retire in the country, and the way all three are
growing older. Japp has checked out some fingerprints for
Poirot, and this brings on a series of nostalgic reminiscences of
their past work. Japp laments that the detective business is not
a nice one, though the official detective's job is not as bad as
that of the private eye—who must often resort to underhanded
methods.

The collection of short stories brought together under the
title of *The Under Dog* (1951) documents many more cases
solved by M. Poirot with the minor assistance of Detective-
Inspector Japp. The murder of the socialite heiress in "The
Plymouth Express" is a contest between two methods, that of
birddog Japp (measuring footprints, collecting mud and
cigarette ash) with the armchair deductions of M. Poirot.
Though Japp researches and gathers evidence on the corpse,
the weapon, and train schedules, it is the brain of Poirot which
leads him to suspect the real culprit. Again, Japp gets the
credit, while M. Poirot's sense of justice is satisfied and his
bank account increased by a generous check written out by the
millionnaire father of the victim.

It is Japp who brings the tantalizing case of "The Affair at
the Victory Ball" to Poirot for solution. Japp is mystified by the
murder of Viscount Cronshaw at a fancy dress ball where all of
his party appeared in a special set of costumes copied from the
personae in the Commedia dell' Arte. Poirot hears Japp's
recital of facts and opinions, and while the Belgian has respect

for Japp's ability as a detective, he deplores his "lamentable lack of method." Obviously, Japp needs help and has come to seek it from his friend. Hastings has a low opinion of Japp's intentions, and Hastings notes that Japp's "highest talent lay in the gentle art of seeking favors under the guise of conferring them."[17] The riddling of this murder-mystery lies in the costumes of the guests; then an inspection of the six china figures from which the costumes were copied gives Poirot the clue he needs for the method and opportunity of the murder—the breaking of the killer's alibi no less. Poirot's love and knowledge of the drama help his deductions of this crime, a knowledge obviously not shared by his low-brow colleague, Japp.

The events leading up to "The Market Basing Mystery" provide the reader with new insight into Japp, the man. The Detective-Inspector is an ardent botanist, loves to study plants, and knows their Latin names. To pursue his hobby, Japp makes frequent visits into the English countryside. He persuades M. Poirot and Hastings to join him in a jaunt to the village of Market Basing for a week-end of relaxation. Constable Pollard, of the local police, comes in to get advice from Japp about a murder. An inspection of the scene of the crime reveals contradictions to M. Poirot's sense of logic, and soon he deduces that the murder before them is a staged affair, a frame-up to turn what is really a suicide into a simulated murder so as to punish a blackmailer. M. Poirot not only solves the puzzle, but he helps prevent Japp from being drawn into the frame-up of an innocent victim.

The friendship of Japp and Hastings is marked by a latent disrespect. When Japp visits Hercule Poirot after the murder of Lord Edgware, Hastings bristles at the way Japp picks his friend's brains for help on the case: "What did annoy me was Japp's hypocritical pretense that he was doing nothing of the kind."[18] The indulgent Poirot laughs at poor Japp: "He has to save his face, so he makes his little pretense."[19] As Poirot gets more involved in this case, Japp assures him that contrary to complaint, the English police are fair. To this Poirot answers: "In my opinion, foolishly so."[20]

During the investigation of the strange events in the murder of Lord Edgware, Japp runs into several problems.

There is the notorious reticence of Poirot who is as closed as an oyster. Japp also runs down a prime suspect only to discover to his astonishment that Jane has an alibi attested to by fourteen people. Japp is warned by the Master-Sleuth to beware of airtight alibis. Both know the history of the old Elizabeth Canning Case, but it is Poirot who points out its moral—the gypsy alibi—which applies to the present case. As Poirot and Japp examine the murder scene, Poirot jokingly notes that the traditional clues of detective fiction are missing—no cigarette ash, no footprints. This strikes a sore spot in Japp who complains: "The police are always made out to be as blind as bats in detective stories."[21]

Japp has great respect for the genius of Poirot, but wonders if old age has impaired his sanity. As a foil, Japp is constantly amazed at Poirot's theories and requests for help. He keeps Poirot constantly informed of all that the police are doing on the case, and even performs special investigations for him. Japp, at one point, accuses Poirot of getting lazy: "You've got to go out to things. They won't come to you."[22] Yet, Japp admits that this armchair detective has gained wealth by this method and guesses Poirot must be a millionaire by now. Japp and his resources are used to full advantage by Poirot: "Japp brings us here the result of the physical energy you admire so much. He has various means at his disposal which I have not."[23] Thus, the reciprocity practiced by the Inspector and the private detective is acknowledged.

In gathering evidence from witnesses Japp runs into an old problem—the reluctance of witnesses to speak: "It's the muddle-headed loyalty of friends and relations that makes a detective's life so difficult."[24] Added to this is the scorn and distrust leveled at the police by some of the rich and powerful, such as the Dowager Duchess of Merton who sees in Poirot's refusal to help her a sign of his being bribed by money. In great indignation she flares out: "Our police force must be corrupt through and through."[25] But the character and actions of Japp are a testimonial to the cheerful, hard-working, honest men in the police force. Japp would prefer that solutions to crimes be simple and definite; unfortunately, Poirot shifts theories as new clues come in. Japp complains that Poirot likes things to be difficult: even when his theory is proven, Poirot is not satisfied but searches about for new explanations.

Aside from criminals, Japp finds that the worst enemies of the police are solicitors and coroners: "I've had a perfectly clear case messed up by the coroner fooling about and letting the guilty party get away with it. As for lawyers, they are paid to use their training and wiles to win cases for their clients; thus, one expects them to be artful and to twist matters to their advantage."[26]

Through the character of Japp, Agatha Christie expresses her growing restlessness with her creation—Hercule Poirot. Japp constantly reminds the readers that the Belgian sleuth is becoming old, senile, and possibly "ga-ga." When the tactics of the Master-Sleuth become too bizarre, Japp is the first to wonder if his genius-friend is "near the border line and liable to slip over any minute."[27]

Ironically, it is Japp, in *The A B C Murders* (1936), who provides a presage of Hercule Poirot's eventual death in *Curtain* (1975). While engaged in one of their favorite criminological discourses, Japp compliments Poirot on being famous and having participated in all the celebrated cases of the day. Japp wonders if his friend has solved all kinds of cases except one: "Shouldn't wonder if you ended by detecting your own death—ought to be put in a book."[28] If ever there was a straw in the creative wind indicating Christie's thoughts on the possible death of Poirot, it is Japp who provides it.

Agatha Christie became impatient with her creations and often infused humor, self-parody, and satirical jabs at her sleuths. Following the lead of Conan Doyle in the Sherlock Holmes' stories, she patterned her Japp after the ferret-like qualities of Inspector Lestrade. A curious parallel developed with Japp and Poirot: as Poirot became older, more enfeebled, and less active, Japp increased in statue, performance, and reputation. One of the funniest episodes in the on-going ridicule against Poirot unfolds in the pages of *Death in the Air* (1935). While traveling on the Paris to London flight, Poirot becomes involved in the murder of a notorious money-lender and blackmailer. While Poirot is asleep in his seat, someone plants a blowpipe behind his cushion. As the plane lands and passengers and crew are herded into a lounge for questioning [and, later, an inquest], the ubiquitous Japp is put in charge of the case since he was at the airport anyway pursuing a "big bug in the smuggling line."[29] Because Poirot picked up a dart near the corpse, because his appearance is most strange, and because the blowpipe was behind his cushion, the jury at the subsequent inquest comes in with the verdict that Poirot is guilty of murder. The coroner corrects the jury. The amused and delighted Japp needles Poirot with the "near squeak of being locked up in a police cell."[30] After all, recalls Japp, detectives do turn out to be murderers—in detective fiction. Again, he is the harbinger of tragic events to come in *Curtain*.

Inspector Japp emerges in *Death in the Air* as a reliable, competent leader of police. He is in strong control, using good logic to sift suspects, evidence, and clues, and thus gains the respect of all colleagues. Japp makes his debut as a fully-developed persona here. In "Murder in the Mews" we again see the efficient, accomplished Japp at work: this is a wise Japp who has become Chief Inspector Japp. Poirot, seldom given to flattering the police, gives Japp high praise: "He is very sound. Yes, he is well thought of. He works hard and painstakingly and very little escapes him."[31] Christie has the great gift of characterizing personae through what they say—those marvellous dialogues framed in English expression, spirit, and psychology. It is exactly through such dialectic give and take with Poirot that Japp is humanized and developed as a more interesting character.

All of Christie's law enforcement officers share positive traits: they are honest, even-tempered, and polite. When they succeed, promotion in rank comes after long years of service and with the respect of their colleagues. They are careful of their relations with the public and mindful of their position with subordinates. Socially adroit, these men move smoothly through the social spheres from the lowly cottages of the poor to the estates of the aristocrats. Any detective may have idiosyncrasies and quirks, but he is still well versed in his work: in collecting clues, interrogating suspects, and penetrating the criminal mind. Christie may treat her policemen with humor or satire, with deference or compassion; but basically she builds respect for them.

Agatha Christie has presented a large gallery of police figures—a variety of portraits painted with different strokes.

Though Inspectors Battle and Japp are the most famous because of their serial appearances and their human qualities, there are several others who appear in one or more cases. Sir Henry Clithering is typical of the old school, much like a knight assisting the Lady Jane Marple. Colonel Race has all the traits of an international agent whose "racy" style enables him to move nimbly through Christie's thrillers. But Christie is more successful with those police officials who are less than perfect and who evince some human qualities, the ones who are less stereotyped and more individualized characters such as Battle and Japp. They are among the most credible of her police officials. Though Battle is closer to the "type" set up by Dickens and Collins, Japp, however, is Christie's own man: she allows him to grow and mature, developing from an inept detective to a leader in the ranks.

Chapter VIII

The Christie Environment

Christie immerses the readers in another world with its own geography, its special lifestyle and rituals. An exotic site in the Middle East, a sophisticated London flat, a luxurious country estate—Christie has conjured up such environments with a facile touch. In fact, the reader moves easily into these milieux because they are so disarmingly simple and non-threatening. Christie achieves her effect through economy of detail, distancing techniques, and a humanistic view—a combination that produces a well-integrated aesthetic structure. In detective fiction, setting (the physical dimension) and atmosphere (the emotional dimension) function together to produce a milieu. The milieu, first of all, must support the puzzle by providing parameters for the crime and its solution; and secondly, it must convey a total environment—offering horizons for studying the psychology of the crime. Christie follows these conventions of the mystery genre, but she adapts them to her own style.

The reader is made to feel comfortable in the setting and is not overpowered by onerous details. Christie accomplishes this by moderating two kinds of descriptive devices: explicit and implicit details. The parameters of the puzzle are presented explicitly, that is with specific details, frequently accompanied by diagrams of the scene of the crime. The reader is thus given direct access to information which permits him to "track" the murderer. The most obvious example of this kind of presentation occurs in the locked room murder puzzle, which relies upon technical data to create tension between the known and the unknown. Although Christie follows the tradition of her forebears in the art of mapping out the field of inquiry, she does not overload the story with such material. Unlike Gaboriau or Conan Doyle, she keeps technical details to a minimum and extends her focus to the larger canvas, focusing on people rather than on objects.

The social environment is Christie's chief interest. Here, she employs explicit as well as implicit methods of development, but sustains an economy of detail. Thus when she wishes to convey a family's financial difficulty, she focuses on a specific area such as the weeds in the garden or the dilapidated shutters on the house instead of describing all the features of the house and garden. Her method is like the poet's use of synecdoche wherein one aspect of the subject is used to signify the whole. The details are explicit in such instances, but the implications are pervasive as the reader makes judgments about the character's social class, integrity, taste, and social consciousness.

Furthermore, by manipulating the reader's perspective through changing distances, Christie provides an added dimension without excessive length. The larger world is remote; there are no extended descriptions of London or the Devon countryside, but the city flat or the country house is clearly realized. For example, in *Death Comes as the End* Christie recreates an ancient cultural unit. Using a kind of synecdoche, she allows the Nile to signify the whole of Egypt. However, the reader is only vaguely aware of the river flowing in the background, for the house and its occupants are in the foreground. The view is distinctly myopic, but functional, as it moves the reader to the heart of the closed community in which the crime occurs.

Within the small social circle, certain kinds of characters embody qualities which reinforce the reader's perception of the scene. Thus the butler or the cook in the country house is as much a part of the setting as the silver tea service or the baize door.

Yet a Christie setting does not support any form of behavioral determinism. Unlike Dickens and other detective story writers who dwell on the adverse effects of social conditioning, Christie treats environment as *place*. And a Christie setting does not support any form of naturalism, for the inexorable forces of fate and nature do not press upon her characters. In fact, nothing could be more contradictory than for Agatha Christie, who loved the garden and the countryside, to portray nature as hostile.

Christie's successful rendering of setting and atmosphere may be attributed to her keen powers of observation and her first hand experience, for she wrote about places she knew well. As we have seen in Chapter One, Christie was a product of her environment, a person concerned about homes and family life, and a world traveler who enjoyed cultures other than her own. Her works reflect these interests in her fictional locales; the English countryside with its small villages and spacious estates; the urban scene, reflecting London's social set; and the exotic settings gleaned from her travels. As we examine Christie's settings, we will move from the exotic locales to the London scene and then to the English countryside—an extensive tour of Christie country.

The Middle East

Having journeyed often through the Middle East with her archeologist husband, Agatha Christie came to know the terrain and the culture of the area well. Professor Mallowan's work brought them to Iraq to the ancient ruins of Nimrud; here Agatha not only assisted her husband in his work but she also discovered another horizon for her writing. Christie put her experience in the Middle East to good account in several detective stories. Her first to reflect this exotic locale is *Murder in Mesopotamia* (1936), which takes the reader to an archeological dig in Iraq; another is *They Came to Baghdad* (1951), a lively account of espionage and murder. While the Nile and its banks set the scene for *Death on the Nile* (1937), the Holy Land is the setting for *Appointment with Death* (1938). But the most unusual work gleaned from her interest in the Middle East is *Death Comes as the End* (1944), an amazing reconstruction of life, love, and murder in ancient Egypt 2,000 years before Christ.

The first of these works, *Murder in Mesopotamia*, describes how a newcomer to this ancient land responds to travel, to the rigors of a trip across the desert, to life at the site of an archeological expedition. Setting is developed here through the point of view of a young British nurse, Amy Leathern, who reacts like a tourist to the spectacle around her. She gives her impressions of the region:

> It took us about four hours to get to Hassanieh, which, to my surprise, was quite big. Very pretty it looked, too, before we got there from the other side of the river—standing up quite white and fairylike with minarets. It was a bit different, though, when one had crossed the bridge and came right into it. Such a smell, and everything ramshackle and tumble-down, and mud and mess everywhere.[1]

The scene is conveyed in hazy outlines; the focus is never close enough to see a particular building or street. But the vagueness creates an atmosphere of romance and mystery, which is reinforced by distancing as the viewer does not confront the more grim realities of the city. To Amy Leathern, "Hassanieh in the distance looked quite fairylike with the setting sun behind it, and the River Tigris flowing between its wide banks looked like a dream river rather than a real one"[2] Then the larger area outside the archeological site, which is the immediate setting for the murder puzzle, is thus remote—its reality merely implied by the river flowing in the background and by the suggesting of Hassanieh.

When Nurse Lathern arrives at the expedition site, she perceives details much more clearly as she enters the small community of archeologists. And far away from the central headquarters are the "digs;" the main locale of action is the Khan or the caravansari, reconstructed to form a complete square with an open courtyard in the center and a series of work rooms and living quarters ranging about the square. Miss Leathern is struck by the fact that although the facade of the building reflects Iraqi architecture, actually the place is more like an English manor, housing international personages who interact along familiar English class lines. Christie, in the Gaboriau manner, provides the reader with a detailed sketch of the khan and its topography: ranged about the open courtyard are the dining room, sitting room, antiquities room, bedrooms, bathrooms, drawing office, laboratory, photographic workroom, and the kitchen. Since the murder which occurs here is of the "locked room" variety, these details are functional as well as descriptive. Very little description of place is gratuitous. The whole setup tends to become a natural setting for a murder because it is well organized, socially oriented, and obviously isolated. Christie provides enough direction and detail to give the reader a feeling for environment, yet not so much that place takes precedence over plot—the essence of a murder mystery.

Christie uses some of the same techniques for developing the setting in *They Came to Baghdad*. Once again, she parlays her knowledge of Iraq and Syria into a background for adventure. The point of view is that of another young British heroine, Victoria Jones, who is swept up by the exotic sights. Although the topographical spread extends from London to Baghdad and from the Iraqi border to Kuwait, Christie's economy of detail and light background touches allow the novel to move at a brisk pace. Thus the palatial Hotel Savoy is used to signify the grandeur and dignity of London, while the noisy and crowded quadrants of Baghdad offer a glimpse of a contrasting culture. The expedition site reflects a cultural admixture with English archeologists encamping in the distinctly Eastern environment.

Imagistic techniques are employed to convey the atmosphere of the "red rose" city of Petra in *Appointment with Death*. The interesting feature of this setting is the singular focus on color as Christie spotlights various shades of rose and red to signify not only the city, but also the emotions of a troubled family. In fact, the natural coloration of the city becomes one with the emotional climate of the characters. Images of the river in *Death on the Nile* evoke implicit responses from readers who have followed the Nile's legend. Consequently, the view of the river seen from the cruise ship is impressionistic: "There was a savage aspect about the sheet of water in front of them, the masses of rock without vegetation that came down to the water's edge—here and there a trace of houses abandoned and ruined as a result of the damming up of the waters."[3] The images foreshadow the dangers ahead. Since a series of murders occur on the ship, a layout of the ship is also presented:

The *Karnak* was a smaller steamer.... The passengers went on board and were shown their accommodations. Since the boat was not full, most of the passengers had accommodations on the promenade deck. The entire forward part of this deck was occupied by an observations saloon, all glass-enclosed, where the passengers could sit and watch the river unfold before them. On the deck below were a smoking room, and a small drawing-room and on the deck below that, the dining saloon.[4]

While *Death on the Nile* presents threatened passengers passing through some of the greatest wonders of the world, another novel—*Death Comes as the End*—traces the perilous journey of a beautiful concubine from Memphis to Thebes into a household ripe for destruction. Both works share landscape similarities: the mighty Nile River, the teeming banks, the green and brown farms, the villages and mighty temples and palaces crowning the high cliffs along the valley. However, this trip takes the reader into the past, to ancient Egypt, as Christie breathes life into the household of a wealthy Egyptian family.

In the preface to *Death Comes as the End,* Christie relates that she began the novel as a challenge from Professor Stephen Glanville, an archeologist on the faculty of the University of London. He gave her the germ of the idea, and she then proceeded to research the details of life in ancient times. This was an enormous task, requiring the reconstruction of an entire way of life. Yet Christie succeeded. She set her stage deftly with details of clothing, furniture, architecture, occupational activities, as well as mundane trivia of daily life. The credibility of the background reinforces the total effect of the plot and provides a realistic framework for the murder mystery.

The focus of the story is on the widowed daughter, Renisenb, who has returned to the security of her father's house. The reader enters the setting with her:

Renisenb turned abruptly and made her way towards the house, passing on the way some loaded donkeys being driven towards the riverbank. She passed by the cornbins and the outhouses and through the gateway into the courtyard. It was very pleasant in the courtyard. There was the artificial lake, surrounded by the flowering oleanders and jasmines and shaded by the sycamore fig trees . . . Renisenb went out to the porch with its gaily colored columns and then into the house, passing through the central chamber with its colored frieze of lotus and poppies, and on to the back of the house and the women's quarters.[5]

Christie takes unusual care to reconstruct the total

environment, rendering a clear plan of the house and its environs. Once inside, the focus is on members of the household as they pursue daily routines. Specific references to food, clothing, jewelry, herbal medicines, and burial customs are integrated into the total picture. When the reader is comfortably settled into the environment, the dynamics of the murder puzzle intensify, as Christie focuses on action and dialogue. As with the other novels having an Eastern background, setting is not just an exotic gameboard for the murder puzzle; it also stimulates drama and heightens emotion. The heat, light, rocky landscape, and desert life-styles function as catalysts for action and emotion. Yet, despite the potential for extended description in this milieu, Christie avoids over-statement.

Christie experimented with another kind of locale, one providing adventure in the form of travel in an encapsulated community—murder on the rails. The train mysteries are hybrid in setting; the aura of the exotic in the form of foreign travel surrounds the train, but within each coach is a small, isolated community. Long before Christie made her contribution to the locomotive mystery category—*The Mystery of the Blue Train* (1928), *What Mrs. McGillicuddy Saw* (1957), and *Murder on the Orient Express* (1934)—trains had been used as a locus for crime. An early variant of the Orient Express is found in Bram Stoker's *Dracula;* Eden Phillpotts' *The Flying Yorkshireman* made use of a crack flyer; and Freeman Wills Crofts (a trained railway engineer) employed the intricate details of time tables and the mechanical operation of trains to set up his murder puzzles.

However for Christie, the train became a drawing room in which international travelers could interact. She was not interested in the mechanics of operating a railway system; her focus is on the interior of the train which *houses* the principals in her novels. The only case in which timetables and rails are scrutinized is in *What Mrs. McGillicudy Saw* (also known as the *4:50 from Paddington).* In this novel, ascertaining the point at which two trains passed each other becomes the basis for discovering a hidden corpse—thus the technical details are functional to the development of the plot. In *The Mystery of the Blue Train* a jewel robbery and murder take place in a compartment of the Calais to Nice "millionaire's train," but only a minor portion of the total action occurs on the train itself.

The famous Christie mystery which takes place exclusively on a train is *Murder on the Orient Express*. The Orient Express was admittedly her favorite: she spent a honeymoon on the train, and she and her husband subsequently traveled over the same line on their yearly expeditions to Nimrud. But the opulence which she enjoyed in her personal travels is *not* recreated in the scenes of this novel. Christie offers only minimal commentary on the train's compartments, its parlours, and its dining service. As one studies the setting of this novel, it becomes apparent that Agatha Christie's aesthetic priorities moderated her use of details, for the focal point of the novel is the characters and their interaction—not the physical attributes of the train itself.

However, when murder occurs, Christie offers explicit information in the form of a diagram of the coach indicating the position and the occupants of each compartment. The topography of the coach becomes important as alibis are dependent upon where each of the suspects was at the time of the murder. She creates a claustrophobic atmosphere which increases tension by confining the passengers to the narrow limits of the coach and then by cutting them off from the outside world with a paralyzing blizzard. This isolation is complete when the train comes to a halt in the heavy snow. This touch is not merely decorative, for it makes the game all the more challenging since the murder puzzle must be solved without benefit of "outside" help.

The reader participates in a vicarious adventure in these novels with exotic settings. The landscape provides a place of intrigue as well as the likely scene for the enactment of murder. However, as in all Christie's novels, place never overshadows action or character, for she creates a living environment in which characters function naturally. By recreating the lifestyle of a culture, she effectively develops a credible milieu for exploring the psychology of the crime.

London

London has traditionally formed the background for

countless novels of mystery and detection. Baroness Orczy's Old Man in the Corner encompasses London in his mind's eye as he unravels the knots of puzzling, unsolved crimes; Zangwills' *Big Bow Street Mystery* makes excellent use of realistic personae, activities, and situations. Mrs. Belloc Lowndes in *The Lodger* brilliantly recaptures the confusion, poverty, and horror of the Jack the Ripper period. Mrs. Belloc Lowndes can also capture the elegance and the luxury of the upper class members of society as they glide from casino to town house to elegant hotels as she does in her novel *One of Those Ways*. But the author who most deftly caught the atmosphere, the ambience, and pulsating dense of quickening life in London was A. Conan Doyle in his remarkable Sherlock Holmes stories, acknowledged by Agatha Christie to be a prime source of inspiration to her. In such stories as "The Sign of the Four," Doyle captured the foggy atmosphere, the street scenes, the chasing back and forth in London's dark streets at night, the interiors of suburban villas, and the complex interrelationships of dozens of Londoners attempting to go on their daily routines while sinister murders and robberies are carried on by foreign agents.

However, unlike many of the writers who preceded her, Christie's presentation of the London scene is highly filtered. Even though she knew London well: she visited the city often as a child, lived there after World War I and then again during World War II, and in later years maintained a flat in Chelsea. Despite this experience, she does not focus on the majestic sights of London. And although she must have seen the slums and knew about brutal street crimes, she never brings these ugly realities into focus. Though she was there during the bombing of London and witnessed vast destruction, her novels of that period do not offer a view of the devastation, the rationing of food, or the more horrific realities. She focuses instead on domestic scenes that reflect stable lifestyles. The view is decidedly myopic as the reader is given detailed descriptions of home furnishings, of breakfast menus, and plumbing fixtures. What emerges through Christie's lens is a comfortable, encapsulated world shaped by homely details or glamorous adventures, but protected from otherwise threatening events.

In order to observe Christie's treatment of the London scene, we have chosen certain novels to examine in the light of areas of interest, descriptive methods, and attention to changes in the urban scene. *Thirteen at Dinner* (1933) and *Cards on the Table* (1936) offer a viable introduction to the early Christie perspective. In both novels the reader is introduced to a character whose very person symbolizes a privileged lifestyle. *Thirteen at Dinner* depicts the aristocratic Lord Edgware through his home: "The house was an imposing one—well built, handsome, and slightly gloomy. There were no window boxes or such frivolities,"[6] The house is presented in quick strokes, leading one to make certain assumptions about the owner and preparing the way for the description of Lord Edgware himself. One becomes aware of the "outside" world more through the pace of the characters' lives rather than through specific landmarks, though the theatre and parties at the Savoy are part of the social schedule. A similar treatment is obvious in *Cards on the Table*. An aura of speed and danger prevail, but details are minimal as action becomes the controlling force.

A bridge between these two extremes, actually in a category by itself, is *At Bertram's Hotel* (1965). This novel, which recreates the ambience of a stay at a first class hotel at the turn of the century, is explicit and rich in descriptive detail. London, however, is implicit in the background as Christie takes one immediately inside the doors of the hotel: "Outside the steps that led up to the big swing doors stood what at first sight appeared to be no less than a field marshall.... Inside, if this was the first time you had visited Bertram's, you felt almost with alarm, that you had re-entered a vanished world. Time had gone back. You were in Edwardian England once more."[8]

Old London comes to life in the hotel's appointments and services. The public rooms contain large chairs designed "properly" for elderly guests. Flowered wallpaper adorns bedroom walls; adjoining baths are "old fashioned" with commodious marble fixtures. Afternoon tea is a work of art: "There were large crested silver trays, and Georgian silver teapots. The china, if not actually Rockingham and Davenport, looked it."[9] Homemade pastries like one's grandmother used to serve—authentic seed cake, scones, and crisp watercress sandwiches—are among the plethora of delights. In fact, the whole scene is just too good to be true, as the wary sleuth soon discovers. Christie conveys this Edwardian atmosphere in such detail in order to heighten the puzzle, for atmosphere is the key to its solution. As in Christie's exotic settings, place relates intrinsically to character and plot. Description is never gratuitous, nor does it impede action especially when reflecting the tempo of urban life.

The Country Estate

But the best of all possible worlds, according to Christie, is the country estate, the large home surrounded by acres of private land. Close enough to London yet far enough from its perils, the estate offers seclusion and comfort. And what better place for a murder? The isolated house filled with family, guests, and servants is the ideal setting for the unexpected. For Christie, who had a penchant for homes and decorating, the estate setting affords an opportunity to create and people houses in her inimitable fashion. In fact, the reader is often taken on a house and garden tour of the great homes of Britain, for Christie is in her element when she provides the details of maintaining a well-to-do household.

Christie also follows a literary tradition in employing the estate setting in detective fiction. Poe, Gaboriau, Green, Leroux, Leblanc, Dickens, Mason, Bentley, Doyle, Rinehart among others—all staged successful murders within illustrious homes. Consequently when Christie entered the field, the role of the country house as a symbol of class existence and as the setting for mystery and detective fiction had already been established.

The country house continues to appeal to the imagination of readers for various reasons: it flatters the readers' interest in the aristocracy; it reflects snobbish tendencies and class-consciousness, latent or overt; and it becomes a psychic symbol of paradise lost, a lost Edenic Golden Age. The mood of this dream is idyllic and feudal. Automatically, the choice of a country house insures maximum space, interesting personae, and intriguing complications. Mystery and crime placed in a large upper-class household, according to Nancy Blue Wynne, provides the best possible combination:

First of all there would be a large house with all its possibilities of atmosphere to use if one wished; lots of servants available as possible suspects, witnesses, comic relief, and as victims of criminals; plenty of family members and guests present to be used in all these roles too.[10]

In the first twenty-five years of her writing career, Agatha Christie wrote at least five major mystery novels centered in a large family gathering within the confines of the country house. Agatha Christie's first novel *The Mysterious Affair at Styles* (1920) is likely to have been inspired by her memories of the elegant lifestyle of the Torquay villas. She uses Styles Court at the beginning of Poirot's career, and again when it came to an end in *Curtain* (1975). Two of her novels, *The Secret of Chimneys* (1925) and *The Seven Dials Mystery* (1929), make use of a venerable historic structure, Chimneys. In 1939, Gorston Hall becomes the location for *A Holiday for Murder*, and in 1944, Gulls Point, another manorial structure is the setting of *Towards Zero*.

In the last thirty years of her career, Agatha Christie released another five novels making major use of the country house motifs. These include *The Hollow* (1946); *A Pocketful of Rye* (1953); *Dead Man's Folly* (1956); *What Mrs. McGilicuddy Saw* (1956); and *Curtain* (written in the mid-1940s but released for publication in 1976).

All of these houses reflect Christie's preference for elegant surroundings and high-toned characters for her murders. Her country homes like Styles Court, Chimneys, The Hollow, are splendid structures, surrounded by terraces, lawns, gardens, tennis courts, lodges, greenhouses, forest groves and, on occasion, a lake for boating. The house itself must contain a study, a library, drawing-rooms, music room, dining rooms, vast corridors, broad staircases, galleries, and servants quarters at the back replete with butler's pantry, scullery, and kitchen. The house, whether U-shaped or L-shaped, usually contains two wings. (Detailed floor-plans are usually provided.) Christie believes the more luxurious the surroundings, the greater the incongruity of crime.

Larmouth also feels that the country house is the best of all murder backgrounds because "it provides the largest canvas; a grand gesture of land, the rumblings and innuendoes of nature, a clearing in the midst of civilization for the interplay of character."[11] Characters reveal themselves through romantic antagonisms, legacy hunting, and upper class ceremonies such as the reading of the will, and the realignment of familial and class loyalties to form a buttress against scandal and shame. Even at the breakfast table with the unidentified murderer in their midst, the family and guests put on the good face that decorum and breeding demand.

The week-end party is the best way to set the stage for an effective murder mystery on the palatial country estate. First of all, the setting is ideal, for the country ambience is natural and helps enclose the community within the manor house. Second, the week-end party is an excellent method of collecting sundry persons under one roof for the ostensible purpose of sociability in the guise of a ritualistic activity—but a sociability which conceals hidden passions, motives, and anti-social proclivities. Third, the week-end party constitutes a closed circle penetrated only by the bona fides of birth and breeding. When everyone knows everyone else personally or by repute, the social benefits of such a gathering are shared only by the in-group; likewise when danger or murder threaten, the innocent and the outsider, as a rule, will not be touched by the malignity making its rounds among the week-end guests. Occasionally though, a stupid maid or hapless villager will be drawn into the vortex of death.

The reader following a crime in the country house is struck by two incongruities: the serene Garden of Eden topography invaded by the murderer, and the seemingly harmonious world which is torn apart by passion, greed, violence, suspicion, and murder. While the family, guests, and staff move through their paces, the reader senses that Agatha Christie has captured a slice of realistic English life. These glimpses of upper middle class England, as Larmouth notes, are documents of social usage, for "these books have become perfect records, not just of social dreams, but of the attitudes that formed them."[12]

Perhaps the most prestigious of all manorial structures in the Christie novels is Chimneys, an estate which is the setting for *The Secret of Chimneys* (1925) and its sequel, The *Seven*

Dials Mystery (1929). Chimneys is the ancestral home of Lord Caterham, Marquis of Caterham, who with his daughter, Lady Eileen, is host to a fatal week-end party. In fact, Chimneys is so esteemed that it is described in *Historic Homes of England,* and busloads of tourists tramp the extensive grounds, ogle the interiors, and envy the life of its inhabitants. The Manor contains expansive spaces, wide halls, a panelled library, and numerous drawing rooms; it not only boasts of a valuable art collection, but it also has two priests' holes, and a secret tunnel leading from the Council Room to Wyvern Abbey. Chimneys is so famous, spacious, and luxurious that it has often been used by the government for diplomatic gatherings. The genial, generous, yet eccentric Lord Caterham's hospitality is easily obtained, and this nobleman becomes "the perfect example of English hospitality among the haute noblesse."[13]

The most dangerous rooms in Chimneys and its sister palaces are the library and the study—for that is where the body will be found! Murders are apt to occur in the library for a variety of reasons: it is open and readily accessible to anyone wishing to get a book; and it is not as social or busy as the drawing room. Libraries tend to be solitary, impersonal, and fully equipped for assault and red-herrings. The long French windows facilitate secret entrances and exits; the book-lined shelves muffle groans and screams; clocks can be tampered with to indicate false time; heavy fire-place equipment can become murderous weapons; innumerable knicknacks are excellent receptors for careless fingerprints, and the fireplace itself becomes the incinerator for destroying incriminating letters, articles of clothing, and other clues. The grisly murder at Chimneys occurs in the Council Chamber, a library with a secret doorway opening on the tunnel leading to the Abbey.

Not only the house, its rooms and furnishings are significant, but also the *servants* who care for the physical site and the well-being of its occupants. Servants add tone and color to the setting, for besides filling character roles, they establish the ambience of the home and their employer's social status. Traditionally, mystery fiction's "hired help" have provided witnesses, clues, and complications for the puzzle, acted as chorus to the tragic events with their exclamations or backstairs gossip, and deepened the human dimension of the setting. While Christie's servants follow these conventions, they also express a genuine appreciation for the rituals of housekeeping and evoke a light, comic quality. One senses that Agatha Christie knows servants and is presenting an inside view of domestic life. Like finely crafted furniture or antique silver, Christie's servants form part of the home setting. By highlighting the background with vitality and humor, servants help to lighten tone and add a touch of color to an otherwise flat scene.

Consider the typical Christie butler who maintains perfect service, order and decorum in the house shattered by murder. The most aristocratic of servants, he is the subtle genius who tends to injured sensibilities, protects the family from intrusion, and maintains calm control. Although usually aged and imposing, he may also be slightly deaf or blind—with just enough imperfection to humanize him. For example, Tredwell, the white-haired butler of Chimneys, deals with unpunctual guests, sees to the utmost comfort of the family, and takes matters in hand when danger threatens. As the nervous servants crowd together at the scene of the crime in *The Seven Dials Mystery,* it is the staid Tredwell who sends them off to their duties with a stiff admonition. Tressilian, the major-domo of Gorstan Hall who has been in service for forty years, is so fiercely devoted to the family and its honor that he lies to the police when the family name is at stake. And so keen is his judgment that he can tell from the way in which a person rings the doorbell whether that person is a reputable visitor.

Should the investigating police ever pierce the green baize door leading to the kitchen, all the family would be greatly alarmed, for the sensitive cook might be intimidated and the forthcoming meal completely ruined. The cook is Christie's conception of earth mother. She is usually large, seasoned in both years and experience, and a "comfort" to the family (second only to Nanny in this respect). Thus nothing, not even murder, is allowed to upset cook and her kingdom. Murders are never committed in the kitchen; in fact, the safest place in the house is the humble kithcen. The next safety zone is the dining room, for few murderers dare to violate the sanctity of the feast board.

Food, an extension of the cook, lends sensual delight to the

Christie setting. In no other detective fiction has food played such a dominant role. For Christie, food is also as much a part of the setting as the furnishings of the home. Without a sideboard covered with the delights of an English breakfast—eggs, kidneys, toast, fruit, tea, coffee—no Christie story is complete. How many souffles or omelets have been served for lunch? And a proper tea served on a silver tray must include cake, biscuits, scones and honey, and possibly fois gras sandwiches. If one completes tea without a murder or related trauma, freshly killed game might be expected for dinner. Given a trauma any time of the day or night, one can count on a soothing cup of chocolate or a bracing cup of tea. Should a murder occur before lunch, thereby delaying the ritual, the hostess is not above preparing sandwiches and coffee for her guests. Food, according to Larmouth, "serves an important function in giving a sense of reality," and it indicates "class."[14]

The most independent of all servants is the gardener—a personage of delicate temperament and autocratic power. The garden is a place for walking, taking tea under the sycamore, keeping a tryst, or simply gathering flowers for decorating the dinner table. But the Christie gardener is usually plagued by footprints in his flower beds, by strangers lurking in the bushes, by sleuths checking footprints, by discarded cigarette ends or matches, and by disappearing ladders. His supply of weed-killer (tins of arsenic) is often tampered with; foxglove is often mixed with salad greens; and poison for spraying bugs or destroying wasps' nests may show up in somebody's coffee. Hostesses frequently have a difficult time with him, however. Even MacDonald, the head gardener at Chimneys, is depicted as princely but despotic.

Another facet of the domestic scene is the decline in the number and quality of servants. Over the years, one notices the changes for Christie's earlier novels are filled with servants, but her later works reflect the sociological changes occurring in Britain's labor force. Between the First and Second World Wars labor was plentiful, and the labor force went into service readily. Servants were always a part of Christie's experience: she had hired-help, and she had watched her grandmother and mother supervise legions of maids, cooks, and gardeners—these experiences gave her some insight into the differences in the servants of the old school and those of the new generation. After World War II, only the very wealthy could afford hired-help on a regular basis; and as wages increased, their numbers in the household decreased. Christie regretted the passing of the old days when servants were plentiful, inexpensive, and knew their place; she often speaks through her characters lamenting the fact that the new generation has a distaste for servitude, submissiveness, dependency, and the old fashioned rules of housekeeping.

The high cost of labor came as a crushing blow to the owners of large estates. In fact, it marked the decline of a lifestyle. Lord Caterham, the owner of Chimneys, perceives the far-reaching effects of immense social change especially in the attitudes of young people, who seem frivolous, irreponsible, and headstrong—especially in matters of love and marriage. He laments the decline of the family, the fall of old standards, the erosion of upperclass influence. A spokesman for the old aristocracy then exclaims, "There are things that should die hard—dignity, beauty, modesty, the sanctity of family life, filial respect...."[15] Lord Caterham is faced with the problem which beset all owners who could no longer maintain their expensive properties: the leasing of his cherished Chimneys (and the abuse of it). Death and violence, and worst of all, the intrusion of the police—all reflect the decline of his ancestral home. Selling is not even a viable alternative, for the monied men are speculators with surplus funds but lacking in class and virtue. The ultimate horror might thus occur to Chimneys: it could be sold and converted into miserable little flats, or torn down to make room for a "development." (Agatha Christie's childhood home, Ashfield, suffered such a fate.)

The Village

All English villages are alike—or so Christie's fictional rural communities may seem to the cursory reader. Admittedly, the communities she creates are based on the same prototype, a combination of Torquay and St. Mary Church which are located in the Devon area where she grew up. Like the fictional Cranford, the Christie village is female-dominated. The many single or widowed women with time on their hands and a natural curiosity about their neighbor's business are the vocal majority. Gossip is as routine as a visit to the green grocer's shop on High Street. Here more than anywhere else in the Christie canon, the influence of the English domestic novel is apparent with its emphasis on the routines of the average householder. In depicting the village scene, Christie captures the rhythm of a lifestyle. *Place* becomes a complete reflection of values, and changing values at that. With the passage of time, Christie's villages record the socio-economic effects of two World Wars. In order to observe the historical development of setting in the Christie village, we will focus on St. Mary Mead, her most famous community.

Agatha Christie's fullest treatment of the village occurs in three Jane Marple detective novels, *Murder at the Vicarage* (1930), *The Body in the Library* (1942), and *The Mirror Crack'd* (1962). It is in these detective novels that we see the genius of Agatha Christie in reconstructing St. Mary Mead as a *total environment*—realistic, peopled with vibrant personalities and alive with human feelings, passions, and actions. In *The Murder at the Vicarage,* we see Christie's technique developing as she slowly establishes the parameters of the village and the circle of upper crust life, and then makes her selection and characterization of the various players in this drama. These characters are types possibly found in small English villages in the period 1914-1941. A high percentage of them are spinsters and gossips.

The village has its High Street with the church, post office, shops, and public house—The Blue Boar. The village of St. Mary Mead, like hundreds of its English sisters, is Cranfordian in attitude: it is restful, quiescent, isolated, and self-contained. It is distrustful of strangers and foreigners, and it views tramps and gypsies with dread. It is a self-contained social microcosm completely surrounded by rural expanses, though seldom does one meet farmers, workers, or toilers of the sod or shop. The religious needs are provided by a wooly-headed Vicar, married to a younger wife, who herself is a notoriously poor housekeeper and worse cook, and who tends to view the parishioners with humor and sarcasm. When passers-by do stay, there are rooms at The Blue Boar, which provide the space for various strangers and detectives who must have rooms overnight; inquests are held in the public rooms. There is always good bus service to Much Benham, the nearest town, and an excellent train carries villagers on London shopping expeditions.

The realism of place is well handled, for Agatha Christie gives us details of houses, furniture, numbers of rooms, and activities of housekeeping. Her sketches of objects are solid, brief, but vivid; she does not overload the description with quantity and purple passages. Her specificity of material details extends to descriptions of the daily life of St. Mary Mead: preparation of meals, household chores, supervising of servants, delicate conversations, adjustment or confusion and disappointments, anger at injustices, etc. Through the portrayal of activities in this one social community, we see the bourgeois orientation, the middle-class materialism, and the basic problems associated with these concerns and problems. Christie's village novels are in the tradition of domestic realism seen in George Eliot's *The Mill on the Floss* and in Charles Dickens' *Bleak House.* Here, preoccupation with domesticity, the preparation of meals, the supervising of servants, tea and supper parties, is all evident. The appeal of the Christie novel comes in part from the simple presentation of basic settings and activities as the reader recognizes and identifies these realities. For example, when the village of St. Mary Mead appears again in *The Body in the Library;* the vicarage, Miss Marple's house, and the Blue Boar Inn at the village crossroads are still part of the scene. The reader thus adapts comfortably to these familiar sights and to familiar characters as well. Griselda, the vicar's wife, puts in an appearance with her young son who is the newest member of the community. The police officials, who played a major role in the murder that occurred in the vicarage, rise to the occasion again; their respect for Jane Marple has grown appreciably since her coup in solving that case. At the same time the reader is struck by two additions to the community: Colonel and Mrs. Bantry's country home, an aristocratic manorial estate called Gossinger Hall; and the latest architectural horror, Mr. Brook's modern house called Chatsworth, which has been rented by one of the swinging cinema crowd. Christie focuses on the different lifestyles which these homes represent—the modest cottage of Jane Marple, the more opulent estate of the Bantrys, the modernistic but tasteless house of the cinema folk become a reflection of values as well as social status. Although the change is subtle, the village of St. Mary Mead is being infiltrated by the nouveaux riches whose lack of taste and good breeding takes its toll on the community. Transients, renters, strangers are traditionally treated with suspicion, but Christie seems to be saying in this novel that the solid villagers have good reason for their prejudices.

More dramatic physical and sociological changes in St. Mary Mead are revealed in *The Mirror Crack'd*. Now, the outward appearance of the village is radically altered. Many of the little Queen Anne and Georgian houses are still standing; along with the Vicarage, the church, some shops, and The Blue Boar. But there are new tenants in the old houses:

...but the houses themselves are little changed in appearance since the people who had bought them had done so because they liked what the house agent called 'old-world charm.' They just added another bathroom, and spent a good deal of money on plumbing, electric cookers, and dishwashers.[16]

New modern shops have sprung up, a supermarket now sits at the end of the High Street, and across from the Vicarage lies the planned development, a new set of residential complexes called Closes, occupied mainly by young families of middle and lower income status. The old inhabitants of St. Mary Mead are gone, only Miss Marple, Miss Hartnell, Mrs. Bantry, and Dr. Haycock remain of the old guard. Instead, a new breed of villager is in evidence: young, fastmoving, modern and scornful of old values and lifestyles. The ladies in the development are fond of modern amenities, do their shopping at the supermarket, do not use servants, shop on the hire-purchase plan, and are often short of funds as a result. Miss Marple has been ordered by the doctor to keep a nurse-companion in her home, but the domestic work is performed by Cherry Baker, representative of the "detachment of young wives who shopped at the supermarket and wheeled prams about the quiet streets of St. Mary Mead. They were all smart and well turned out. Their hair was crisp and curled. They laughed and talked and called to one another. They were like a happy flock of birds."[17]

Among the changes are new buildings, new ways, and strangers everywhere. One is apt to blame both wars, the younger generation, and women going to work in factories for the drastic social shift. It is reported that gangs of Teddy Boys armed with knives haunt the development, and it is accepted that the Mayor is corrupt, deep in graft, and just one shade this side of the law. It is natural that Miss Marple should think kindly of the old days when maids really knew how to wash dishes and clean house properly, when lads worked as shop assistants, and when officials were noted for their honesty. An astonishing physical transformation has overtaken the manor-house, Gossinger Hall, where the Bantrys found the body in their library. The death of the old Colonel led Mrs. Bantry to put the estate up for sale, reserving just a small garden and the lodge for herself. Gossinger Hall has recently been purchased by a famous movie star, Marina Gregg and her current husband, prominent movie director, Jason Rudd. The modernizing of the old hall reflects the history and the fate of numerous old lovely country homes in England after the war: original families no longer able to afford the upkeep sell to wealthy owners who renovate and alter the character of the property.

Amid all the changes occurring in St. Mary Mead, the salient factor remains the personage of Jane Marple. Christie personifies Miss Marple as the embodiment of solid, middle class values. Though old and weak, Marple refuses to become an invalid. In order to maintain her home, she invites Cherry Baker and her husband to move in with her in return for assistance in running her house. Though the manor house on the hill fails, Miss Marple's house is revitalized with new blood and youth. We assume that Agatha Christie through Jane Marple extends a legacy to future generations—a respect for life, personal integrity, and support for religion, justice, and humanity.

A survey of all the lands and communities that Agatha Christie depicts—the exotic, the London scene, the estate, and the village—reveals a basic concern for social environment. It is the people and their lifestyles that matter, for crime is inherently anti-social, an assault upon the community. Christie treats the scene of the crime with explicit details, which provide parameters for the puzzle but yet enough ambiguity to maintain the mystery and the challenge of the game. Less specific and more impressionistic is her treatment of the total environment where she is more apt to rely upon selected aspects to convey the whole scene.

Christie's settings provide a social experience for the reader, not merely a background for the detectival challenge. The terms "cozy" and "comfortable" are often applied to her settings because the reader feels at ease. The integrity of the atmosphere reflects Christie's personal interest in homes and lifestyles. This focus on the human condition is complemented by Christie's skill at capturing the essence of a scene: light touches of detail, clear and concise comments on the garden, the house, or the breakfast menu are informative without being ponderous. Thus the reader enters a scene quickly and easily, becoming an insider privy to homely rituals as well as to exciting and glamorous escapades.

A desire to reclaim the past, to settle into a well-ordered environment accounts for the large readership who enjoy Christie's works not only for the challenge of the puzzle or the delight of the game, but also for the ambience of the experience. Although Christie's settings reflect the impact of world events and changes in societal structure, still there is a timelessness that is as vital as the well worn grass of the village commons and there is a nostalgia for by-gone days when life was sweeter in Christie's world—if no where else.

Chapter IX

Christie's Legacy

When Agatha Christie was interviewed in 1974 by Lord Snowden, he asked her what she would most like to be remembered for in the next century. She replied, "I would like it to be said that I was a good writer of detective and thriller stories."[1] Whether Christie will be remembered or whether her reputation will fade before the onslaught of time remains to be seen. But, we feel that Christie's detective fiction will endure.

Agatha Christie was virtually unknown when her first book, *The Mysterious Affair at Styles,* appeared in 1920. Since then, however, she has skyrocketed to fame as the world's most widely read detective fiction writer.

In quantity alone, Christie's accomplishment staggers the imagination: 60 detective novels, 15 volumes of short stories— "more short stories than O'Henry, Ernest Hemingway, and Damon Runyon combined."[2] Since 1923, forty-eight million hardback Christie's have flooded the market: to date, more than 200 million (or is it billion?) paperbacks have been sold around the world.[3] So enormous are the sales that even her publishers have lost count. And the end is not in sight!

How did this shy, unschooled, middlesclass matron manage to corner the market on detective fiction? Actually, these very "limitations" became the means to her success. Because she was so shy, Christie preferred to observe and listen rather than express herself orally. From childhood, she developed an eye for mannerisms and an ear for speech patterns. Christie encountered lords and ladies, vicars and soldiers, spinsters and actresses, professors and cooks—and she learned *how* they talked and *what* they discussed. Her editors claim that she protested the altering of any words in her manuscripts lest the characters begin to sound the same. Basically, Christie's method of composition was oral—she talked her stories into being. If a character did not *sound* right, she changed the dialogue.

Lack of formal schooling freed her from constraints and pretensions. She taught herself to read and write. And though she did not attend any educational institutions, she read constantly and acquired particular literary tastes. Christie came from a family of readers; she was encouraged to write out her fantasies and kept notebooks recording her imaginative adventures. What gradually emerged is that distinctive style that is purely Christie's— simple, direct and conversational.

Her insulation in England's comfortable middle class fostered her stalwart Victorian views. While others of her generation became more "liberated," Agatha Christie found sustenance in the well-worn values of the past. Far from rendering her passe as a writer, her perspective shaped a nostalgic Eden out of England's Victorian and Edwardian past. Readers continue to be drawn to Christie's stories seeking that halcyon environment of the posh home with its comfortable ambience and its reassuring housekeeping routines. Nostalgia provides nurturance as Christie feeds the public's appetite for security and stability.

Yet cozy though the setting may be, the detective story requires the hard core of the mystery puzzle. Surprisingly enough, Agatha Christie met this challenge too—despite being shy, unschooled, and sheltered. She possessed a natural flair for games of wit like bridge, backgammon, mahjong, crossword puzzles—and murder puzzles. Though she is sometimes criticized for being "formulaic" with her puzzle designs, the fact remains that she continued to invent new variations to the murder theme, creating unusual twists and shocking dénouements.

The greatest paradox in Christie's astounding success is that amid all her so-called "limitations" she worked out the perfect combination. Refusing to become part of a particular school of writers, she followed her own inclinations and then proceeded to set the tone and pattern for the Golden Age of detective fiction. In the process she forged a style so simple, so artless and natural, that even today it baffles critics and charms readers. Other writers have tried to imitate Christie but with little success; publishers seek the "new Christie" among the budding generation of writers, but yet no one has been able to duplicate Christie.

Simple though her style may seem, Agatha Christie achieved that delicate balance of romance and realism, mystery and homespun wisdom, which renders her work eminently readable. And unschooled though she was (or perhaps because of it), Christie understood people—their motivations and values. Out of her own culture, she constructed a commonsensical, down to earth fictive world— most assuredly English but essentially human. Consequently, Europeans, Americans, Asians, Africans—of all ages and backgrounds—have become "hooked on Christie." Her works have been translated and marketed all over the world, so universal is Christie's appeal.

Agatha Christie was a dedicated and professional writer who worked hard even in her last years. The promised "Christie for Christmas" kept her busy and committed to writing within a specific time frame. Still, she conjured up unusual and challenging plots—despite the confines and well-worn grounds of the genre. She once commented, "It's not so difficult to think of something new after all. And, of course, as you get older you change, you see things from another angle."[6] (If you have Christie's talent!)

Though Agatha Christie's personal image may fade in time, her characters and their remarkable, murderous worlds will endure. Jane Marple, Hercule Poirot, Inspector Japp, Superintendent Battle will carry on when the "game's afoot," and the gossip fills the shopkeeper's ears on High Street as deadly nightshade spices an unsuspecting victim's tea!

Notes

Preface

[1]Willa Petschek, "Agatha Christie: The World's Most Mysterious Woman," *McCalls,* 96 (February 1969), 80.

[2]Obituary, *New York Times,* 13 January 1976, p. 16

[3]Nancy Blue Wynne, *An Agatha Christie Chronology* (New York: Ace Books, 1976), p. 262.

[4]Wynne, p. 262.

[5]Max Lowenthal, "Agatha Christie, Creator of Poirot, Dead," *New York Times Biographical Service,* January 1978, VII, 29.

[6]Wynne, p. 262.

[7]Francis Wyndam, "The Algebra of Agatha Christie," *London Sunday Times,* February 27, 1966, p. 25.

[8]Jeffrey Feinman, *The Mysterious World of Agatha Christie* (New York: Award Books, 1975), p. 20.

[9]See References.

[10]Derrick Murdoch, *The Agatha Christie Mystery* (Toronto: The Pagurian Press Limited, 1976), p. 9.

Chapter I

[1]   Unfinished Portrait (New York: Dell Publishing Company, 1971), p. 69.

[2]*An Autobiography* (New York: Dodd, Mead & Company, 1977), p. 198.

[3]Personal Interview with Adelaide Phillpotts Ross, daughter of Eden Phillpotts, 17 April 1977, Bude, Cornwall.

[2]*Autobiography,* p. 32.

[5]Ibid, p. 34.

[6]Ibid.

[7]Ibid, p. 33.

[8]*Mallowan's Memoirs* (London: Collins, 1977), p. 199.

[9]Ritchie Calder, "Agatha and I," *New Statesman* (30 January 1976), p. 128.

[10]*New York Times,* 17 December 1926, p. 4.

[11]*Daily Mail,* 17 December 1926, p. 7.

[12]*New York Times,* 16 December 1926, p. 7.

[13]Calder, p. 128.

[14]*Daily Mail,* 11 December 1926, p. 9.

[15]*Memoirs,* p. 311.

[16]Ibid, p. 201.

[17]Ibid.

Chapter II

[1]Julian Symons, *The Detective Story in Britain* (London: Longmans, Green, 1962), p. 3.

[2]*Autobiography,* p. 198.

[3]*Hickory Dickory Death* (New York: Pocket Books, 1975), p. 113.

[4]For a discussion of detectival references see George M. Dove, " 'Shades of Dupin,' Fictional Detectives of Detective Fiction." *Armchair Detective,* 8 (November 1974), 12-14; and R.W. Hays, "More 'Shades of Dupin'!", *Armchair Detective,* 8 (August 1975), 288-289, 274.

[5]*Partners in Crime* (New York: Dell Publishing Company, 1957), p. 211.

[6]*Autobiography,* p. 198.

[7]Nigel Dennis, "Genteel Queen of Crime," *Life,* 14 (May 1976), 98.

[8]Lord Snowden, "Grande Dame of Whodunit," *The Los Angeles Times,* Calendar Section, 15 December 1974, p. 64.

[9]Snowden, p. 64.

[10]*Autobiography,* p. 12.

[11]Ibid, pp. 183-184.

[12]Adelaide P. Ross, daughter of Eden Phillpotts, believes that Naoke was a likely prototype: Personal Interview, 17 April 1977, Bude, Cornwall.

[13]W.H. Auden, "The Guilty Vicarage," *Harpers,* 198 (May 1948), 409.

[14]Howard Haycraft, *Murder for Pleasure* (New York: Biblo & Tannen, 1968), p. 132.

[15]John D. Cawelti, *Adventure, Mystery, and Romance* (Chicago: University of Chicago Press, 1976), p. 119.

[16]David I. Grossvogel, *Mystery and Its Fictions: From Oedipus to Agatha Christie* (Baltimore: Johns Hopkins University Press, 1979), p. 41.

[17]*The Mysterious Affair at Styles* (London: Pan Books, 1954), p. 10; hereafter references to the novel will be included in the text.

[18]Grossvogel, p. 44.

Chapter III

[1]Marcelle Bernstein, "Agatha Christie: 'Queen of Crime' is a Gentlewoman," The *Los Angeles Times,* 8 March 1970, p. 60.

[2]For a discussion of detectival games, see Jane Gottschalk, "The Games of Detective Fiction," *Armchair Detective,* 10 (January 1977), 74.

[3]*Partners in Crime* offers a treatment of such games.

[4]*Cards on the Table* (New York: Dell Publishing Company, 1964), Foreword.

[5]Ibid, p. 53.

[6]For a discussion of tangible and intangible clues, see Marie Rodell, *Mystery Fiction* (New York: Heritage House, 1952).

[7]*A.B.C. Murders* (New York: Pocket Books, 1976), p. 163.

[8]Cawelti, p. 2.

[9]Robert Champigny, *What Will Have Happened?* (Bloomington: Indiana University Press, 1977), p. 81.

[10]Champigny, p. 81.

[11]*Autobiography,* p. 329.

[12]For a discussion of mystification structure, see Cawelti, p. 110.

Chapter IV

[1]Colin Watson, *Snobbery with Violence* (London: Eyre & Spottiswoode, 1971), p. 167.
[2]Haycraft, p. 131.
[3]"Hercule Poirot—A Companion Portrait," *Agatha Christie: First Lady of Crime,* ed. H.R.F. Keating (New York: Holt, Rinehart and Winston, 1977), p. 216.
[4]*Murder on the Links* (New York: Dell Publishing Company, 1964), p. 52.
[5]*Lord Edgware Dies* (New York: Dell Publishing Company, 1969), p. 224.
[6]*Curtain* (New York: Pocket Books, 1976), pp. 254-255.
[7]Ibid, p. 279.

Chapter V

[1]*Lost Man's Lane* (New York: G.P. Putnam's Sons, 1898), p. v.
[2]*Hilda Wade* (New York: G.P. Putnam's Sons, 1900), p. 4.
[3]Gordon Ramsey, *Agatha Christie: Mistress of Mystery* (New York: Dodd, Mead & Company, 1967), p. 59.
[4]Bernstein, p. 60.
[5]*Sleeping Murder* (New York: Bantam Books, 1977), p. 179.

Chapter VI

[1]Symons, p. 11.
[2]*Autobiography,* p. 420.
[3]*The Mysterious Mr. Quin* (New York: Dell Publishing Company, 1957), p. 5.
[4]Ibid, p. 10.
[5]Harley Quin makes a final appearance twenty years later in a single story entitled "The Love Detectives," published in *Three Blind Mice and Other Stories* (1950).
[6]*Parker Pyne Investigates* (London: Fontana Books, 1965), p. 7.
[7]Ibid, p. 8.
[8]*Partners in Crime,* p. 162.
[9]Ibid, p. 163.
[10]Ibid, p. 183.
[11]*Cards on the Table,* p. 12.
[12]*Parker Pyne Investigates,* p. 34.
[13]Ibid, p. 34.
[14]*Cards on the Table,* p. 33.
[15]Ibid, p. 54.
[16]Ibid.

Chapter VII

[1]Alma Elizabeth Murch, *The Development of the Detective Novel* (London:

P. Owen, 1958), p. 248.

[2]Joan M. Mooney, "Best Selling American Detective Fiction," *Armchair Detective,* 3 (January 1970), 110.

[3]*Murder at the Vicarage* (London: Fontana Books, 1961), p. 43.

[4]Ibid, p. 75.

[5]*The Body in the Library* (New York: Pocket Books, 1973), p. 16.

[6]Ibid, p. 18.

[7]Charles Reith, A Short History of the British Police (London: Oxford University Press, 1948), p. 105.

[8]*The Secret of Chimneys* (New York: Dell Publishing Company, 1967), p. 81.

[9]*Cards on the Table,* p. 43.

[10]Ibid, p. 66.

[11]Ibid, p. 67.

[12]Ibid, p. 103.

[13]*Towards Zero* (New York: Pocket Books, 1947), p. 106.

[14]*The Mysterious Affair at Styles,* p. 100.

[15]*Murder on the Links* (New York: Dell Publishing Company, 1964), p. 13.

[16]*The Big Four* (New York: Dell Publishing Company, 1973), p. 74.

[17]"The Affair at the Victory Ball," *The Underdog and Other Stories* (New York: Dell Publishing Company, 1975), pp. 89-90.

[18]*Lord Edgware Dies* 13 at Dinner (New York: Dell Publishing Company, 1969), p. 41.

[19]Ibid, p. 41.

[20]Ibid, p. 45.

[21]Ibid, p. 64.

[22]Ibid, p. 128.

[23]Ibid, p. 133.

[24]Ibid, p. 128.

[25]Ibid, p. 145.

[26]Ibid, p. 154.

[27]Ibid, p. 160.

[28]*A.B.C. Murders,* p. 8.

[29]*Death in the Air* Death in the Clouds (London: Fontana Books, 1974), p. 24.

[30]Ibid, p. 52.

[31]*Murder in the Mews* (London: Pan Books, 1976), p. 19.

Chapter VIII

[1]*Murder in Mesopotamia* (New York: Dell Publishing Company, 1964), p. 21.

[2]Ibid, p. 36.

[3]*Death on the Nile* (New York: Bantam Books, 1978), p. 81.

[4]Ibid, p. 80.

[5]*Death Comes as the End* (New York: Pocket Books, 1977), p. 2.

[6]*Thirteen at Dinner* (New York: Dell Publishing Company, 1964), p. 32.

[7]*Cards on the Table,* p. 18.

[8]*At Bertram's Hotel* (New York: Pocket Books, 1976), p. 10.

[9]Ibid, p. 12.

[10]*Nancy Blue Wynne, An Agatha Christie Chronology* (New York: Ace Books, 1976), p. 13.

[11]Jeanine Larmouth, *Murder on the Menu* (New York: Scribners, 1972), p. 3.

[12]Ibid, p. xii.

[13]*The Secret of Chimneys,* p. 22.

[14]Larmouth, pp. 156, 157.

[15]The Seven Dials Mystery (New York: Bantam Books, 1964), p. 133.

[16]*The Mirror Crack'd* (New York: Pocket Books, 1976), p. 3.